DETOUR FROM NORMAL

Ken Dickson

The events of this book are true and based on medical, mental health and court records, Beth's journal, interviews with friends and family, and the author's recollection. The names of people and places were changed to protect privacy.

ISBN: 1491248637
ISBN: 13: 9781491248638
Library of Congress Control Number: 2013914431

CreateSpace Independent Publishing Platform,
North Charleston, SC

DETOUR FROM NORMAL

Ken Dickson

DEDICATION

I dedicate this book to Beth. During my time of need, you were my constant angel. As I wrote my story, you were my biggest fan and toughest critic. In my life, you are my best friend and the one person I never wish to be without.

TABLE OF CONTENTS

PREFACE

Mania is a psychological state that can be brought about by medical procedures, adverse reactions to medications (notably steroids and SSRIs), drug abuse (such as cocaine and methamphetamines), trauma (physical or psychological), or persistent mental illness such as bipolar disorder. Once experienced, it is something that one will never forget.

Detour from Normal is a true account of medically induced mania resulting from a lifesaving surgery, associated medications, and improper treatment. Because of the liberal use of medications, and their singular and combined side effects, mania is becoming increasingly more prevalent among postsurgical patients, commencing as long as several weeks after their release from the hospital.

Mania manifests itself in some of the following ways:

Physical changes—increased energy, insomnia, catatonia, heightened senses, and improved memory;

Behavioral changes—hyperactivity, increased socialization, keen interest in new ideas or projects, rapid or excessive speech, overspending, increased sex drive or risky sexual behavior, poor judgment;

Mood changes—optimism, happiness, euphoria, irritability;

Thought changes—avalanche of ideas, uncharacteristic self-confidence, difficulty with focus, grandiose thoughts, delusions, hallucinations, loss of sense of time.

It is critical to detect these changes early and seek treatment, or the patient will become incapable of recognizing his or her disorder and may refuse treatment.

Because of the little information available on medically induced mania, its treatment, and its prevention, the author's family, friends, and relatives had no experts to turn to for help. In the hands of uninformed professionals to whom they entrusted his care, his condition rapidly deteriorated. *Detour from Normal* not only awakens readers to the potential pitfalls of our medical and mental health systems, it also provides important information that could change the lives of loved ones potentially heading toward similar fates.

Beyond that, *Detour from Normal* is an incredibly human story told from the author's heart, which is bound to affect anyone who reads it.

INTRODUCTION

Before April 14, 2011, I was just an average citizen, with a job, a house, a wife, kids, and a few pets. I was fifty-five years old and extraordinarily healthy. I'd never had any major surgery or mental health issues. If I ever did see a doctor, I left my medical forms almost completely blank: I had no medical history. I exercised regularly and had even recently completed a grueling hike up the Flatiron, one of most difficult hikes in Arizona.

After April 14, everything changed. What began as an emergency surgery to remove a damaged portion of my lower intestine quickly became something much more complicated. Over the next few weeks, my family rushed me to emergency rooms, hospitals, and psychiatric facilities; doctors administered over thirty different drugs, some against my will, and I suffered paralyzing seizures. I received six CAT scans—the radiation equivalent of three hundred standard X-rays. I had an MRI of my head, EEGs of my brain, and EKGs of my heart. Police delivered me to a high security facility where staff observed me continuously, and I stood up to fight for my rights and safety in court.

This is the true story of my ordeal; an insane snapshot from a life that I could never imagine would be my own. It was a time when no one who loved me or cared for me knew who I was or what to do with me. It was a time when everyone harbored identical concerns: what was wrong with me and would I ever be the same again?

Part 1

MISERY

Chapter 1

DESERT HOPE

It was late on Sunday afternoon, April 10, 2011, and I'd been swinging a rusty pick for what seemed like hours. Despite the fact that it was only seventy degrees, perspiration mottled my gray t-shirt. I removed my baseball cap, wiped the sweat from my brow, and replaced it; then I took a long drink of water from the red-and-white Coleman water jug sitting close by. Years earlier, I promised my wife, Beth, a lemon tree, and it was well beyond time to deliver on that promise. The day before, we finally went shopping for that tree. Somehow, after all that time, one tree just wasn't appropriate. We ended up instead with two fruit trees, which we scheduled for delivery later in the week. I could have arranged for holes to be dug and the trees professionally planted, but with the poor economy, four job losses, and months of unemployment in the previous five years, I wasn't eager to spend more money than I had to. After resting for a few minutes, I once again hefted the heavy pick by its sun-bleached wooden handle, raised it high over my head, and drove it with an audible chink into the hard caliche.

Throughout my life, I often had times when I felt I needed to prove my manhood—if only to myself. This was one of those times. I put every ounce of effort into each swing of the pick; despite the negligible response of the earth to my best efforts, I was determined that when I finished, there would be two twenty-four-inch square

3

holes where I stood, each two feet deep, just large enough for each of the two trees to be planted.

Unbeknownst to me, a disease had compromised my lower intestines. Tissue from weakened bowels bulged through muscle fibers in several places. With each stroke of the pick, one of those bulges stretched beyond natural limits. By the time I proved to myself that I could still do the work of a much younger man, the damage was done. Though it would take days before I realized the full impact of what had transpired, my fate was sealed: the ride of my life had begun.

On the morning of Thursday, April 14, 2011, I drove east on Highway Loop 202 on my way to work, '80s rock and roll blaring from the tinny speakers of my aging Kia. In my right hand, I held a Hostess Mini donut from the open six-pack sitting on the passenger seat. My left hand vibrated gently on the steering wheel from the unbalanced tire that I always meant to fix but never did. I shoved the entire miniature donut into my mouth, chewed for a bit, savoring the rich cake and cinnamon flavor, and then washed it down with some Diet Coke. The construction for the new carpool on-ramp was finally complete, and the myriad of cones, barricades, and reduced-speed-limit signs were gone. The effect was like an asthmatic taking a hit off his inhaler and suddenly having his lungs open up. Instead of tensely waiting for the brake lights of the car ahead to come on, now there were no cars in sight. The road was breathing again, and my mind was free to wander as it often had before all the construction.

As I drove, my body complained loudly to me about how badly it needed to use the restroom. I wondered what could possibly be wrong. Since April 10, I hadn't had a normal bowel movement. I didn't consider that it could be something serious since both Beth and my children had been sick for days with similar symptoms. It had to be stomach flu of some kind. In any case, there wasn't much I could do about that now, so I attempted to distract myself from my discomfort—my inability to relieve myself despite the fact that I felt a desperate need to do so. I forced myself to think about something more pleasant: my anniversary—my twentieth anniversary, to be exact. It was coming up in August, and I had been trying to figure out something special to do for Beth. That led me to daydream about when I first met her.

When I first saw Beth in the spring of 1990, she had just walked through the door of Old Chicago's in Colorado Springs. It was a blustery day and she was bundled in a heavy coat, scarf, and hat. I could see nothing of what she looked like but something drew me to her nonetheless. Unbelievably, she walked across the room and took a seat directly across from me. She then proceeded to unravel her many layers of protection. It reminded me of a moth wriggling out of a cocoon. I had no idea who she was, but she mesmerized me. As the evening wore on, I found that I loved the way she interacted with her friends. I loved her laugh and her smile, and, on top of everything else, she was gorgeous. She had dark, shoulder-length wavy hair, beautiful skin, a slim athletic build, and glasses. For some inexplicable reason, I had always been partial to women with glasses.

I was single at the time and really wanted to get to know her, but I was there that night to celebrate the college graduation of a female friend of mine. I was sitting at her side that evening in a kind of position of honor. I didn't want to disrespect that by using the opportunity to pursue another woman, particularly someone I didn't know. Therefore, I spent the evening spying on my future spouse. What followed was a kind of cat-and-mouse game over a period of weeks that I won only by tenacity and sheer luck.

We married just over a year later. Our early years together were full of adventure, and wherever we went, we were always hand in hand. If ever we were apart for long, all we could think of was the other and we'd talk on the phone every day until we were together again, even if we were half a world apart. We were soul mates, and I couldn't imagine anyone I'd rather be with. As time passed, life blessed us with two wonderful children, Kaitlin and Hailey. Beth had a new mission once they came into our lives, and her focus shifted toward motherhood. Beth was a terrific mother. She taught our children compassion and good manners. She instilled in them confidence and a zest for learning. She was a dedicated cheerleader and knew when to comfort, and when to say, "Get out there and try again." Though I was no longer the center of attention, I deeply admired her dedication to raising the children right, and through her, I learned how to be a good father.

Reminiscing about our life made me smile. The smile quickly faded, however, as painful cramps rippled through my midsection. I took a deep breath and arched my back in hopes that would stop them. Eventually they faded. I took that to mean that perhaps things were on the move inside me and relief from my days of gastrointestinal torture was on its way.

After the cramps subsided, I took stock of where I was and realized I was about to miss my exit. I gritted my teeth and swerved quickly, barely clipping the tip of the gore triangle. There's a huge fine for cutting through the gore triangle, but I never heard of anyone actually getting a ticket for doing so. Still, I glanced nervously in the rearview mirror, expecting to see flashing lights. That quick decision saved me from having to drive another mile down the freeway to the next exit to turn around, something I had to do a few too many times because of daydreaming.

With my reverie interrupted, I was back to where I started thinking about going to the bathroom again. I really was making many trips to the restroom lately. It was one of those things that, though uncomfortable, wasn't bad enough to convince me to miss work, stay home or (God forbid) see a doctor. The strange thing was that every time I rushed to the restroom feeling that disaster was imminent, I couldn't go. Lord knows I tried, but I just couldn't do it. I was a little concerned about what would happen if I didn't go to the bathroom for several days or even a week. Would I explode? Would I start rotting from the inside out? I let it rest there. It was bad enough feeling the way I did—no need to make matters worse.

I arrived at work just after 8:00 a.m. I rushed straight into the three-story building, and leaping several stairs at a time, covered the flight to my office level in no time. Instead of heading to my desk, I went straight to the men's room—much as I had on previous days.

Again, I was unable to relieve myself, but this time I couldn't urinate either. *This can't be good.* Still optimistic, I continued trying. I pressed and poked my abdomen, twisted my shoulders to the left and right, stretched to either side, held my breath, and pushed harder, all to no avail.

Giving up, I headed to my desk, powered up my laptop, and checked my e-mail. I was pleased to see that from a work standpoint at least, everything was under control. I checked my calendar and made a mental note of the 10:00 a.m. meeting with my boss. Just as I finished with my e-mails, I felt as if an unseen assailant punched me in the gut. "Ow," I moaned as I doubled over in my chair. The pain quickly escalated, and within moments, I felt as if I someone knifed me to the hilt and twisted the blade for good measure.

I should have stayed put and called 911, but my parents raised me to be strong and independent: I rarely asked for help. I stubbornly stood from my desk and staggered toward the stairway I'd sprinted up only a short time before. Once there, I leaned against the railing and let it slide through my grip as I stumbled down the stairs, swiped my ID badge over the badge reader, and exited the building.

Once outside I was in so much pain that I could hardly stand, let alone remember where I parked the car. I reached into my pants pocket, retrieved the car keys, and pressed the key fob repeatedly until the Kia responded with two familiar beeps. Although I effortlessly made the trek a short time before, the car now seemed impossibly far away. I meandered toward it, sliding along one car, and bumping off the next as I went. I held my belly with both hands as if trying to prevent it from exploding. When I finally reached the car, I opened the door, collapsed into the driver's seat, and retrieved my cell phone to call Beth.

"Beth? It's me."

"What's the matter? You sound out of breath."

"Something's wrong with my stomach. I'm in terrible pain. I need to get to an emergency room. Where should I go?"

Rather than ask numerous questions, or try to convince me to call an ambulance, Beth cut right to the chase. Having visited countless emergency rooms with her mother, she was intimately familiar with emergencies, and with most of the local hospitals.

"Don't go to Chandler General, go to Desert Hope—they have the shortest wait time."

I winced at that reply. Chandler General was only two miles away and Desert Hope was nine. "OK, I'll call you when I get there."

As we spoke, Beth headed to her van to meet me there—or perhaps find me slumped over the wheel somewhere along the way on the 202.

The pain lessened but came in waves. Sweat ran off my head and stung my eyes. I frequently wiped it away with my shirtsleeve, soaking it in short order. My pulse raced and my vision blurred as I finally arrived at Desert Hope. I drove frantically around the main building looking for the ER entrance. When I found it, I drove right up to it, screeched to a halt, swung the car door open, and waited expectantly for someone to save me.

If this were television, two young, strapping male nurses or perhaps doctors complete with lab coats and stethoscopes would rush to my aid. I'd collapse in their arms, and they'd load me onto a gurney and proceed posthaste to the emergency room. However, this was the real world: no one came. I took a deep breath, stood, and walked through a set of automatic doors, past black leather and shiny chrome wheelchairs that looked brand new, and through another set of automatic doors. I looked around the unfamiliar facility wondering what to do next and spotted a sliding glass window to my right with the words "Check In" above it. I made it to the window by sheer willpower and then lowered myself, breathing heavily and drenched with sweat, into a chair in front of it.

"Can I help you?" asked a young woman dressed in olive scrubs with blonde hair pulled back tightly in a ponytail. Her ID badge indicated that she was an RN.

"Yes, please. I'm in terrible pain," I replied.

"Where does it hurt?"

"My belly. I need to see a doctor right away."

"When did the pain begin?"

She questioned me incessantly. At a point when I doubted that I could answer another, she finished. "That's all I need for now. Please take a seat in front of the second counter to your left where it says Emergency Registration. Someone will be right with you to take care of your paperwork."

Paperwork? I'm dying and I have to fill out paperwork? Despite my despair, I thanked her and followed her instructions. I rose in agonizing slow motion, shuffled to the registration counter, took a seat in front of it, and waited. After considerable time, it was clear that nothing would happen if I didn't take action. "Excuse me?" I called out weakly. A plump brown-haired woman in a dark blue lab coat appeared seemingly from nowhere and proceeded calmly toward a chair on the other side of the counter. "I'm sorry about that," she said as she plopped her large frame down in a chair and donned the reading glasses that hung from a cord around her neck. "It will just take a few minutes to get you registered; then we'll get you some help." She was very pleasant, but pleasant didn't make me feel any better.

"Is there much paperwork? I really need help. Could I just sign a few things and finish the rest later?"

"It won't take long. Do you have your health insurance ID card and a driver's license?"

"Yes." I reached for my wallet and pulled the yellow insurance card and my driver's license from it, then handed them to her. She took the cards and passed me a small stack of papers.

"Now if you'll just fill in the top section here with your personal information—you're just giving us permission to treat you. The next form is regarding your insurance coverage, and the last is about the HIPAA Act and your right to privacy. I marked everywhere that you need to sign with an X. Please read all the forms before signing them."

I groaned and started filling in my address. I made it through half the paperwork and buckled in pain.

"Are you OK?" the woman asked.

I didn't reply. I just took a deep breath and attacked the paperwork again, determined not to die while completing it. I skipped reading anything else and went directly to signing at the Xs.

"Thank you. Here are your cards back. Please have a seat in one of the chairs and someone will be with you shortly."

I collected my insurance card and driver's license and made my way to the nearest row of chairs, noticing that all the chairs faced a television. I picked up a magazine from the closest one, tossed it to another chair, and sat down. The television and magazine were hints that I could be there awhile—I prayed that wasn't the case.

Thankfully, Beth was right about the ER at Desert Hope. I was one of only three people there, and before long, a patient transport arrived with a wheelchair. He helped me into it, folded down the footrests, and then helped lift my feet onto them. He then wheeled me back into the ER. A male nurse arrived and helped me out of my clothes and into an ill-fitting hospital gown. I was barely able to make it into the gown before the worst pain so far racked me. It felt like someone thrust a fistful of red-hot pokers into my abdomen. I sought out the wheelchair with my hands and fell backward into it. As I fought the pain, I doubled over in agony and screamed through clenched teeth. Before long, involuntary tears mingled with the sweat running down my face.

Seeing my extreme agony, the nurse said, "I'm going to get you some morphine to ease the pain." I nodded in acknowledgment but felt concerned. I'd never had morphine in my life and didn't know what to expect.

"Could you just give me a baby dose and give me more later if I need it?" Most people would beg for all they could get, but I was adamant. He agreed, and a short time later I felt a prick in my arm as he injected a half dose of morphine. I waited patiently for the painkiller to kick in, but nothing happened. I was in so much pain by then that I imagined my death was imminent.

A short time later, a lanky Indian man in a white lab coat got behind my wheelchair and pushed me out of the area. "I'm Dr. Chandra; I'm an ER doctor. I'm taking you to get a CAT scan so that we can determine what's happening inside you. Hang in there. It will just take a few minutes."

Once we arrived at the CAT scanner, I was unable to do anything but writhe around on the table in pain. It was impossible to hold still long enough to complete the scan. After nearly twenty minutes, the morphine took effect. I relaxed and they completed the scan. Afterward the doctor helped me off the table and back into the wheelchair. "We should have results shortly," he said and wheeled me back to the ER.

***

"Where is he? Where's my husband?" Beth yelled from the entrance of the ER.

"Here," I replied weakly.

She saw me and ran to my side. "Are you OK?"

"I'm better. They gave me some morphine that just kicked in. The pain was terrible before that; the worst I've ever felt. I had a CAT scan, but haven't heard the results yet."

"Does anyone know what's going on?"

"I don't know. No one's said anything."

A few minutes later, Dr. Chandra returned. "Are you Ken's wife?"

"Yes, I'm Beth."

"I'm Dr. Chandra, the ER doctor. I reviewed Ken's CAT scan. He has diverticulitis. There's a micro-perforation on his sigmoid colon, which allowed a gas bubble to form outside of his colon. That micro-perforation is what's causing all the pain. In addition, his colon is most likely infected."

"Is it serious? What can you do?" Beth asked.

"The best course of action is to treat it with IV antibiotics and see if we can stop the infection. If we can, he could potentially go home and might only have to make some dietary changes to prevent future infections."

That was a relief to hear. I would relax in bed for a few days, recover, and get back to normal life. I was glad it wasn't anything life threatening, although based on the severity of the pain, I was inclined to differ with the doctor's optimistic prognosis.

I couldn't stay in the ER indefinitely. Eventually, they wheeled me to room 247 in the southwest wing of Desert Hope. Luckily, I had a private room where I could suffer in solitude. For the moment, the pain was manageable with regular half doses of morphine, which made me feel somewhat nauseous. I was glad that I opted for the half doses or I'd be vomiting and making things really complicated.

A nurse wheeled an IV cart into my room with two IV pumps attached to it. Each pump managed dosages of two different medications. One pump was for saline, a saltwater solution given to ensure that I remained properly hydrated and that my electrolytes stayed in balance. The other pump was for Levaquin and Flagyl, two powerful antibiotics to kill the infection. The nurse hung the bags of saline, Levaquin, and Flagyl on the hooks on the top tree of the rack. Each of the three bags of chemicals had a small drip chamber to monitor flow rate and to prevent air from entering my blood and causing a deadly embolism. The nurse placed a PIV (peripheral intravenous catheter) into a vein on the inside of my left forearm to administer medications. After connecting everything to my single IV line, the nurse adjusted the individual flow rates on each pump, making sure that all the drip chambers indicated good flow, and then left.

I napped fitfully through much of that afternoon. In the evening, I turned on the television to see if there were any shows or movies to watch. I found that I needed to view several mandatory videos before I could watch anything else. The videos painted Desert Hope as a premier state-of-the-art medical facility, and covered the general rules and regulations related to my stay. What interested me most was the description of the pain chart. The pain chart had ten round black-and-white cartoon faces with the leftmost having a beaming smile and the rightmost having a horrified frown with tears squirting from its eyes. Beneath the faces were the numbers one to ten from left to right. The purpose of the chart was to help people better explain their pain to the hospital staff. The number ten was supposed to be like getting your arm cut off with no anesthesia. I couldn't imagine how excruciating that would be. Based on the chart, I figured the pain I experienced was bad but not like getting my arm cut off, perhaps an eight or eight-and-a-half, tops.

After watching the videos, I completed a quiz on them and passed with 100 percent. I imagine that if I couldn't pass, a nurse would help me. Exhausted, I turned off the television and room lights after that and continued my fitful tossing and turning throughout the night.

The next day, April 15, I lay in bed watching movies and resting. Everything looked positive. My white blood cell count was 10.3, which was within the normal healthy range of 4.3 to 10.8. It was a good indication that my infection was under control. My pain had subsided and there was talk of sending me home in a day or so.

April 16 started out uneventfully, but as the day progressed, I felt more and more uncomfortable. By early afternoon, my original pain unexpectedly returned in its full glory, and a new pain sent fire across my abdomen, groin, and upper legs. The new pain was so intense that I had to hold my bed sheets away from my skin. The combined pains were the worst imaginable, without a doubt a ten. I could imagine nothing worse. Pain consumed me; I could think of nothing else and could do nothing else but fight it—not even call for help. I sat there, alone in my agony, grimacing, yelling through my teeth, and holding the sheets away from my body.

In the middle of the episode, a nurse opened the room door, took one look at me, and rushed for morphine. After twenty more minutes of intense suffering, the morphine kicked in and things settled down. A short time later, they performed another CAT scan to investigate what happened. I got on the machine with a little less effort than before, but could feel a pressure in my abdomen: a warning of worse yet to come.

The CAT scan showed more damage. I exacerbated the perforation by grimacing, yelling, and the contractions of my abdominal muscles. The bubble on my colon had grown. No one could explain the new pain. I requested my doctor, but could only see a hospitalist. Thankfully, he arrived quickly. He was a tall Asian man with gold wire-framed glasses, sharply dressed in black slacks, a white shirt, and a black tie. He had an air of professionalism about him.

"Hello, Mr. Dickson, I'm Dr. Hou. Tell me a little about what's been going on." I told him everything I could about the first pain, the first CAT scan, the burning, and the second CAT scan. He said "hmm" often, but didn't communicate anything helpful. When he left, I felt no more encouraged than when he arrived.

After a few hours, I sensed the start of pain again as the morphine waned. I braced myself for what I expected would be the worst pain imaginable when another doctor came in. He seemed the polar opposite of Dr. Hou right from the start. He was perhaps forty-eight years old and of Indian descent, stocky and around five foot seven. He wore a colorful reddish-brown print shirt with an open collar, no tie, and dark brown casual pants. His most endearing quality was his jolly, straightforward demeanor.

"Hi, Ken, I'm Dr. Bonjani. I'm a hospitalist working with Dr. Hou." He extended his hand, and I shook it as firmly as I could manage. "Dr. Hou and I conferred about your condition, particularly the new pain you are experiencing."

"Have you figured anything out?"

"Yes, your prostate is irritated in reaction to everything happening and is so swollen that it squeezed your urinary tract closed. Consequently, your bladder is about to burst. When was the last time you peed?"

"I don't really remember. It's certainly been days. I assumed I was dehydrated. Why does it hurt so much? I've never felt such intense pain in my life."

"When I said your bladder was ready to burst, what I meant is that it can't hold one more drop of pee. Ken, you're going to have to man up and get that pee out, or I'll have to put a catheter in. Do you know what that is?"

"Isn't it just a tube?"

"Yes, but more to the point, someone has to take hold of your penis in one hand and force a tube up into it with the other—all the way to your bladder." As he explained, he gestured vividly, leaving nothing to the imagination. "Once it's in, they'll inflate a bulb with saline solution so it won't slide out. You'll be stuck with that tube hanging out of your penis and a Foley bag full of pee that you have to lug around with you wherever you go until I tell someone to take it out. Is that what you want?" he asked sternly.

"Since you put it that way, no. I'll try to pee. Can I use a commode so I don't have to deal with all these tubes and the IV rack going to the bathroom?" I asked, pointing to all the IV tubes connected to me.

"Sure." With that, Dr. Bonjani fetched the commode from the bathroom and placed it beside my bed. "OK, let's see how manly you are. I want you to fill that commode to the rim."

"OK," I said doubtfully.

Carefully, I disentangled all my tubes from the IV rack and made my way to the commode. Since the slit in my gown was in the back and I didn't want to expose my naked bum to the nice doctor, I stood by the commode, carefully lifted only the front of the gown, and gave it my best shot. I grunted and groaned; I pressed in different areas of my abdomen with my free hand and stretched my body in different directions.

"Come on, you can do it. Don't be a wuss. Get that pee out!" cheered Dr. Bonjani.

I never had a pee cheerleader before. Perhaps my mom cheered for me when I was young. If she had, she never told me about it. Having Dr. Bonjani cheer me on didn't exactly put me in the optimum frame of mind to accomplish the job at hand. I was in limbo somewhere between embarrassment and laughter. After trying everything I could while standing up, I sat down, thinking that perhaps I might be more relaxed in that position.

"What? That's a sissy way for a man to pee, but I'll give you a break. Go Ken, go Ken, you can do it, yes you can," Dr. Bonjani chanted, clapping in time.

I forgot all about being embarrassed at that point. Perhaps that had been Dr. Bonjani's intention all along. I cooperated fully as he tried every "man" trick he could to convince me that I had it in me to defeat whatever prevented me from peeing. Ultimately, it didn't happen. In exasperation I finally said, "Put the catheter in, please."

"OK, I'll get the nurse. I still think you could have done it, though."

"Dr. Bonjani, since you're here, can you explain what's wrong with me? I don't understand what happened. What's diverticulitis?"

"Certainly, when the food you eat moves through your intestines, it's very wet so that it moves readily and the intestines can more easily absorb nutrients. Once the food is digested, all that remains is a kind of soggy waste. Your colon is the last stop before you have a bowel movement. To conserve water in your body, your colon squeezes excess water out of the waste, kind of like wringing water out of a washrag, and then recycles it.

"If you ate enough fiber and drank plenty of fluids, your waste would be like chopped, cooked spinach. In Arizona, people tend not to drink enough water and are often dehydrated. In addition, Americans in general don't eat enough fiber. Your waste was probably more like sticky bread dough. The chopped spinach would move easily through, and your colon wouldn't have to work at all. The bread dough on the other hand sticks to everything and is difficult to push through. Being unable to move it readily, your colon expands to make room as it piles up."

As Dr. Bonjani spoke, I realized that as an engineer, I spent a lot of time in laboratories and clean room environments where water bottles weren't allowed. In addition, whenever I was in those places,

I tended to focus on what I was doing and went for hours without a break, and consequently anything to drink. *Is that the sole cause of my problem?* I also wondered if there would still be a place for the finer things in life, like donuts, when I got through this, or if I was going to have to spend the rest of my life downing bran cereal and vegetables.

"Your colon is like a mesh of muscle fibers that can expand a great deal." Dr. Bonjani placed the fingers of one hand over those of his other at a right angle then spread his fingers to show how the colon can expand in a sort of web fashion. "With the spinach, the mesh is tight and there are no issues. With the bread dough, the mesh expands. As the muscle fibers contract to squeeze out the water and move the waste, the tissue between them balloons out. Over time, permanent pockets called diverticula form. This condition is called diverticulosis."

"Why didn't it show up on any tests I've had? I just had an ultrasonic body scan only a few months ago."

"The pockets don't have to be very big to cause a problem, so they can be hard to spot. In addition, you can live your life with those pockets and never have a symptom. Something just happened to one of yours. The pockets can plug with food or seeds and become infected or even rupture. If a pocket becomes infected, we call the condition diverticulitis. That's what you have now."

"Can you remove infected diverticula?"

"The infection generally spreads beyond the diverticula. We're trying to treat your infection and see if the diverticula will heal on its own. If it doesn't heal, we'll have to surgically remove part of your colon."

I thanked Dr. Bonjani for being my cheerleader and for the detailed explanation. He left with a smile, and I waited for a nurse to come to my rescue and install the catheter before my bladder exploded.

I felt embarrassed again as a pretty, young nurse came into my room to perform the procedure. I wished I could do it myself. It was one thing to listen to Dr. Bonjani describe the procedure and quite another being faced with the reality of it. Once the catheter was in place, however, all feelings of embarrassment vanished as I experienced instant relief. It was unbelievable how wonderful it felt to let go of almost a liter of urine in only a few seconds. I could actually feel my belly shrink as the Foley bag filled. "That's the best feeling I've felt in days!" I exclaimed to the nurse.

The next two days were a blur of misery. After my extraordinary pain on April 16, my body reacted fiercely. My white blood cell count shot up to 17.3, and I spiked fevers as high as 103. I hadn't eaten or drank anything since April 14; I was starving and thirsty all the time. The doctors continued to flood me with chemicals, and by April 18, my fever subsided, and my white blood cell count returned to 10.3. No longer was anyone talking about me going home. Instead, they scheduled me for surgery on April 19. It was a certainty that I would lose part of my colon.

On April 18, four days after my admission, I started preparing for surgery by drinking Golytely. Dr. Bonjani returned and explained in technical terms how Golytely draws large amounts of water into your bowels, quickly and thoroughly cleaning them. All I could think about was how badly my gut would hurt every time I went to the bathroom.

I drank eight ounces of Golytely every ten minutes until I finished a gallon of the salty, metallic-tasting concoction—the same as drinking four thirty-two-ounce Big Gulps sold at the convenience store.

It took an hour and a half before the Golytely kicked in. At that point, chaos ensued as I repeatedly snaked through all my various tubes to make it to the commode before having an accident. I had many narrow escapes negotiating that vinyl spider web every ten minutes. Sure enough, the pain was unbearable, and I required a fresh shot of morphine before I was halfway through. A few hours and a raw behind later, I finished, and was ready for surgery. Unfortunately, the surgeon postponed it until April 20. The next day, I did it all over again: another round of Golytely, fighting the vinyl spider web, and the pain. My surgeon either wanted to ensure I was extra clean, or he was a sadist.

That night, the movie *Invictus* played on my room television. It starred Morgan Freeman and Matt Damon. Morgan Freeman played Nelson Mandela, who, after spending twenty-seven years in prison, regained freedom in 1990. Through a twist of fate, he became president of South Africa. Matt Damon, on the other hand, played Francois Pienaar, captain of the downtrodden and hated rugby team, the Springboks. After Mandela attended one of the Springboks' games, he decided to support the team and met with its captain. He convinced Francois that a victory in the World Cup, then almost a year away, would inspire and unite the nation. He also shared the poem "Invictus" with him, a poem that was special to him during his trials and tribulations in prison.

What followed was a lot of hard work, broken bodies, sweat, and grunting as the Springboks brute-forced their way up from the bottom of the rugby ladder. Unfortunately, I don't remember much after that. I wanted to watch more, but the day took too much out of me. Before I knew it, *Invictus* was playing to a sleeping audience of one.

Chapter 2

UNDER THE KNIFE

In a hospital, sleep comes in broken pieces. There's always a nurse wanting to check your vitals, an IV bag emptying and setting off an alarm, or a shift change, requiring someone to come in and check off boxes on their never-ending paperwork. A constant stream of people randomly entered and exited my room. If I was lucky, they closed the door behind them. Otherwise, I listened to the night-shift sounds in the hallway, too. Eventually the night ended, and, although the sun wouldn't ever peek through the north-facing blinds of my room, the light of day shone around them.

It was April 20, the day of my surgery, and I was ravenous. I would die for a nice breakfast of waffles or pancakes and bacon, maybe some milk with ice, too. I hadn't eaten in six days, and for two of them, my digestive tract was completely flushed out. My stomach would rumble if it could, but it was now as equally dead as my intestines. Everything automatically shut down days ago to protect my body from further damage. Though I still felt hunger and thirst, it would literally kill me to give in to those cravings.

Shortly, Beth arrived to be at my side when they took me to surgical prep. I pressed a button on the side of my bed to raise it so that I could see her better. I couldn't raise it very much due to my distended belly, which increased in size every day. My intestines were swelling, and, without muscle peristalsis, gas accumulated inside them as well.

"What do you think?" I said. "They say I'll give birth any minute. Do you still remember those breathing exercises?" I tried to make light of my distended belly, but this close to the knife, nothing could transform something that serious into a laughing matter. Beth feigned a smile. I was proud of her. She held strong through everything, and was a little dervish in the background making sure that no details were missed and only the best folks were on my team.

"I always wanted another baby," she said. "Maybe we'll have a boy this time." She reached out from the bed and patted my belly.

I took her hand and held it against me, looking into her eyes. "I know this looks like crap, but I'm going to be OK. I just know it. I have absolute faith, and besides, we have Dr. Demarco on our side. He sure went overboard to save your mother when she had her perforated bowel. In my book, he's the best. I can't believe our good fortune to have him as my surgeon."

"I know," she said, but I could see she was holding back tears.

I squeezed her hand reassuringly. We shared an uncomfortable quiet after that. It was difficult to have a conversation in such an unusual situation. I had been in such good health all my life. What I was experiencing was completely alien to me. If I hadn't already personally known the surgeon, I'd fill several tissues with tears and snot. My only experience with surgery was sitting at my mother-in-law's side in intensive care units on multiple occasions, watching her erratic heartbeat on monitors, and wondering if she would die right in front of me. It was never a pleasurable experience, but at least she always pulled through and I forget the bad parts. I hoped that was how it would be with me.

Soon, hospital staff trickled in, a nurse, an aide, and a patient transport person. The patient transport person was young with blond hair in a ponytail, wearing a black shirt and khaki pants. "I'm Susan," she announced. "I'll be taking you to surgical prep. Do you need to go to the bathroom before we go?" I nearly laughed—one end of my body didn't work and the other end was connected to a bag. Before I had a chance to respond, a red glow crossed her young face. "I'm sorry about that. Let me take care of that Foley for you."

The pumps went silent as the aide turned them off, and the vinyl spider web vanished as the nurse disconnected all the lines. Aside from the Foley and catheter, I was free of everything and ready to go. Susan released the brakes on my bed, pulled up the guardrails, and reclined it. Before I knew it, the electric bed was moving at a good clip down the hallway with Beth trailing close behind. I savored a cooling breeze in my face. It's funny how at traumatic times you still appreciate such simple things. I counted the florescent light banks as we rolled smoothly down the industrial carpet of the hall—thirteen of them. It calmed me to count them as I rolled toward my uncertain future.

When we arrived at the entrance of surgical prep, Beth joined me at my bedside and smiled; despite her best efforts, it was but a half smile filled with worry and dread. I took her hand. "Thanks for being here with me."

She leaned down and kissed me. "I love you. I'll be waiting for you."

"I love you, too. I'll see you in a while."

With that, Susan rolled me through the automatic door of surgical prep. There were no walls in surgical prep, just curtained partitions. We rolled past a few and then finally turned into one. Susan parked me there, wished me luck, and left to get Ms. Santos, the anesthesiology technician, pulling the curtains closed behind her.

There wasn't much to do at that point. I tried not to think about what lay ahead. If everything went well, I'd have a cut and be done. If not, I'd have a colostomy bag and with luck, I would come back in a few weeks for another surgery to reattach my intestines. If things went poorly, I'd be stuck with an external plastic bag permanently, and have to empty it and wash out the remaining excrement several times a day for the rest of my life. I told myself it would be better than the alternative, but I crossed my fingers that I wouldn't need one.

I closed my eyes and tried to think pleasant thoughts: my kids, my dogs, even my kids' pet rats. I remembered all the wonderful times we shared and hoped those were what everyone would treasure if I didn't make it. I mentally scratched that last thought. Of course, I would make it. After a half hour or so revisiting my lifetime memories and trying to convince myself that I wasn't having a "life flashing before my eyes" moment, the anesthesiology tech arrived. She introduced herself as Mary and explained what she would do. I was under anesthesia a few years before for a minor hernia surgery, and the anesthesiologist asked me to count back from one hundred. I made it to about ninety-seven. That's what I expected when Mary gave me the shot. I thought I still had some counting to do, that I'd get to remember a little more, but that was it. I watched her start to inject the anesthetic into my IV, and was gone.

According to Beth, a six-member surgical team worked on me for four grueling and tense hours before moving me into recovery.

Chapter 3

TWILIGHT

"And what can I do for you today, my son?" someone asked. I knew that voice, but it wasn't my surgeon. I looked over to see a man in a colorful Madiba shirt and black slacks washing his hands with his back to me. After he cleaned them, he turned to me, his fingers facing up at chest level. A nurse pulled a white latex glove onto each hand, letting loose a puff of powder as each glove hit home. A surgical mask covered his face, but I recognized those calm, wrinkled, wise eyes: Dr. Nelson Mandela. Actually, it was Morgan Freeman, but to me he was Dr. Nelson Mandela.

"Ah, I see," he said, looking intently at my freshly shaven Betadine coated belly, so racked with infection that I looked nine months pregnant. He walked toward me, eyeing a rolled white cloth on the stainless steel cart beside me. He approached and within plain sight unrolled it. An unmistakable clanking of steel against steel followed as it unwrapped to reveal four knives.

Deep, asymmetrical gouges from years of hacking into bone marred the sides of the butcher's knife. Next to that lay a bread knife, its serrated teeth polished so finely from years of sawing through flesh that they sparkled like gems in the room light. The third knife, designed for boning, had kissed the grindstone so many times that all that remained was the sharpest sliver of steel I've ever seen.

He examined each of the knives carefully before picking up the fourth: a carving knife. Unlike the others, its virgin edge was razor-sharp. "Ah, this will do just fine." He then turned to everyone in the OR. They bowed their heads and spoke in voices so low that I couldn't make out what they said.

In time, Dr. Mandela turned toward me and continued speaking. As he did, I recognized the final words of the poem "Invictus" that empowered him with its message of self-mastery so many times during his imprisonment at Robben Island Prison.

… It matters not how strait the gate,
How charged with punishments the scroll,
I am the master of my fate:
I am the captain of my soul.

"Are you ready, son?" He asked, the knife flashing in the glare of the operating table lights. Instead of replying, I held my breath and blinked at him like an animal at slaughter. "Well then, let's see what we've got." With that, he raised the knife in both hands above his head.

"No, Dr. Mandela, don't!" I yelled. He looked at me with a sadistic gleam in his eyes, then plunged the blade below my ribs and ripped me open to my groin.

***

I gasped and opened my eyes. I was cold, shivering despite several blankets laid across me. I looked around, wondering where I was.

"Hi, hon." I turned my head to the side. It took a moment to recognize Beth in a chair by my bed. My throat hurt from an airway recently removed from it. I cleared it and tried to speak, but my voice was weak.

"Where am I?" I croaked.

"You're in your room. You awoke about four hours ago in recovery. Don't you remember?"

"No, the last thing I remember was being in prep." It was dark in the room except for a fluorescent light above my bed. The sun had clearly set. "How did I get here?"

"After you initially came around and they determined you were OK, they released you from recovery. You fell asleep again after that. Everything went well. You didn't need a colostomy." I reached down and felt a long, thin pad on my belly, glad that there was no plastic bag there.

"Thank God for small favors"

"Why did you just say 'No, Dr. Mandela'?"

I didn't want to tell her the truth—she'd think I'd lost my mind. "It was just something from the movie *Invictus*. I started watching it last night before surgery but fell asleep partway through. It was very inspiring."

To me, there was meaning to the dream. It foretold bad times ahead. If I persevered, everything would work out: I'd be the master of my fate and captain of my soul, but if I did not persevere? There seemed no answer to that question. I often dreamed vividly but never knew how to interpret the dreams until after the fact, so I wasn't about to tell Beth that things were going to get worse before they got better; it already seemed bad enough. Despite my prophetic dream, I couldn't begin to imagine how bad it would really get.

Chapter 4

ON THE MEND

I took stock of my changed surroundings. There were a few new bags hanging on my IV racks. There was also a tube releasing oxygen into my nostrils held in place by a plastic shield that partially covered my mouth. A rubber band around my head held the shield in place. It was part of a monitoring system used to measure CO2 in my breath, tied into what I called the Michael Jackson Pump or MJP for short. The MJP was a morphine delivery system that allowed me to dose myself as needed, no more than once every six minutes. On the bed lay a push button that I could press to inject morphine into my IV. The shield monitored CO_2 as I exhaled to make sure I didn't overdose. I called it the Michael Jackson Pump because I envisioned that he might not have died were he connected to such a safeguard: it made a real racket if you stopped breathing or if the CO_2 was too high.

I noticed something surprising after my surgery: I had no pain. I had a ten-inch incision, my innards were all shifted around or cut up and sewn together, I had thirty-six staples and several feet of sutures holding me together—but no pain. I knew that morphine depressed the respiratory system. I was very concerned that weakening my respiratory system could lead to respiratory infection. Hospitals are notorious for fostering superbugs; that was the last thing I wanted. Without pain, I didn't need morphine. I raised my point to the nurses and doctors and asked to remove it. They insisted that I keep the pump in case I needed it.

Stuck with it, I decided to see what it could do for me. I knew that morphine through a needle worked wonders for pain, but had no idea what to expect from a pump. The first night post-surgery, I gave the system a test drive, intending to evaluate the effects of dosage, hopefully, culminating with a deep, restful sleep. I pressed the button once and waited. Six minutes later, I pressed it again and immediately began to hallucinate. Bright colors and soft shapes twisted and floated peacefully, but then the colors grew dark and sickly, and the soft shapes morphed into hideous metallic orbs peppered with sharp, steely barbs. Instead of floating peacefully without a care, they now seemed self-aware and purposeful. I couldn't help but think what their purpose was. I held my thumb over the button, tempted to press it a third time and get beyond the disturbing visions, but fearful of what might happen, I couldn't do it. I suffered through the hallucinations until they burned themselves out and ended the experiment there.

During my hospital stay, I tried my best to be a good patient, partly to be respectful and partly because I wanted to get out of there as quickly as possible. Among other things, I was very dedicated about using my spirometer before and after surgery to keep my lungs clear while spending so much time on my back in bed. A spirometer is a plastic device consisting of a hose and a graduated tube with a plastic disc that floats up during inhalation. To use it, you inhale hard for as long as possible, and then hold the air in for at least five seconds, after which you exhale and rest for a few seconds. I was expected repeat that procedure seven times every twenty minutes to keep my lungs clear. It was very effective, and I could feel the difference after doing it.

With my CO_2 monitor, I could only inhale twice before the MJP alarm went berserk. I tried everything to trick it unsuccessfully. Again, I asked the nurses and doctors if they would remove the morphine pump, but they still refused. I hadn't used it at all since trying to put myself to sleep with it. I was genuinely concerned that all the days on my back were going to be my demise if I couldn't keep my lungs clear.

Sure enough, my respiratory concerns proved valid. The next day—April 22—I went down fast. My white blood cell count shot up to 17.3 again, and my temperature rose to 103. As the morning wore on, it became more and more difficult to breathe: I was drowning in my own mucous, and my vital signs were in steady decline. The flow of nurses, then doctors, to my room increased. Like me, everyone focused on my lungs. At their command, I wheezed air in, and wheezed it out. They listened intently at the four quadrants of my back with their stethoscopes. They tapped on my back and listened again. Each would leave with a look of concern.

Eventually, the flow of staff stopped, leaving me alone in my suffering. It was worse than when I was young and had asthma. At least asthma attacks ended. This only got worse. I never felt I was done for in my life, but that day I did for the first time. That hospital would be my last stop.

Just then, a nurse and an aide scrambled into the room and removed the IV lines. In seconds I was counting fluorescent lights on the ceiling again as they rushed me to get another CAT scan. After making the journey to the first level, I found myself outside the CAT scan room once again. Because of my fever and high white blood cell count, the doctors worried that my re-sectioned bowels were leaking, spreading infection throughout my body.

All the activity helped clear my lungs a bit, making it easier to breathe for a change, but more bad experiences were just around the corner. Everyone seemed in a terrific rush with little concern for my comfort. I'm sure they explained everything they were about to do, but in my condition, my focus was elsewhere. The technician rolled me over onto my side and suddenly jammed a cold enema nozzle into my freshly stapled and sutured rectum, filling me with equally cold contrast fluid. The pain was horrific. To make matters worse, once he filled me to near bursting, he asked me to hold the fluid in for several minutes while the machine created the images.

I didn't know until then that during my surgery just over a day before, they stretched my anus to extra-large proportions using a dilator in preparation for the EAA (end-to-end anastomosis) stapler that would pull my rectum and shortened colon together, and apply two neat rows of titanium staples to reconnect them. In the process, things tore a bit down there. I hadn't gone to the bathroom since my last round of Golytely before surgery and had no way of knowing. That couple of minutes in the machine felt like a year. Finally, they finished and drained me like a water balloon. They then wheeled me back to my room and hooked me up to all the machines again. A while later, a new doctor with a very grave look on his face entered my room.

"Mr. Dickson," he stated in a somber voice, "my name is Dr. Edwards. I'm an infectious disease specialist. I have some good news and some bad news. The good news is your resection is sound. The bad news is you have a nasty infection in your lungs. I'm not going to try to paint a pretty picture: you are seriously ill. I wouldn't be here otherwise. We're going to do our best to help you beat it, though. I'm going to start you on Diflucan, a powerful antifungal that we'll administer through a PICC line. I'll get you set up to have one installed. Do you have any questions?"

So many questions spun through my mind that I didn't know where to begin. I could literally feel myself getting worse by the minute and knew that this was a life or death situation, but the questions that came to mind all involved my wife and children living without me and of things beyond death, for which no doctor could provide answers. "No," I managed to wheeze.

"Hang in there. We'll get you squared away." With that, Dr. Edwards smiled reassuringly and left the room. Shortly afterwards, a patient transporter arrived, and a nurse again unhooked me from my IV rack. I counted the lights again, this time ending up in what looked like the surgical prep I was in in prior to my surgery. One last turn parked me. The transporter locked the wheels of my bed and pulled the drapes around me. A few minutes later, a nurse pulling a cart of medical instruments parted the drapes.

"Good morning, Mr. Dickson. And how are you doing today?"

"I've definitely felt better," I replied.

"Aw, it'll be all good from here, I promise. I'm Donna, and I'm going to install a PICC line for your Diflucan and so that you can get a square meal." Donna was very cheerful, very blond, and very chubby. I liked her immediately.

"How's that?"

"Once we get your PICC in, we can feed you intravenously."

"That sounds yummy: I'm really hungry."

"Sorry, it doesn't go to your stomach. You'll feel as hungry and thirsty as ever, but at least you'll have more energy and stop losing weight."

Donna wore the most colorful getup I saw at Desert Hope: floral-patterned nineteen-fifty glasses and a flower-print bouffant cap that nearly matched her glasses if I squinted hard. "That sucks. I like your glasses and hat. They're very cheery."

"Donna has a whole collection of those glasses," someone remarked from outside the curtain.

"But sadly they only make this one bouffant," Donna said, pointing toward her head.

"What's a PICC line?" I asked.

"It's a peripherally inserted central catheter."

"Why can't they just put the stuff in my IV?"

"Since we can't feed you any real food with your intestines shut down, we're going to give you TPN: total parenteral nutrition. You'll also receive Intralipid. Those are equivalent to meats and veggies. You could live for years on them. Unfortunately, they're both toxic to your veins. Diflucan is also very nasty. The PICC line will go right into your heart, bypassing all those delicate veins. There's such a flood of blood in there that everything we put in will immediately get diluted and therefore be safe for your blood vessels from then on."

"You're putting a tube into my heart?" I asked in disbelief.

"Yes, this little tube." She wiggled a thin, floppy blue piece of plastic tubing. "It will go into your arm, across your chest, then all the way down into the old superior vena cava and say 'hello, baby' to your tricuspid valve." As she explained the procedure, she manipulated the thin blue tube as if it was a puppet, making me laugh.

"Will I feel it inside?" I asked worriedly, imagining that it would tickle flopping around inside my heart.

"Fortunately, there aren't any nerves in that area, at least not the feeling kind." She hummed as she picked up some things from her cart, then she turned and draped a sterile paper-like blue sheet over me. "I need to put one of these down for the blood spatter—it's a real mess putting a PICC in." My eyes widened. "Just kidding, honey, this isn't a surgical procedure, but we need to keep clean. Wouldn't want you to get any infections in your condition, would we?"

"You're funny, but I think I've already got that covered," It was nice to hear humor. Most things, in fact, everything about me had been purely business for a while, *at least since Dr. Bonjani was my pee cheerleader*. She retrieved a pair of scissors, cut a hole in the sheet, and placed it over my arm. She taped around the hole so that, in the end, it looked like a circle of skin unattached to anything. It didn't seem like my arm when I looked at it. Next, she turned on a machine attached to her cart.

"All right, I'm going to check out your lovely veins and see if we can't find a good one to poke." With that, she applied some cold jelly to my arm and began to move an ultrasonic wand against my skin. As she observed the instrument's display, several thick, noodle-like veins became apparent. "Ah, there's a real beauty. You get the prize for best vein of the day. Of course, you're my first vein of the day. Now, I'm going to introduce a very sharp needle into your arm. I'll watch the needle with my ultrasound to make sure I poke it in the center of a big, fat vein. It will sting a bit. After that I'll feed a wire into your vein."

I winced as a needle broke my skin and felt pressure as it bit into the vein, but I noticed nothing as she snaked the wire through the needle tip into the vein. "There, that looks marvelous," she said, pulling her wand away. I looked down and noticed a piece of wire sticking into the air from my arm. It vibrated like a spring with the slightest movement of my arm. A few drops of blood trickled away from it, and were promptly absorbed by the sterile paper cover.

Donna turned the ultrasound off and wiped the gel up. "How are you doing?"

"Hanging in there, what's next?"

"I'm going to numb you with some Lidocaine." She pulled out the "big gun," an enormous needle used for Lidocaine. "This is going to feel like a bee sting, and then it will burn, but not for long."

"Ouch." It hurt, but the pain quickly subsided.

"Are you still with me?"

"Yeah."

"Good. You might want to turn your head away for a minute. I have to cut you with a scalpel to enlarge the site for the inducer. After that, I'll slide the inducer down the wire and press through the vein with it. Then we'll remove the wire and feed the catheter through the inducer and into your heart."

"OK. You just do your job and I'll try not to think about it." I didn't feel the incisions at all, but felt the pop when the inducer broke through my skin, and again when it penetrated my vein.

"Pops are good. You have tough skin and veins. Of course, you're just a young pup, so I guess that's to be expected."

"Hey, when you're done here, can you come back to my room and make me laugh all day?" I chuckled.

"I would, honey, but you know how it goes. I have so many other people to save. OK, we're on the home stretch." She set her measuring tape on the sterile paper and held the blue tube near it. "That was a close guess," she said as she snipped about an inch and a half off it.

"When we're done, can I have that little piece you cut off? This has been very fascinating, and it will help me remember you."

"Sure," she said with a wink and set the small piece aside. "Now I'm going to remove the wire and feed this tube in, but before I do, I want you to turn your head and tuck your chin on your shoulder. It could easily go up your jugular vein instead of down into your heart. Holding your head like that closes off the jugular a bit and discourages the tube from going up that way."

I immediately did as she requested. "OK, here goes...got it. Now I'll flush the PICC with saline. Look forward while I inject it into the tube." She connected a big syringe filled with clear saline solution to a connector on the end of the blue tube. "All right, tell me if you feel any coldness in your neck or hear a popping sound in your left ear. That would mean that the tube went up the wrong way, up your jugular. Here goes...nothing?"

I didn't hear or feel anything. "Nope."

"Then let's get you cleaned up and out of here." She cleaned the PICC insertion area; dressed and bandaged the wound with a clear, skin-tight bandage; stabilized the line with an adhesive mount; and taped down a second PICC line that split off from the first at a joint. After that, the paper sheet came off. "That's it, young man. I just need to get you off for an X-ray to make sure everything is in the right spot, and then you're on your way. Oh, one more thing, Mr. Dickson," she paused, looking at me sternly. I had no idea what she was about to do, which was the great thing about her. She reached toward me, holding the little blue piece of PICC line. "I don't know why on earth you want this, but here it is."

I smiled and took it from her, clutching it in my hand. "I have a treasure box at home with weird things that only have meaning to me, like the clamps that held my daughters' umbilical cords while I cut them at their birth. I'm going to put it in there."

"That's a new one. Well, it's been great, Mr. Dickson. I hope you recover soon."

"Me too."

"The technician will be here shortly to take a chest X-ray. I'll check it, and if everything looks good, we'll send you back to your room."

She patted me on the arm and smiled, then took her cart and disappeared through the curtains again, pulling them closed behind her. Everything went well with the X-ray, and a transporter wheeled me back to my room. I placed the piece of PICC tube on the cart next to my bed and kept a close eye on it until I could figure out a better place to keep it. Ultimately, it did end up in my treasure box.

Shortly after my return, a new bag appeared on my IV rack: Diflucan. As soon as the Diflucan made its way through my PICC and into my heart, a burning filled my chest. A battle for my life raged inside me, and I hoped that the infectious disease specialist made the right choice.

Sometime later two additional bags appeared on my IV rack: a small one filled with white Intralipid and a larger one with yellowish TPN. Another pump controlled the flow of nutrition, and two tubes ran from the pump to my PICC line. I looked forward to my first meal in over a week. I didn't know it at the time, but I lost over twenty pounds, and to everyone who knew me, I looked like death. When the fluids rushed into my heart, the feeling was overwhelming, like a sugar rush times ten. My whole body flushed as nutrition arrived almost instantaneously to every cell. From that day forth, I referred to the bags as my meats and veggies. They would be my constant companions until my bowels began to function again.

One final matter of business remained. I reached for the push button that I insisted they disconnect and pressed it every six minutes until the pain in my behind went away. Soon, I slept like a baby.

***

I opened my eyes as morning light crept around my curtains the next day. *I'm alive!* I tried to fill my lungs with air, and they filled effortlessly. *I can breathe!* I felt rested, had no pain—everything looked good except for my belly: distended beyond belief. *How can I live with my intestines shut off?* When I asked the nurse when they would turn on, she said, "It's up to God whether or not your intestines turn on again and when. If everything goes well, it could take anywhere from two to nine days." In the meantime, they gave me Protonix, a proton pump inhibitor, to control gastric acid secretion. Without food in my stomach, it helped to prevent stomach acid from digesting my insides.

Aside from Beth, who visited several times every day, few other people visited before my surgery. Not because no one wanted to see me, I reminded everyone of how fragile life is: I was too close to the edge. Once word spread of how bad I looked, everyone relied on Beth to keep them informed. It was actually fortunate; I was too busy fighting for my life to entertain them. After my lungs cleared and I received three square meals a day through my PICC, I really perked up. After that, more friends and relatives visited. People gave me blessings and gifts or just sat and talked with me. Since my daughter Kaitlin was old enough to drive, she and her younger sister, Hailey, even stopped by several times. I enjoyed seeing everyone, knowing that I was on the mend, and feeling much better. The only problem remaining was my ever-growing abdomen.

I finally had enough and called the nurse. Since I felt better, I began to learn everyone's name, which was difficult for me with all the turmoil and my medical condition in previous days. That morning, Maggie, my favorite nurse, responded. Maggie was like a mother to me. In looks and manner, she reminded me much of Beth: always concerned for me and dedicated to solving problems.

"What's the matter?" Maggie asked as she entered the room.

"Is there something we can do about this?" I asked, pointing to my big belly.

"I don't know if it would help or not, but I can talk to the doctor about inserting an NG tube and see if it will drain some fluid." She explained that an NG tube would go up my nose, down my throat, and all the way through my esophagus into my stomach, allowing any fluid trapped there to escape.

"Let's do it."

Maggie left and returned a while later with tubing that was larger and harder than I envisioned. "You still want to do this?" she asked. I didn't know if that was a question or a challenge, but envisioned a gallon of liquid gushing out and the instant relief it would bring, exactly like when they put the catheter in.

"Yes." I exclaimed. With that, she lubed up the tubing and slid the gooey thing up my nose. *That was tolerable.* Then it rounded the curve somewhere behind my eyes. *That was very weird.*

"Are you OK?"

"Yeah."

"I need you to swallow for me, and don't stop until I tell you to." With that, she drove the tube home. When the slimy thing slid past the back of my throat, it felt awful. I followed Maggie's orders and kept swallowing, but it took everything I had to not vomit the tube out. "OK, you can stop swallowing, it's in." It felt huge and hard, like a jumbo pencil lodged in my throat. It hurt and nothing I did provided any relief.

Just then I felt warmth as the contents of my stomach rose, went somewhere behind my eyes, and then out my nose. I looked cross-eyed at the green liquid flowing through the tube, anticipating the relief I would feel when my belly deflated. Maggie had connected a bag to the end of the tube and it was slowly filling. In no time it stopped, after only draining a few ounces.

What? That's it? All that trouble for that? "Can I take it out?" I begged.

"No, let's leave it in for today and see what happens. Besides, the doctor has to approve taking it out."

"Agggh,"

"Sorry,"

That was the last bad thing to happen to me at Desert Hope, aside from waiting for sounds of life from my belly. It was April 23. My insides had been quiet since April 16. On the different shifts, nurses Maggie, Joan, and Yasmine arrived with their stethoscopes to listen to my belly, smiling as they came in and shaking their heads as they left. Yasmine gave me a body wash, which felt very nice after all that had transpired, and I'm sure that I desperately needed it. Joan suggested walking to stimulate my bowels to work. So walk I did.

I'd like to think that I burned holes in the carpet of my tiny route around my wing, but the truth is that I staggered like the sick man I was—inches from death's door, my cheeks hollowed from weight loss, mostly from starvation, but a little from the section of colon removed. With my sickly colored bags of fluids and all my contraptions and hoses, I was certain to scare off any children in my path. The tube of vile green fluid dangling from my nostril alone would be enough to send them screaming.

My lack of strength limited me to a few passes around the hallway at a time. It was difficult pushing the heavy rack of fluids and pumps, which operated off backup batteries as I walked, half of them beeping in complaint from want of wall power. Even the MJP alarm gave an occasional chirp.

Nothing worked to switch my insides back on, so I resorted to desperate measures: praying. Prayer is something that doesn't come easily to me. I've always felt there was a cost for anything I received through prayer. But what else could I do? That night, as I lay on my back listening to the late-night sounds of Desert Hope, I closed my eyes and prayed: *God, please turn my bowels back on, Amen.* Then I picked up the large remote by my side and pressed the button to turn off my light.

The next morning was Easter, April 24. I lay in bed wondering if the kids were running around in their pajamas frantically searching for hidden plastic Easter eggs full of candy at that very moment. I knew it was true—my sickness wouldn't get in the way of that tradition. As I lay there swirling my hands around my belly, I realized why pregnant women did it all the time: not only is it particularly soothing, it's hard to ignore such a prominent feature. Just then, Maggie arrived with her stethoscope. It was no mystery what her intentions were. I cleared everything off my big belly to make way.

"Happy Easter," she said.

"Happy Easter to you, too. How are you today?"

"Wonderful. Let's see how your tummy's doing." I jumped a little as the cool stethoscope touched my skin. She listened, moved it a little, and listened some more. Finally, a big smile spread across her face. "You've got a real party going on in there today."

"Hallelujah!" I yelled. God had answered my prayer. Things happened quickly after that. The first thing to go was the catheter. I can imagine that many people might wince at the concept of catheters. I can tell you that as long as they use generous amounts of lubricant, having one inserted isn't a big deal. On the other hand, removing it is a different story: all that nice lubricant dries up over time and you have no choice but to tough it out. Upon deflation of the saline bulb inside my bladder, Maggie gave a swift pull on the catheter. A few moments of pain later, it was over. The good news: that part of my body worked just fine again.

Next came one of the best experiences I've ever had: removing the NG tube so that I could swallow better things. When Maggie pulled that hose out through my nose in one fell swoop, I swear it was like having an orgasm. I can't recall many things that felt better in my life.

Then it was time to eat. I could hardly wait to eat and drink again after ten days of being unable to do so. At first, they gave me clear liquids: beef broth and Jell-O. I never realized just how wonderful beef broth and Jell-O could be until that day. When that hot, salty, beefy broth passed my lips, every salivary gland in my mouth leapt into action as if I'd eaten a lemon. As the broth met my tongue, my taste buds let out a mighty scream of joy. That broth was pure heaven, but the cool cherry Jell-O with its sweet, fruity taste and comforting texture was the real icing on the cake. Nothing could be a more pleasing contrast to the hot beef broth. Sometime later, I tried regular food but vomited it back up and had to continue with clear liquids. It was a stop-and-go process teaching my insides their old job, but I soon ate a regular meal again.

After that, the IV bags disappeared one by one until there was nothing left beeping and whirring beside my bed. I was down to one last tube that I didn't even recollect—my Jackson-Pratt drain.

The Jackson-Pratt drain removed blood, puss, and other fluids from inside my body around the area of my surgery. It consisted of a tiny, clear plastic squeeze bulb on one end, a drainage tube, and a foam drain on the other end. The surgeon placed the foam drain in my abdomen at the end of surgery before suturing and stapling me closed. A tube exited through a small incision on the lower left side of my belly. He then squeezed the bulb to create suction and attached it to the end of the hose to pull undesirable fluids from the wound area through the foam drain, and into the bulb. Nurses constantly monitored color and quantity of fluid to ensure everything was OK at the surgical site.

It was time to take out the Jackson-Pratt drain. There is no science to doing so—you just remove the bandages around the incision and pull it out. However, over time the drain adhered to the tissues in my body, making it difficult to remove. Maggie made a vain attempt, and then called for someone more experienced. Another nurse, Denise, made a go of it next. She likewise failed to make headway.

"I'll get Mark," Denise said. "He can always get these out." She left the room and returned with a male nurse: a thin young man of average height with tousled sandy hair and light green scrubs. I was dubious that he'd meet with better success.

"Hi, I'm Mark," he announced.

"I'm Ken. So you're the king of drain removal, huh?"

"Well, there hasn't been one yet that I couldn't remove. Let me take a look."

He cleared the nurses out of the way and began fussing with it, tugging firmly to no avail. He tried twisting it and pulling harder, still without results.

What he did next shocked me tremendously. I have a hard time believing that it's in any medical book in the world. He put his foot on the side of the bed, grabbed onto the tube with both hands, and instructed me to, "Hang on to something." With that, he gave a mighty pull, and it felt as if my entire insides ripped out.

"Jeeeesus!" I screamed at the sudden burst of fire across my abdomen when the drain tore free of all its connections. Mark stumbled backward and the soggy drain nearly whacked Maggie in the head as it flew by. A moment of strained silence followed, and then, unable to hold back, we all burst into laughter. It was such an outrageous scene that none of us could help it. That night was my last at Desert Hope. I was finally myself again, free from all the hoses and contraptions and working as good as new. My sleep that night was one of silence and comfort.

Chapter 5

HOME AGAIN

They released me from Desert Hope on April 25. I was excited to be well again and able to go home. Beth came to pick me up and walked beside my wheelchair as the patient transport person wheeled me from my room. I waved good-bye to Maggie, Denise, and Mark at the nurses' station as we passed them, and then I rode in the public elevator for the first time ever. It was strange to go down an elevator I never came up. As I crossed the huge entryway near the exit, I looked up three stories to the steel and glass dome meant to mimic that of a cathedral. It looked much grander from this angle than from the 202. Having entered through the emergency entrance, everything I experienced was brand new, making my exit seem all the more special.

Once outside, Beth left me at the entrance with the patient transport person while she retrieved the van. Before me was a grand circular drive comprised of concrete and paving stones. Beyond that was a beautiful garden with a water feature built from several tall, irregularly cut granite stones. Water flowed over their surfaces from hidden plumbing. Behind, the garden continued to the hospital exit, with date palms lining its length on both sides. The exit beckoned and I couldn't wait to drive through and past it.

After being in the hospital for twelve days, it was immensely freeing being outside again, totally separated from the people, machines, sights, and sounds of the hospital, which over time became a part of me. However, it also made me feel naked without them. I had a strange yet hopeful feeling that perhaps I would do just fine on my own, that my job would be waiting, the kids would remember me as I was before I got sick, and my pets would still recognize me.

I didn't want people to think I was fragile glass and that they needed to protect me, so when Beth approached, I pushed myself up from my wheelchair and stepped away from it. Those first few steps with no help and without machines or tubing connected to me were more liberating than anything I could imagine. I stood straight and strong, and then turned back to look at the hospital that was my home for what felt like an eternity. I would never see it the same way again. Instead of simply a building next to the freeway that I gave no consideration whenever I passed, it would now be an indelible part of the story of my life. As we drove home on the 202, I leaned forward in the passenger seat of the van and watched Desert Hope shrink until it blended in with everything else.

Arizona was never my dream place to live, or Beth's. I moved to Phoenix to escape painful memories of a divorce and to pursue a new career. Beth followed, but her story is that she came for a job as well. I couldn't believe that was twenty-one years ago when we'd barely started dating. Back then, I never imagined that we'd marry and have a home and a family together. You'd think the worst thing about Phoenix is the summer heat. It's responsible for three of every four people moving here eventually leaving. Personally, I think the dust storms, or haboobs, are the worst. They rise from the desert and then roll like gargantuan, mile-high tumbleweeds across the city, leaving a coating of dirt everywhere. Just when you've cleaned up from one, another one blows through. Though Phoenix was never our top choice, we learned to accept the bad with the good, and surprisingly, we've lived here longer than anywhere else.

I've come to love many things about Phoenix: firstly, it's the home of our friends or, I should say, my wife and children's friends.

With many hobbies, I have few friends of my own. Like a parasite, I feed off their friendships. Fortunately, unlike me, they attract many quality friends. The kids' friends visit our home so often that some of them seem like my own children. Even dogs stop in for a visit. We've had as many as nine dogs in our home at once.

I love our comfortable home. Beth is big on making it that way. Through dedication, she keeps everything clean and in its place—as much as is humanly possible with two teenagers and their friends routinely sabotaging her efforts. She decorates inside the house for every holiday, and when the holiday ends, many photos of the family and interesting interim knickknacks replace decorations.

Then, there are the pet rats. I feel so sorry for them because gruesome tumors frequently shorten their already short lives. Scientists intentionally genetically altered domestic rats to be susceptible to cancer for our own selfish needs. They are the sweetest animals, though. We love our rats so much that they stay in the family room with their cage right behind the sofa where they can see and be part of everything going on. They frequently scamper around on the sofa with us, using our legs for ramps to the coffee table or the love seat next to it. When we let them out, before exploring, they always come to us first to say hello, licking our ear lobes like dogs with their tiny tongues, or tickling our cheeks with their long whiskers. They often snuggle under our arms or sit on our laps and groom themselves.

There are other things about home: the convenience store clerk with short black hair who always has a kind word; the mom-and-pop neighborhood hardware store run by the oldest people I know, which holds its own against the big retail chains only because those old-timers can tell you how to fix anything. Not to mention my favorite ice cream shop, Chinese restaurant, gas station, movie theater, and knowing the quickest routes to get to them. It's comforting knowing all the speed limits, where speed bumps and school zones are located, and what traffic is like at different times of the day. My favorite thing is to be with my family inside my home or tinkering on a project in the garage. I'm not much of a yardman, much to Beth's chagrin. All these things make my home what it is. I was so happy to be back to enjoy it.

After returning home, no one pampered me or treated me like an invalid; they treated me like me, which was exactly what I needed. I was eager to resume a normal life. I had no problems getting around, but was very weak, having lost much of my former strength. I slept well, but could only sleep on my back due to the staples on my belly. I couldn't imagine what they looked like and hadn't yet built enough nerve to look at them.

Several days later, my incision ached. It was time to remove the bandage that had remained on my belly since my surgery. I gently peeled off the tape holding it in place, leaving a rectangle of glue. For the first time, I saw the ten-inch zipper on my belly. It was ragged, red, and angry looking. Halos of inflammation surrounded each staple puncture. It was clear that I needed to take action. I showered in the hospital a few times, wrapping myself in plastic wrap to protect my bandages, IVs, and PICC, but this was the first time I showered without protection. The warm water soothed the long incision. I patted it with a soapy sponge to clean it as best I could, which seemed to ease the irritation. I became expert at rebandaging myself, and stayed on top of the health of my incision from then on.

I couldn't wear my old clothes yet, partly because I was so thin that half of them fell off, but mostly because much of the incision was below the beltline. It was too uncomfortable and probably unsafe to wear regular pants. I had to find a way to protect it. Beth found me some black pants that were like pajamas. That still didn't solve the problem but some ingenuity did. To prevent anything from touching the incision, I placed two pairs of socks inside the elastic waistband of my new pants, one on either side of the incision. I referred to them jokingly as my six-shooters.

Chapter 6

BAD SLEEP

After only a week, I felt stellar. On May 4, my surgeon, Dr. Demarco, gave me his stamp of approval to return to work. I was on short-term leave, but with four job losses in five years due to three layoffs and a company going out of business, I didn't want to give any reason for my new employer to let me go. On May 9, I returned to work. Initially, everyone greeted me excitedly, asking many questions, but things quickly settled into familiar routines.

Apparently, no one noticed my odd pants or the telltale lumps from my six-shooters. What they particularly noticed was my weight loss. I can't imagine seeing someone and then seeing him or her again only a few weeks later nearly twenty-five pounds lighter. As the week continued, work seemed progressively easier, and I quickly caught up. By the end of the week, I exhibited so much energy and enthusiasm that fellow employees wondered if I was OK. "Of course I'm OK. I feel fantastic," I responded. Concern grew, and unbeknownst to me, word got back to Beth. Of course, she noticed things, too: I was talking more rapidly and sleeping less. I was abuzz with ideas and filled with vigor.

I slept spottily through May 11. By May 12, sleep was impossible. Overwhelmed, my racing mind collapsed, reduced from its recent brilliance to a barely flickering candle. Increasingly scatterbrained and incapable of functioning as an engineer, I left work early on May 13, unsure when I'd return. The next six days seemed the longest of my life.

Attempting to function without sleep was unimaginable. With a freshly repaired colon, I was overly cautious with medication, but on May 16, I took a Dramamine, two Benadryl and drank two mugs of Sleepytime Tea over the period of an hour and a half in a desperate attempt to induce sleep. From those I managed only three hours of slumber. Normally, any single one of those would knock me out for the night. Fearing overdose, I refrained from trying anything else.

Beth scheduled an emergency appointment with Dr. Demarco to discuss my dilemma on May 17. Aside from the few hours the day before, I went five days straight without sleep and several more with only a few hours of sleep. We met with him at his Scottsdale office, which was a lengthy drive for us. As we spoke, he was very standoffish and reluctant to help. He stated that I was sound from a surgical standpoint and would have to see a general practitioner for my sleep issues. We left no better off than when we'd arrived.

On the drive home, Beth and I were both astonished that a medical doctor would turn his own patient, clearly in a crisis, away. There must be something within his power: someone to whom he could refer me, or somewhere he could admit me for help. We surmised that he feared legal repercussions or that he suspected mental health issues and wanted no part of that.

Later that afternoon I took my daughter to the dentist's office for a routine teeth cleaning. I traveled the route regularly for well over ten years and knew it by heart. By then, my mind was so impaired that during the two-mile trip to the dentist's office, I missed two turns. Frustrated, I asked my daughter to navigate for me. The simple act of driving required my full concentration. I was unable to even carry on a conversation and hope to make it to my destination.

Before that day, I behaved like someone on amphetamines. Now, burned out from whatever coursed through me, I was a shell of my former self. While I waited for the dentist to finish, that changed in an instant. The fog that enshrouded my brain vaporized and I was once again whole. To test that conviction, I attempted a conversation with the receptionist—something that was impossible only minutes earlier. We conversed comfortably for over fifteen minutes until my daughter returned from her teeth cleaning. On the way home, I further evaluated my abilities by executing a random and convoluted route, speaking with my daughter the entire time. I easily drove and conversed, confident of my exact location at every turn. For a brief moment, my life seemed normal once again.

***

Recalling this incident later, I recognize it not as a return to normal but as my first brush with mania. It was so subtle that, even now, I cannot identify anything sacrificed for that brief moment of clarity. Indeed, there were no identifiable negative consequences whatsoever. The improvements I experienced, however, were not at all random; they were in direct response to my disabilities, everything I had difficulty with earlier was a breeze after I transitioned to that first level of mania.

***

Unfortunately, as the day wore on, I found that I still couldn't sleep. That night, knowing that it was imperative that I somehow rest my brain, I took desperate action: I lay perfectly still on my back with my hands crossed over my chest and my eyes closed. I focused on an imaginary black spot in my mind, inhaled slowly, exhaled more slowly, and paused before repeating. Beth taught me the breathing technique just that evening. In no time, I was able to drop my heart rate by twenty beats per minute. I was confident the technique would induce sleep or prove the equivalent of it, providing the rest my brain desperately needed.

I lay immobile and continued the practice for four hours straight, nearly driving myself insane. I can imagine it was the equivalent of placing me in an isolation tank. As dawn approached on May 18, I bolted from bed like cornered prey, pacing and growling as imaginary captors closed in for the kill. My world compressed rapidly, and the heat of that compression reached a boiling point. I rushed downstairs and outside to breathe, to cool, but met no relief. Beth came to my rescue, and I tried to explain that something was wrong, that something bad was going to happen. "We need to go to the ER," was all that she said.

Part 2

CHAOS

Chapter 7

PINECREST

Soon, we retraced the route to the ER, the same one at Desert Hope where everything began. Instead of experiencing a déjà vu moment when I arrived, I was beyond recognizing it at all. I followed Beth blindly, allowing her to deal with the paperwork. Meanwhile, I paced, my agitation growing by the minute. They quickly admitted me and directed me to a bed. They must have thought me a mad man. I couldn't stay still; every jazzed-up nerve in my body felt ready to self-destruct.

Suddenly, I yawned. It was strange to yawn when it was impossible to sleep. I couldn't help but notice, certain that it foretold danger. Beth's cell phone rang and she walked away to take the call. "Don't go," I pleaded.

"I have to. A therapist is taking over for me at a meeting and he's in a panic. He already called several times."

At that very moment, something rushed over me like the enveloping darkness that precedes a tornado. I felt as if my soul left me, leaving a hollow shell. I slumped lifelessly into the bed. Frightened, Beth called out, "Ken? Ken?" I could no longer reply, my lips, tongue, and vocal chords were paralyzed. My eyes still saw, my ears still heard, but all muscle tension melted away and I lay perfectly still on the bed. I wondered if I was dead and experiencing the last fleeting moments of consciousness.

Though it was only for a short time, it seemed an eternity before I felt the first spark of life return. Then electric sensations raced from my torso through my extremities, like a thousand pins piercing my flesh. As my facial muscles reanimated, they automatically contorted from the pain. My eyes squeezed tightly shut and my teeth gritted. As my hands returned from the dead, they clenched into fists of agony. Finally, the sensations faded and my body once more was my own.

Meanwhile Beth managed to attract the attention of the ER nurse. I received an immediate X-ray of my chest and a CAT scan of my head. Neither showed anything unusual. The ER nurse left and shortly afterward, a social worker arrived to speak with us. She informed us that they were going to send me to Pinecrest where they could better address my problems.

"Will I be able to get some sleep there?" I asked in desperation.

"Yes," she answered. I was elated about the prospect of help. I had no idea what or where Pinecrest was, but if they could help me sleep, that's where I wanted to go.

Before I knew it, I was saying good-bye to Beth. A paramedic helped me from my bed onto a waiting gurney, which bumped down an outside ramp to an ambulance shortly thereafter. As the ambulance left, my excitement grew over the possibility of finally sleeping. The paramedic questioned me along the way, taking copious notes on his indestructible Panasonic industrial laptop. Suddenly, I yawned and seconds later yawned again. Fear overtook me as I remembered that was how the strange seizure started earlier.

I warned the paramedic that something would happen. I don't know if he heard me: things progressed much faster than I expected. This time the shapeless darkness coalesced into a monstrous form, that reached into me and snatched my life in a suffocating grasp. My puppet strings went slack, and my limbs fell lifeless once more. Soulless eyes watched me as countless seconds ticked away, increasing the potential of my suffering with each tick. When confident that my pain would be unbearable, the monster released his grasp. Life rushed back into me, only this time, the pain was magnitudes worse: a thousand bees stung me from my torso to my extremities. I gasped in despair as I awaited relief, flexing my arms, legs, feet, and hands to speed the process, but the pain was unrelenting.

We arrived at Pinecrest and the paramedics rolled my gurney through the main entrance, helped me from it, and then shockingly left me standing alone while they filled out paperwork at the receptionist's desk. With my muscles still partially numb and in terrible pain, I could barely stand. While swaying, staggering, and trying not to fall, I continued to flex my extremities to ease the pain.

Beth followed the ambulance, and by the time she arrived at the reception area, the paramedics were on their way out the door. My pain finally subsided, but left me with the memory of two seizures—the second much worse than the first. I knew it was only a matter of time before another started, and I dreaded how painful and debilitating that one would be. I feared for my life.

"I need something to help me sleep right away," I insisted to Beth. An ominous feeling overtook me, and I knew that danger was imminent. Beth entered a side room where a social worker asked her questions and filled out forms. "Can we skip the paperwork? Can someone help me?" I pleaded anxiously. It seemed that no one was sympathetic to my desperate plight.

I didn't know it then, but at Pinecrest, I was no longer an emergency room patient; I was simply one more mentally ill person to whom no one paid much attention. Pinecrest was a psychiatric care facility. There, they witnessed people like me acting out like clockwork. I was a television rerun that everyone had seen a hundred times.

I was outraged at how long it took to fill out the forms. In short order, time for me ran out once again—the warning signs multiplied until there was no doubt of my impending doom. My life would change in moments without quick thinking.

"Beth, I need help right now!" I insisted. The monster came for me, but with memories of the paralysis and pain still fresh in my mind, I refused to go without a fight. A plan formed in my mind as his heavy footsteps approached. He was less of a specter and more real with each visit, and this time, I could almost feel his hot breath as he lunged for me. The plan went into effect: I ducked and dodged; I avoided his grasp any and every way I could. I never rested, never sat, or stood still for fear of becoming his easy prey. I never thought about or repeated the same action long enough for him to decipher the pattern. I paced and I chatted with people in the lobby, never quite able to finish a conversation before I had to change tactics or "change up" as I called it. One by one, I scared them all away with my erratic behavior. I grimaced and strained my muscles in the corner of the room, trying to beat the monster by sheer brute strength. I walked into the side room and interrupted the paperwork to have Beth play patty-cake with me or put ice on my neck.

Though I tried to explain to Beth what was happening, it was incomprehensible to her. No rational person could understand what I was going through. It meant so much to me that she would do the things I requested. It saved my life, from my perspective. Hours after the paramedics dropped me off, the paperwork was finally finished, and all that remained was for me to sign it. I had no idea what I was signing, nor did I care. Stopping the monster and sleeping were my only priorities. With a few quick strokes of the pen, I qualified myself to enter Pinecrest and face whatever awaited me there.

***

Beth's journal, May 18, 2011:

Ken struggled to sleep all night. He complained frequently of cramps in his arches. In the early morning, he got up and plugged in my hot wax machine (which I use for softening my very dry hands). When the wax melted, he dipped his feet into the hot liquid one at a time. Once the wax hardened, he pulled thick white athletic socks over the warm wax on his feet to hold the heat in. That eased the cramping, but he still could not sleep. When I awoke, I saw Ken pacing outside. He was very agitated. He kept repeating that something was wrong; something bad was going to happen. As soon as the girls left for school, I took him to the Desert Hope ER.

The triage doctor at the ER noted Ken as being hypomanic. Shortly after arrival, Ken had some kind of seizure. He was talking to me from the emergency room bed when suddenly his head dropped to his chest and he became unresponsive. I yelled for help, and they rushed him out of the ER for a CAT scan and X-ray, both of which came up negative. The doctor never returned to discuss Ken's case. Instead, a social worker appeared and recommended transferring Ken to Pinecrest, a behavioral health facility where they would manage his sleep deprivation and monitor his postsurgical health. I asked that they instead admit him to Desert Hope, but she said that he didn't qualify medically.

They transferred Ken to Pinecrest by ambulance. When he arrived, he reported that he had another seizure in the ambulance. The admission wait at Pinecrest was excruciatingly long. Ken remained very agitated and in constant motion. His behavior was very odd. He begged me to walk with him, play patty-cake, rub his neck with ice cubes, etc. When we finally met with an admissions person, she told me that Ken's treatment at the facility would primarily address his insomnia. Ken wasn't considered mentally ill when he was admitted. He signed all the necessary paperwork to allow the facility to release information to me and allow staff to discuss treatment.

***

At 4:15 p.m., they escorted me into Pinecrest. A young man offered me a white pill in a paper cup and a small cup of water to wash it down.

"What's this?" I asked.

"It's Ativan. It will help you sleep."

I swallowed the pill and washed it down without further questions. In no time, the medication took hold and the monster withdrew. The man showed me to a bed: a three-inch-thick, vinyl-covered foam pad perched on top of a wooden frame with an uncomfortable pillow, some sheets, and a blanket. I quickly lay on the bed. It was the worst bed I ever encountered, but at that moment, it felt like heaven. I pulled the thin blanket around me and finally slept as if I hadn't in a lifetime.

***

"Mr. Dickson," a voice called out faintly. "Mr. Dickson...," it repeated more insistently. I tried opening my eyes. They refused my efforts, begging me to let them remain closed. However, behind those eyelids I was fully awake, my perfect sleep destroyed. I forced an eye open and peered at my watch. An hour and a half had passed since I took the Ativan. I sighed, rolled over, and took stock of my tormentor. He was of small stature with a full head of black curly hair, a close-trimmed beard, and brown eyes staring through dark, plastic-rimmed glasses. His overly sincere grin spread widely across a squat, chubby-cheeked face.

"Hello, Mr. Dickson, I'm Dr. Alverez. I want to ask you a few questions."

"I was dead asleep. I haven't slept for nearly a week, and you woke me. Why did you do that?" I asked in frustration. He ignored my question and replaced it with one of his own.

"Have you ever wanted to kill yourself?"

"No."

"Have you ever wanted to kill anyone else?"

"No."

"Have you ever had racing thoughts?"

"Well, I never really thought about it. I guess not."

"Have you ever been depressed?"

"No. I never get depressed."

The questions continued relentlessly. I answered them to my best ability, but I don't actually remember much of how I responded. I just wanted to finish and go back to sleep before the drug wore off. Before Dr. Alvarez left, he offered me a new pill, Seroquel. I accepted it without question, chased it down with water, then rolled over in bed, closed my eyes, and thankfully succumbed once more.

Two hours later, the door to my room opened and another man called my name. He produced yet another pill for me, Restoril. I swallowed it without making a scene and went back to sleep. I managed a few more hours of sleep after that before fully waking. Though my mind revved up again, my body remained numb and sluggish from the drugs. I lay in bed for a time, waiting for my body to catch up to my mind, and then investigated my new home. I already knew that I had a roommate: his snoring helped terminate my drugged sleep. I couldn't see him in the dark, but I could make out his form in the sliver of light that crept under our room door. He was tall, thin, and had the raspy snore of a lifetime smoker.

I rose from my bed and walked to where I expected the bathroom to be. I guessed correctly. Yawning, I took care of business, washed my hands, and splashed water on my face. I searched for a towel finding only a soiled one hanging on a hook behind the door. After drying my hands and face with my T-shirt, I made a mental note to locate clean linen later. Instead of returning to bed, I cracked the room door and peered out. It was quiet. I couldn't see or hear anyone, so I stepped out.

I anticipated that exploring my surroundings might take some time, but quarters were tight in this section of Pinecrest. The unit was an H shape with rooms on the outside of both the "legs" and "arms" of the H. I estimated from the number of rooms that there must be twenty patients with two to a room. Above the crossbar of the H sat the staff office, a large room with a single door. In front of the door stood ten feet of open area filled with roll-around chairs. A low counter filled with computer monitors, keyboards, phones, and printers surrounded the open area with a high counter surface outside that to separate patients from staff. Below the cross bar of the H, a partially glassed-in room contained chairs and a flat screen TV high up in a corner. A corded touch-tone phone hung on the outside wall of that room. The late-night staff seemed small; I noticed only two people working at the low counter. They appeared uninterested in me. I walked toward them, leaned on the high counter, and said "Hi."

"Please step away from the counter," one of them said without looking at me. I backed a foot or so away, and they continued working.

They aren't very friendly, but at least they don't mind me walking around.

At the tips of the arms of the H, were two sets of unmarked steel doors. At the tips of the legs of the H were similar doors marked Emergency Exit. All the room doors were heavy, solid wood with a thick oak veneer. The walls were painted light sand and the baseboards were a darker sand color. The flooring was an oak-like wood laminate.

That was it. That was my new home. I walked for a while longer and then sat on a chair outside the glassed-in room across from the staff's counter. The counter was so high they couldn't see me. Occasionally, one or the other staff member bobbed up to see what I was doing. I amused myself trying to guess which one would bob next.

I returned to my room and lay in bed again. To pass the time, I reflected on the many odd things happening to me but could make no sense of them. Before long, morning light crept through the room window and the world of Pinecrest awakened. My roommate let out one last, harsh snore, sat up in bed, coughed heartily, and rubbed his eyes.

"Hi, neighbor," I said.

"Uh, hi," he replied in a gruff smoker's voice. I sat up and stretched. My back cracked. I rotated my head. My neck cracked as well. That reminded me of my youngest daughter, Hailey, who can crack any joint loudly at whim.

"I'm Ken. I just arrived last night."

"I'm Ray. Nice to meet you. What are you in here for?"

"I can't sleep. I started having some kind of seizures, so they sent me here. They gave me pills last night and I finally got my first rest in nearly a week, and guess what? Some doctor woke me up right in the middle of it with a bunch of questions."

"That sounds par for the course. Good luck getting sleep in this place; there's always some kind of ruckus going on. Myself, I'm an alcoholic. I'm trying to get clean though. It's strange that they sent you to a psych unit for sleep. Aren't there sleep clinics or something for that?"

"What are you talking about? Isn't this a hospital?"

"Yeah, for whackos and addicts."

That confused me. I shouldn't be in a place like that, but if it helped me to sleep, I'd be better and back to normal life in no time.

As we continued our conversation, I learned that this wasn't the first time Ray tried to get clean. Unfortunately, his lifestyle was taking a toll on his brain. He could hardly remember from minute to minute. If I forgot something he said, there was no point worrying: we'd repeat the same conversation again in a few minutes.

Ray rose from bed and stretched. Like me, he wore street clothes. I noticed later that all of the patients at Pinecrest save one wore street clothes and from the look of it, they wore the same clothes every day. No one appeared to notice or care, even if the patients smelled atrocious. As far as I knew, there were no mandatory shower, hygiene, or laundry policies. No one informed me about anything when they admitted me; they simply threw me into the population and left me to fend for myself. I was not alone in this fate, but was perhaps the highest functioning patient there, and possibly the only one to wonder about it.

As Ray and I chatted, the doorknob unexpectedly rotated. The door creaked open, and a patient shuffled into the room. Unlike everyone else, he wore a hospital gown, which was so oversized that it dragged on the floor, its edge ragged and filthy where it touched. Soiled and faded, the rest of the gown hinted of a hard life. Hidden beneath the gown, the patient's feet sported equally discolored and threadbare formerly white socks that occasionally peeked out from under the gown when he moved. Most noticeably, the patient stank to high heaven. The door swung fully open, he stopped shuffling, and stood, squinty-eyed and grinning.

"Who is this?" I asked.

"Caaarrrlllos," the patient announced barely audible through thin, ventriloquist-like lips, one of a very few times I would ever hear him speak.

"It's time for breakfast." Ray announced. Apparently, he and Carlos connected at some primitive level and joined each other for breakfast. Perhaps Ray enjoyed talking without criticism, and Carlos liked to listen without having to respond. They could have a worse relationship, I supposed.

We left the room and headed toward the tip of the left arm of the H. There, PAs (psychiatric assistants) corralled the three of us and other patients into a pack by the steel security doors. I turned to Carlos and joked, "Hey Carlos, maybe they'll have huevos rancheros for breakfast. Would you like that?" He smiled and nodded.

The PAs opened the doors and herded us like cattle down a hallway. We turned into a cafeteria filled with small, square tables, each with a speckled, earth-toned Formica top supported by a black metal pedestal with four matching black metal feet protruding from it. Four Shaker-style oak chairs surrounded each table. Unlike the inside of our unit, matted and framed paintings hung on the walls that looked like stock selections from a retail craft store. I later realized that the paintings were hung only there because that's where family visited patients, and they wanted to give a good impression. Once everyone was inside, a PA locked the doors, turned, and stood guard in front of them.

As I fell into line with Ray to get breakfast at the food service area along half of one wall, Carlos disappeared. I knew that he couldn't go far, however, and shifted focus to breakfast. The kitchen staff for the food line was as crotchety as the PAs who escorted us to the cafeteria. With the passage of time, I discovered that everyone working at Pinecrest seemed miserable. I filled my tray remembering after the fact to get utensils and milk. It was quite a job convincing the mentally unstable patients to let me through the line to fetch those few items. They insisted that I should go to the end of the line, but I persisted and they grudgingly gave way.

As I joined Ray at a table, I noticed Carlos shuffling around the cafeteria with an apple in his hand. I watched him curiously as Ray and I ate and talked. Ray's story, if it were true, was that he was once a lawyer. He hoped to return to the legal profession once he got a handle on his drinking. If Ray offered me a business card, I would accept it politely, and later toss it in the nearest wastebasket. He was a likable man, but not a lawyer I would hire. He shared details of his family and his life, and then repeated that he was once a lawyer. It continued that way, him repeating the same stories, until we both finished eating.

After breakfast, the cafeteria literally emptied, except for me, as everyone went to a small patio surrounded by eight-foot high tan-painted cinder block walls topped with inward curving steel spikes to smoke. Monstrous clouds of cigarette smoke billowed into the open sky. It looked as if someone was having a cookout. The smokers packed tightly into the small patio and silently inhaled every molecule of nicotine they could in the short time allotted. There was no time for chitchat. Getting a fix was serious business for that crowd.

Next on the agenda was "group" which everyone was expected to attend. There were group meetings at 9:00 and 10:30 a.m., and 1:30, 4:00, and 8:00 p.m. That day, a depressed counselor led the 9 a.m. group. He seemed barely better off than many of his patients. During roll call, he asked Carlos his name, Carlos replied, "Fred." I laughed until I noticed the rest of the group glaring at me in uncomfortable silence. After roll call, the counselor asked the group what they did to prevent stress. The unanimous answer was "Get high!" From there the meeting fell into chaos. Some patients heckled the counselor ruthlessly as he tried to share his required tidbits of information. Others who genuinely wanted help added to the din by expressing their frustration. They were sick of inept and burned out counselors. I left the room feeling worse than when I arrived.

After the 9 a.m. group, a PA approached me with two pills in a cup. I refused the medication. I didn't want to sleep just then, and I didn't want to take anything that made me feel like Jell-O.

The 10:30 a.m. group took place in a different room upstairs that was larger and seemed like a recreation room. It had parquet wood flooring and a Ping-Pong table on one side of the room and several oak cabinets, tables and chairs on the opposite side. There was a large open area in the middle. The topic for the meeting was "coping skills." We played a game called Traffic Jam, which required critical thinking and cooperation to move players (physical people) from one side of a set of imaginary boxes to the other. It started with an empty box in the center with patients filling boxes in a line on opposite sides of the center box, all facing the center. The object was to work together to get everyone from both sides to the opposite sides without violating some basic rules. It was hilarious watching patients of various levels of functioning try to fathom the relatively complicated game. I don't think anyone understood it aside from me, and the frustrated counselors ended up moving people themselves as patients turned in many directions in bewilderment. The point of the game was lost to that group. It was, however, the first interesting and challenging thing I did since arriving. I complimented the staff on the game afterward and asked where I could find more information about it. They ignored me.

During the day, I ran into Carlos everywhere. I took him on as a kind of pet project, determined to crack his shell and get to know the real man behind the quiet, reserved mask. Whenever I saw him, I gave him a high five, a low five, or some goofy handshake. I laughed and he grinned each time. I never saw anyone else interact with him, and I don't think anyone ever imagined interacting with him at that level, but Carlos was game if someone took the time. I'm sure he got a kick out of it even though he never said anything. The standard big grin was no clue, but the fact that he was always willing to participate was all the feedback I needed.

At lunchtime, I joined Ray and Carlos in the lunch herd. Carlos disappeared from view upon entering the cafeteria, but I later saw him shuffling around the outskirts of the cafeteria with an apple again. *Does he ever eat it? What does he eat?* I never saw him eat anything—including that apple. I couldn't imagine how he survived.

The group at 1:30PM involved "the day's events and feelings." Again, people shared their frustrations at not getting the help they needed, sometimes standing, and yelling directly at the female counselor facilitating the meeting. I shared a little about my medical experiences and got the group off on that tangent for a bit. I was surprised at the level of interest of these supposed mentally ill people. In the middle of the meeting, the door to the room opened and Carlos shuffled in. Seeing him bumble into the room and watching people's reactions to his horrific smell made me laugh aloud. Not surprisingly, he had his pick of chairs and the benefit of plenty of room to stretch out. That scene was all I could think of for the rest of the meeting.

Every group meeting was broken. It was impossible to have effective treatment if the people running groups couldn't care less about what they were doing. They all seemed frustrated, disconnected, and exhausted. After the third meeting, I "no showed" subsequent meetings, deeming them pointless. I was there to get sleep. I didn't have behavioral problems, a drug addiction, or any of the other issues the rest of the patients had. No one seemed to notice my absence.

During the first meeting, however, I couldn't help but notice how much some patients really wanted—indeed *needed*—help and how incapable the staff was of providing it. It made me wish that I could provide that help. I realized immediately that this was just the tip of the iceberg: there were many others like them in the world. A small fire began to flicker within me. I felt compelled to find a way to help all these poor, suffering people.

After each of the second and third meetings ended, I picked out a few patients and tried to strike up a conversation with them as PAs herded us back from the group room. I found that most were approachable and eager to have someone listen. I easily saw a way to help them: accept them as they are and listen to them with compassion and empathy. I quickly learned to spot the best prospects as well as those who were toxic: too infuriated or sick to approach. By the end of the day, I had a little gaggle of followers. They didn't know me by name, but they loved that I was perhaps the only person at Pinecrest who sincerely listened, reassured, and comforted them. They rambled more often than not, but it made them feel better having a friend who treated them like a normal person. I think the secret was that I was not staff: I was just like them. I had no agenda, and they had nothing to fear from me.

That evening I joined Ray for dinner. As usual, Carlos paced around the cafeteria with his apple. I decided to invite him to sit with us. When I did, he didn't answer but he followed me back to our table and sat down. With several different items on the dinner selection that night, I asked Carlos what he would like. He wouldn't answer, so I had to do it his way: I presented a menu item to him and he either nodded yes or no. Then I stood in line once more and filled a tray for him, again forgetting milk and utensils as I had every other time.

After struggling to get the milk and utensils, I returned to the table and placed the tray in front of Carlos. He stared at it for a moment and then set his apple down and dug in. He ate as if he were a Labrador retriever puppy, stuffing food in faster than he could swallow. His cheeks filled like a hamster's as his teeth struggled to keep up. Most surprising of all, he never picked up that apple again. He just left it sitting on the table. He didn't say anything, but I could tell that he was satisfied for the first time in a long time. It was the first meal I ever saw him eat.

***

Beth's journal, May 19, 2011:

As soon as the girls left for school, I drove to Pinecrest to drop off clean clothes for Ken and to obtain release of information documents allowing Pinecrest to obtain medical records from Desert Hope. I spent over two hours waiting for someone to assist me, only to learn that Ken needed to sign the release forms even though I had power of attorney. After I got home, I called Pinecrest five times throughout the day and left messages to have someone contact me to discuss Ken's treatment plan.

I visited Ken at 6:30 p.m. He seemed better and reported that he slept well except when a doctor woke him from a sound sleep for an interview. At that time he still had not been given the medical release forms to sign nor had he received the clothing or personal belongings that I had dropped off that morning.

**

At 9PM, a PA approached me with medication. I decided to take it to help me sleep. He offered me a Seroquel tablet, which I'd had the night before. Unfortunately, I didn't know that it was twice the dosage. I will never know if that triggered the events that followed or if it was just time for the next part of my ride. As a doctor would later describe, it was perhaps a "paradoxical reaction" to the Seroquel.

**

In 2002, Beth's father, whom she loved dearly, was diagnosed with stage-four lymphoma and within weeks was near death. Right before he died, knowing she was the most dependable of her siblings, he asked her to take care of her mom. That proved to be a turning point in Beth's life. Although the youngest sibling, she assumed the huge burden without hesitation. Right away, her mother suffered horrific medical problems. Beth spent a good deal of time over the next years as her mother's medical advocate. At times, she literally saved her mother's life. To Beth it was a way of showing her love—both to her mother and in honor of her deceased father.

Unfortunately, things sometimes overwhelmed her physically or emotionally. However, instead of throwing in the towel, she cried briefly, wiped her tears away, and then headed right back to the trenches. Nothing stopped Beth until she was unable to function. She was relentless to the point of putting herself in jeopardy. To her, the people she loves are more important than anyone, even herself. Now, she was going to put all that experience to another use. Never in my life have I needed someone to look out for me as I did from the moment I took that pill. From then on Beth was going to be my advocate, my champion.

Chapter 8

INSIDE THE BIG MACHINE

Between the late hours of May 19 and the early hours of May 20, 2011, my mind ramped to a new level of mania. Consequently, it disconnected hurtful memories and desensitized me to negative emotions. Apparently, that was the first step in the creation of an emergency state of mind that allowed me to solve problems many times more rapidly without such things as worry, fear, self-doubt, and old baggage hindering me. Much knowledge also disconnected as my mind streamlined itself to best deal with the perceived emergency at hand: coping with continued sleep deprivation and medications, and surviving along with other sick people in a psychiatric unit. The following is a description of the most dramatic phase of my change: losing my negative emotions. Whereas this change was for some reason interactive (possibly because negative emotions have to be unlearned), all other changes were automatic and out of my control.

***

In the late evening of May 19, an avalanche of thought filled my mind. If I didn't find relief, it seemed that my head would explode. Intuition led to an idea. I sought out my rock-hard bed, lay down, and relaxed as much as possible. I closed my eyes and my racing thoughts transformed into the roar of a huge diesel powered machine bearing down on me. I spread my arms in invitation. *Come, I am ready.* The roar increased until it shook me to the core. *Take me.* Sensations overwhelmed me as a massive invisible machine rushed through and enveloped me, sweeping me with it toward an unknown destination.

It seemed I was in the heart of the big machine—the very core of its immense engine. The din should have been unbearable, but instead it comforted me. All around, explosions burst from invisible combustion chambers so rapid-fire that I couldn't discern them. Intuition informed me that each explosion contained something sinister. When I grew fearful of them, the speed of the great engine increased noticeably as if fear fueled it, and when I ignored them, it perceptibly slowed. I wrestled with emotions for what seemed hours, ignoring them one by one in an attempt to bring the engine to a standstill, feeling that it was my destiny to do so. Eventually, the explosions slowed to a point where I could study them closer. When I tried, parts of my mind waved warning flags and I grew fearful. The engine accelerated once more.

Through sheer determination, I slowed the engine to a point where I could see the explosions with my conscious mind. What I saw shocked me. Each one contained a vision of an act committed against me. The first visions angered and enraged me. When I gave in to those feelings, the engine accelerated madly. When I ignored them, they faded and the engine slowed. I faced another barrage of visions that made me feel loathing and disgust. When those emotions carried me away, the engine raced with joy. I ignored them and made it through to a third wave that brought me great sorrow and grief. Again, I battled the emotions, succeeding in reducing the speed of the engine even more.

Next, I faced the worst visions: nightmares of fear and terror. They played all around me with each explosion of diesel in the massive combustion chambers: beheading, hanging, strangulation. I learned to ignore them by repeating to myself, *it doesn't matter; nothing matters.* Eventually, the machine slowed to the point where seconds ticked by between visions, and they grew ever more horrible: mutilation, dismemberment, and disembowelment. *I submit. I submit completely. I am unafraid of what awaits me.* The machine continued slowing until minutes passed between each vision: slicing, flaying. *I have no fear; nothing can harm me.*

Finally, the most horrific vision of all played steadily before my eyes: I was upside down and naked with my hands and feet bound to rough-hewn wooden poles buried in the earth. My clothes lay shredded and strewn on the ground beneath me. Men with black hoods covering their faces wielded a large, two-man tree saw. They commenced sawing my body in half, beginning with my genitals. *It doesn't matter; nothing matters.* The ghost of me let out a blood-curdling scream as saw teeth ripped through my genitals and raked my pelvic bone. *It doesn't matter; nothing matters.* A crowd of relatives, friends, and strangers cursed and threw garbage at my body, and then cheered in unison with each stroke. *It doesn't matter; nothing matters. It doesn't matter; nothing matters.* With a hiss of air brakes and a groan of steel wheels against rails, the big machine ground to a halt, punctuating the end of my racing thoughts. A feeling of peace and serenity overcame me.

I lay there breathing heavily, sweating and exhausted. That moment changed me forever. It was sometime after midnight on May 20, a day I will always remember in wonder. As I lay in bed, mystified by what happened and trying to deduce the purpose, a thought filled my quiet mind: *negative emotions are the source of all dysfunction.* I pondered that for a time, and the liquid thought crystallized. If emotions such as guilt, shame, hatred, jealousy, confusion, and anxiety—all the negative emotions—are removed, there will be no more dysfunction, no mental illness. I had my answer to what was wrong with the people in Pinecrest and in similar institutions throughout the world. The big machine had provided it to me.

There was another outcome of my once-in-a-lifetime interactive session with the mysterious big machine: my own negative emotions were blocked or gone. I didn't need testing to confirm it; I knew it beyond a doubt. In any case I was about to experience life without negative emotions for real. If there were doubt, it would soon be gone.

Chapter 9

UTOPIA: DREAMING

After my encounter with the big machine, I had a dream. I was flying, not like a bird, but flying just the same, moving along at a decent clip. My shadow skittered across the bristled tops of pine trees a thousand feet below, looking like a ragged varmint fleeing from an unseen predator. As I flew silently through the air, I reached out and my fingers met resistance. The harder I pressed, the more the air resisted. An invisible flying machine made of air surrounded me, taking me to an unknown destination.

As I flew, I breathed in the clean, refreshing scent of pine trees and alpine meadows. Mountain peaks sprang into view. The last snows of winter covered the tallest of them like dollops of whipped cream. Abruptly my invisible craft slowed and then dropped, slipping cleanly through pine trees to the ground. It landed with the slightest bump and dissipated like fog, leaving me standing in lush grass, well-groomed despite no evidence of human attention. I reached down and felt it. It was strong, thick, cool to the touch, and perfectly content growing in the shade of tall pines where grass normally didn't grow. No pine needles or pinecones marked it, despite the fact that the trees were laden with both.

Suddenly, the ground ascended into the air in front of me: grass, then dirt and finally a panel several inches thick. The grassy disk rose to a height of eight feet and hovered there, unsupported. A sleek, silver-and-gold two-passenger vehicle reminiscent of a Polaris ATV rose beneath it on an invisible platform. If it had doors or a roof, they were currently missing. A young couple seated in the vehicle smiled and waved at me as it rose. When the vehicle reached ground level, it emitted a slight whine and accelerated smoothly across the invisible surface onto the surrounding grass. I noticed that it said "Polaris" on the left and "Orion EV" on the right of its tail end.

The couple climbed out, walked toward me and the man greeted me. "Ken Dickson, how are you doing, buddy? We heard you might show up but weren't sure when." He turned away and spoke softly, as if letting someone know I had arrived, and then faced me again. "I'm Roy, and this is Kathy."

"Do I know you?" I asked, thinking they looked vaguely familiar.

"You certainly do, but I'll let you figure it out. Hey, you wanna see our digs?"

"OK, but first, how is that grass floating in the air? As a matter of fact, how was I floating in the air?"

"I can't give you an exact answer to those questions. That's someone else's passion. Nevertheless, we use it for everything here. I call it a rain curtain for my garage. People call it different things depending on how they use it. The thing you flew in is an airplane. Get it? It's made of air," he chuckled. "It has a lot of great uses as you'll learn: keeps the weather from getting into our place when we crank the garage door up, among other things. Of course, nowadays the weather is predictable: it's on a schedule here at least, so it's not as necessary as it was when we first got this place up and running. Come on in," he said, beckoning me onto the invisible platform. I hesitated at first, expecting to fall into the ten-foot-deep hole. I tentatively tested the invisible surface with my foot and felt resistance, then cautiously joined them on the platform. It smoothly descended toward the floor below. As we neared the floor, lights automatically illuminated as the grass panel locked back into place above us.

The enclosed living space was small but comfortable, roughly forty feet in diameter. There were no walls aside from those around the perimeter, only occasional supports between the floor and ceiling. The floor looked solid but felt soft when I walked on it. I lifted my foot and it left no impression. A warm, natural glow from the ceiling lit the home.

"Check this out," said Roy. The area around us came alive with the sights of the forest. "That's a live view of the forest above us."

It was beyond TV or projection—we were literally in the forest right above us with the Orion sitting on one side.

"We can crank this whole room up like the garage if we feel like a real outdoors experience, but you can't do this in that case." The view changed to that of a beach, with all the accompanying sounds of crashing surf and seagulls. "There are thousands of live feeds and simulated ones too that are just as real. Of course, this is just one of the models. Most people aren't really into this kind of thing anymore. They're either with family or friends or involved in their passions. There's nothing really like TV or movies either. People that have those passions live them out for real or in simulations. There isn't any news per se anymore because of how the world is, and you know how that is, buddy." He peered at me and then poked me on the forehead.

"Ow!" I exclaimed, stepping back and rubbing my forehead with no clue what he meant.

"You know how it is because it's how *you* are. But, keep the faith and keep dreaming or none of this will happen, and we don't want that, do we?" he asked, smiling at his wife.

Suddenly it dawned on me. "I know who you are—you're Skip, the dune buggy guy." He and his wife were at least thirty years younger. Gone were his handlebar mustache and wire-rimmed glasses and his hair was no longer gray. He more closely resembled his son than himself, but I was sure of it. Skip was helping me build a sand rail back in my world.

"Bingo!" he exclaimed, a big grin on his face. It occurred to me that it was a grin I would see often if my Skip didn't have that mustache. "How did you become so young?" I asked.

"That's the million-dollar question. In this world, anything and everything is possible. That's all I'm gonna say or I'll spoil the surprise."

I kept quiet and let him conduct the tour. There was a large, simple bed at one end of the room with no header or footer, a stand-alone shower next to it, which I guessed had its own rain curtain and a toilet minus the tank next to that. I saw no mirror or obvious medicine chest. A sofa and chairs filled the middle of the room opposite the carport. A kitchen along the wall opposite the bed contained a small pantry; a refrigerator, or at least something that looked like one; a stove with what might have been an oven; a dishwasher; and some counter and cabinet space. That was it. There were no knick-knacks, collectibles, or artwork. "Sure is a lot smaller than your old house," I said.

"Yeah, things are different here. We're not of a mind to collect stuff, and like I said, you're either with friends or family, or working on your passion with others who have the same passion. So we pretty much just sleep here and maybe eat if we aren't eating out somewhere."

"What's behind that door?" I asked, pointing to a large door at the front of the carport that appeared to be an entrance into the dwelling.

"Everything and everyone," he said. "You just gotta think it all out, buddy."

I wasn't satisfied with that answer, imagining there were other homes, people, and more on the other side of that door, but changed the subject instead of pressing the issue.

"Hey, I was wondering about the Orion. Is it really a Polaris?"

"Well, you know how I used to work on all that sand rail and buggy stuff? I just can't get that passion out of my system, so that's what I do now. Polaris used to be a company, but now it's a community, like this place, only it's a manufacturing community of people like me. There are people who live and work there—people who really need a hands-on experience—and there are people like me: satellites, who work on designs remotely. The Orion is a model T by today's standards, but it's the first electric buggy I worked on, so I kept it. Been driving it ever since. Most people here don't drive, but there are a few old-timers like me who still like to feel the wind in their face."

With that, I sensed the tour was over. "Well, I don't want to hold you guys up. I can see that you were heading somewhere when I arrived. What's next on my agenda?"

"I suggest you use your wings and find out."

"Uh, OK." I replied, unsure what that meant exactly. The three of us walked back to the carport, and suddenly, were moving upward. "That's just freaky," I said looking down and watching the room drop away. "How do you do that? How do you make everything work? It all seems so automatic."

"Like I said, anything and everything is possible."

As the platform—or should I say air form—stopped smoothly at ground level, I stepped off and offered my hand to Roy. He shook it briskly. "Good to see you again," I said. "I almost have that old sand rail that you were helping me with running, you know."

"That old thing? Feels like a lifetime ago. Hmm, I guess it was. It turns out really well, by the way. You have fun with that and keep the old me posted on how it's going. I enjoyed working on that buggy with you."

I turned to Kathy and hugged her. Although I remembered little of her from my old life, I had to admit that she was a fine-looking woman in this place and time. "I hope I'll look as great as you two someday."

"Maybe you will. I'll see you around, buddy." They both got in the little car. Before departing, Roy turned and added, "Now would be the time to try those wings again. We'll see you at the party."

I waved as they drove off, wondering what he meant. As they motored smoothly through the forest, I noticed that all the trees were spaced in such a way that they could drive anywhere. I was sure it was no coincidence.

With no idea what to do next, I sat cross-legged on the lush grass, closed my eyes, and thought of flying above the forest. Abruptly, I accelerated upward, and then horizontally. Trees whipped silently by below me. I lay back and placed my hands behind my head. The trees thinned, giving way to green fields. Cattle, pigs, goats, chickens, turkeys, and even a few horses roamed freely. Odd farm machines stood at the edges of fields. Rectangles of color filled one area: vegetable gardens. I wondered if invisible greenhouses made of air protected them. Beyond the fields, rows of solar panels tracked the sun hungrily and small wind turbines danced in the breeze. Apparently, these were sources of food and power for this place.

My airplane banked sharply carrying me over the pines again. It slowed, and as it did, the trees unexpectedly ended, revealing a beautiful alpine meadow not far from a pristine lake. Sailing vessels and powerboats of all shapes and sizes dotted the lake, many pulling skiers, wake boarders, or children on brightly colored tubes. Ski runs slashed the forests of distant snowcapped mountains, but I could make out no lifts, a technology most likely obsolete.

A crowd of people filled an area of the meadow, and I headed right smack for the middle of them. I scanned the crowd during decent and recognized family, friends, coworkers, and neighbors. Some looking as I expected, others looked younger or older. Everyone gazed up at me, and all of them wore the broadest smiles. I knew at that instant what this place was. I opened my eyes and blinked the welling tears from them. "Utopia," I said. "The name of the place is Utopia."

Chapter 10

MY CHANGED WORLD

When I awoke early in the morning on May 20, I didn't know what to make of the dream or much else from the night. Somehow, it seemed that my loss of negative emotions, Utopia, and the fate of the patients intertwined, but I was unable to make the connection. After a time, my mind drifted back to concern over the mentally ill patients. It dawned on me that perhaps I *could* make a difference in their lives. From that moment forward, that's what I would do. I didn't know exactly how I would help, I'd just have to learn as I went, but it filled me with purpose and made me feel alive.

That morning I again joined Carlos and Ray for breakfast. While waiting in our herd by the security doors, I joked with Carlos about huevos rancheros again. *Someday, I'll get Carlos some huevos rancheros.* When we entered the cafeteria, Carlos shuffled toward the fruit. People in line parted like the Red Sea around him, some of them holding their noses to fend off the stink. He picked out his apple and headed back to his habitual trail, sweeping the cafeteria floor clean with his oversized hospital gown as he went.

I made it through the line and noticed that for the first time ever, that I didn't forget my utensils and milk. I felt like jumping for joy. While in line, I couldn't help but notice how fantastic I felt: fresh, rebuilt—I nearly started hugging everyone. *What happened to me? Why do I feel so wonderful? Why do I have so much energy?*

After filling my tray, I sat by Ray. The food even tasted better. I pounded my breakfast down and then hungrily went back for seconds. I was so overwhelmed with all the wonderful changes that I felt breathless. I was like a teenager with no cares or responsibilities in the world, except that I wanted to help people. That became my driving desire. I finished my breakfast and started by listening intently to Ray's same stories.

I don't know if that helped Ray, but I wanted to help him. I wanted him to face his demons and rid himself of his alcoholism. I wanted to will it out of him. It was then that I realized that perhaps I could give him a piece of what was in me. Perhaps I could help him by just being with him. I liked that idea: the good in me contagious to people like a common cold. I wished it to be true. I wished I could heal all sick people, and if someone wasn't sick, I wished I could take away their fears and worries and give them a better life—a life of passion instead of drudgery, a life of anticipating the future with joy instead of rehashing the past with sorrow.

Maybe that's it: if I can somehow shut off those things in others as were shut off in me, Utopia is what we can achieve. People will live together in harmony, with no threat of war. People of similar passions will unite to eradicate starvation, disease, and poverty, and make our lives better and longer. As soon as the idea formed, I knew that it was true. Utopia wasn't a place or a destination; it was a journey—a journey to a better human race.

After breakfast, I promptly discovered that my memory was better than ever. I immediately took advantage of that to memorize all the staff's names with whom I interacted. I never possessed that ability before. I was terrible with names. Even though none of them responded in kind, I cheerfully greeted them by name every chance I could.

Shortly after breakfast, Dr. Alverez literally ran into me while staring at his papers and walking down my side of the H. I hadn't seen him at all since May 18 when he woke me.

"Excuse me," he said, almost dropping his stack of papers. "Oh, hi," he continued gradually recognizing me. "I've been meaning to talk to you. Come over here and sit down." He directed me to the chairs facing the staff counter where I sat on my first night.

"How are you doing?"

"Not bad. I could use more sleep."

"I wanted to tell you that I've decided to double your medication. Then, I want to keep you for another week and see how you progress."

That ended my great mood in a single heartbeat. There was no way I was staying another week or more, and I wasn't going to take additional medication. I didn't need to be a zombie. I just needed sleep. *A better bed and some peace and quiet is what I need, thank you.* I didn't respond to Dr. Alverez. My mind was too busy trying to determine a way to avoid his plans for me.

Chapter 11

ON THE RUN

After my conversation with Dr. Alverez, I tasted a bit of freedom: a PA escorted me to a small courtyard on the side of the building. I didn't know what qualified me to be there, but it must be a special privilege—there were only a handful of others there. The circular courtyard was literally a cage, surrounded by brown, ten-foot-high bars spaced about four inches apart. I casually approached them and shook them to test their strength. The stout bars were solid steel. "Get away from the bars, please," the PA demanded. I strolled around the concrete pad, taking in the roughly sixty feet of bars. There were benches and picnic tables bolted to the concrete, all made from steel tubing and expanded steel mesh, protected by a dark green epoxy powder coating. At the center of each table stood a bowl filled with ash-discolored sand and hundreds of suffocated cigarette butts standing filter up at random angles.

It wasn't refreshing outside; it was stuffy with hardly a breeze or nice smell. If I stood upwind of the few smokers, I sometimes caught a whiff of wet grass as the last moisture evaporated from the lawn, which was watered every morning and evening. In Phoenix, the sky is nearly always blue with upward of 320 days of sunshine per year. I sat on the end of one of the benches and gazed at the sky. Sure enough, it was blue, without a cloud in sight. Blue sky spelled freedom in my book. I breathed in the aroma of damp grass and savored the idea of freedom. At that instant, I knew what I needed to do: escape.

Without a real plan, I made one up on the fly as soon as I was back inside. First, I would body slam an emergency exit door at the bottom of the H. If I made it through that locked door, I hoped that I would have time to formulate what to do next. It wasn't much of a plan, but in my mental state, quantity of opportunities was more important than quality. I charged the door, succeeding only in making a racket. The latch on the door failed to budge. No one bothered to investigate the commotion.

As I rubbed my aching shoulder, I noticed a map of the building on a wall a few feet from away. *A gift from God. Anyone planning an escape should be so lucky to have a map of his prison.* I approached the map excitedly, and then stared blankly at it. I knew what it was, but I no longer remembered how to use it. The knowledge was either blocked or missing from my mind. Apparently, I lost more than just negative emotions, but I didn't let that derail my mission.

Although I was no-showing groups, the 9 a.m. group presented another opportunity for escape. I joined the herd, and just as the counselor opened the door to the meeting room to let everyone in, I slipped away unnoticed. *This is already going better than my last plan.* With one level of security behind me, I walked briskly, alert for the next opportunity. After passing a few dead-end hallways, I found one with an automatic sliding glass door at the end. A black man in dark green scrubs, possibly a janitor, mopped an area of the floor about halfway to the door. I considered moving on, but the automatic door proved irresistible. I walked confidently toward it, saying, "Excuse me" as I passed the janitor. As I neared the door, it remained closed. Frustrated, I stood in front of it, looking out longingly at the green lawn and blue sky just a thickness of glass away.

"The keypad is on the wall behind you," the janitor said.

I turned and looked at it, clueless of the combination.

"Oh, I missed it. I assumed the doors were unlocked," I replied, thinking quickly. "I'm here for new hire orientation. I must have taken a wrong turn. Can you direct me to the main entrance?" When I arrived at Pinecrest, my clothes were nice. Perhaps they added credence to my fabricated story, for he replied without hesitation.

"Certainly, follow me." He escorted me through the final security doors to the main entrance lobby and asked me to take a seat. From where I sat, freedom was but a few feet away. I waited for the janitor to reenter the facility. Just as I was about to make my move, the receptionist requested that I follow her into a side room where I assumed I would meet a human resources person. As she opened the door and walked in, I calmly turned and headed for the entrance. The door opened. Unfortunately, the janitor had not returned to mopping. Somehow, he continued to watch me.

"Sir?" he called out.

I turned my head slightly and yelled back, "I left some paperwork in my car. I'll be right back." *I missed something.* Then I remembered the black object hanging from his belt—a radio. Perhaps he was a security person who just happened to be cleaning up a spill when I stumbled upon him. *Of all the dumb luck.* Without missing a step, I continued through the door.

I might as well have been on an alien planet then—I had no clue where I was or where I should go. I was, after all, in the middle of a seizure when I arrived. I kept moving, however, keen for the next opportunity. I walked several yards, and instead of crossing the parking lot in front of me, turned left and followed the sidewalk to the end of the building. I then cut across the grass to a large parking lot. Halfway through the parking lot, I glanced back to see if the janitor had followed. He appeared at the end of the building at that very moment.

"Is your car parked in this lot?" he asked.

"Yes, it's right over here, the red Jeep Cherokee," I said, walking toward the vehicle. I reached into my pocket for nonexistent keys and pretended to unlock the door with them. I glimpsed back again and he hadn't moved. *Crap.* I was as far from him as I was ever going to get—less than fifty yards, and I was out of options. I bolted.

At first, I sprinted at full speed, but with only a few sutures holding my abdominal wall together, I knew that put my life at risk. I placed one hand on my belly to prevent my insides from spilling out and slowed my pace, opting instead to outlast the janitor. I spent a good part of my life running and had no problem finding a sustainable rhythm. In addition, I felt no pain whatsoever and my muscles cooperated fully. It was a true testament to the resilience of my body, and that fact alone fueled my belief I might actually pull off the escape.

I looked over my shoulder one last time. The janitor was a hundred feet behind me with his radio in-hand to communicate my whereabouts to Pinecrest. It would only be a matter of time before a vehicle joined the pursuit. I strategized as I ran: *nearly everything in central Phoenix is on a one-mile grid. If I can lose this man and make it to a major cross street, I'll know where I am. There are always gas stations or shopping centers at major intersections from which I can call Beth. If worse comes to worse, I'll walk home once I have my bearings. There are plenty of places to get water, the temperature is in the low eighties, I don't need sleep, and I've lived without food before. I'll avoid the main streets so they won't spot me.*

I cut to the right, running along the side of the facility on 35th Street, and then turned left onto Harl Avenue. I crossed the street and continued, keeping close to the curb. I maintained my rhythm by counting as I took in all of my surroundings: cracks in the asphalt, short chain-link fences separating yards, swamp coolers on roofs of the sixties-era, ranch-style homes, Chevys and Fords in the carports. *One, two, three, four, one, two, three, four: I can run all day.*

The crackle of a radio cut through the air, reminding me of reality. "Sir...sir...please stop running!" the janitor yelled. I felt like responding *not on your life,* but the crackle was undeniably closer. I was losing ground and running out of time—fast. The janitor was clearly in better shape than I anticipated. Continuing my straight path would be suicide. If he didn't catch me, a car couldn't be far behind. My mind switched to desperation mode, evaluating every possible option at lightning speed.

A plan quickly formed in my mind. *I'll turn right onto 34th Street just after passing the house on the corner. Once out of the janitor's field of view, I'll run at full speed to find cover. The janitor will miscalculate where I am when he rounds the corner, thinking that I maintained the same speed as before. That will create confusion, and he'll waste time looking in the wrong places. At the first opportunity, I'll bolt to a new location, putting more space and obstacles between us. I'll make my way from hiding place to hiding place, and then house to house, until I'm far enough away to run again in a new direction. I'll keep moving and find a main intersection.*

When I passed the house, I turned, maintaining the same speed until I was out of sight. Then, I ran at full speed. A few houses down, I saw a perfect spider hole: a short, white, block fence about two feet high. On the other side of it was a scrubby hedge that followed the fence to the sidewalk near the street. At the end of the hedge nearest the house was a gap between the shrubs and the house of just a few feet. The gap and wall provided a workable minimum of cover so impossibly small, that no one would suspect its potential as a hiding place. From there I could crawl back over the wall and backtrack if necessary as the janitor walked by the hedge. The hedge was tall enough to cover such a move if I remained low.

I felt like a kid playing hide-and-seek, but this was serious business. If they caught me, I feared what the increased medication would do. I dashed for the wall, placed my hand on it, jumped over, and assumed a tuck position on the other side, my face inches from the dusty ground.

By the time the janitor rounded the corner, I was gone. Although I couldn't see him, I kept track of his location by the sound of his radio. My plan had potential, but there was an unforeseen problem: a woman raking her yard witnessed my mad dash and my disappearing act behind the wall. When she saw the man in green scrubs with a radio, she pointed in my direction. It was over. I was no longer the glorified fugitive I fancied myself to be. Instead, I was simply an escaped loony. As he approached, I stood, brushed the dirt from my clothes, and to defuse the situation, placed my wrists together and offered them for handcuffing. He laughed, the first and only laugh I ever heard from a Pinecrest employee. "I wish I could cuff you for making me run my ass off," he exclaimed.

Just then, a black SUV pulled up to the curb. Moments later, I was beside the janitor in the back seat of the SUV.

"Why did you try to escape?" he asked.

"I just wanted to go home and be with my family," I replied.

He subtly nodded. It was a rational thing to say, and I think it struck a chord with him. As we turned onto 35th Street and drove alongside Pinecrest, I had my first good look at the place. It was much larger than I imagined. My little H was a small fraction of the two-story building. We passed the parking lot with the red Jeep. It seemed smaller than earlier. The cage with the brown bars and green steel furniture bolted to the concrete slipped quietly by next. It was devoid of smokers and looked like something you see animals in at a zoo. Then, I saw my room window—second from the end. We turned left and then left again and arrived at the main entrance. It shocked me to discover that the most memorable journey of my life was, in fact, less than half a mile.

***

As I sat alone on my thin mattress in my darkened room, I noticed that my left hand burned. I turned it palm up. It was scraped and bloody, as if I took a dive onto asphalt and tried to stop myself with it. The left side of my face stung as well. I touched it and my finger came away wet with blood. The injuries must have been from jumping over the wall. I had no regrets. Perhaps I was crazy, but I was sane enough to protect my body from medications that were making me this way. If I scarred from my wounds, those scars would be worthy reminders of my battle against a system bent on destroying me. At a minimum, they'd make for a great story: if I survived. Despite my predicament, I smiled with pride.

Chapter 12

DOWN THE RABBIT HOLE

No one bothered to treat the wounds on my hand and face once I was back at Pinecrest. I just walked around with dried blood and dirt on them. I did manage to command another kind of attention though. If ever I got too close to one of the exits, a menacing team of PAs would block my way. No longer could I go to the cage, although I couldn't imagine how anyone could possibly escape from there without a cutting torch or explosives. I spent the remainder of the morning and much of the afternoon in my room. I wasn't allowed to go to lunch or dinner.

Later in the afternoon, Dr. Alverez followed through with the increased dose of Seroquel he promised. I wasn't exactly sure of the purpose of Seroquel, but I imagined it would make me less able to plot future escape attempts. I was done with that in any case. If I got out of there, it would be by the power of my wife's pen, not by me running through the streets holding my guts in. I called Beth around 5:00 p.m. using the wall phone by the glassed-in room and pleaded with her to get me out of Pinecrest.

After that next dose of Seroquel, my mind went to unimaginable places. Perhaps the step-function leap my mania had taken in the early morning hours compounded matters. Everything suddenly took on a completely new character. It became increasingly difficult to discern whether I was awake or dreaming. I asked questions I never before considered such as *Can I become invisible (and cause panic)? Can I walk through walls (and escape)? Can I fly on a magic carpet to Hawaii (with my family)? Can I teleport (anywhere)?* I actually believed these things could be possible. It was as if I had suddenly lost the concept of limitations.

In response, I set about reestablishing the boundaries of the real world by trial and error. I started by testing the invisibility theory by sitting very still in a familiar chair across from the staff counter, willing myself to disappear. The staff popped up and down just like before, only more frequently as they wondered what the escape artist was scheming.

Next, I tried walking through an exit door at a decent clip so I could beat the PAs to it and conduct a "walking through barriers" experiment before they could get to me. I was actually surprised when I didn't slip cleanly through the door and complete my plan of giving them a sly grin and the finger from the other side. I bounced off with a resounding thud. PAs quickly surrounded me. I decided then that I was not, in fact, some kind of superhuman, and the wild ideas subsided. I put off exploring more boundaries for the time being.

About that time, Beth arrived to set me free. They allowed her to visit me in the cafeteria. She immediately noticed strange behavior and became quite concerned. Then she saw the cuts on my face and hand and inquired about them. I didn't say anything. I don't know why, I wanted to, but the words wouldn't come out. I instead informed her that I was hungry, having had neither lunch nor dinner. She asked the staff to bring me something and they presented a brown paper bag with a sandwich, chips, and an apple. It seemed odd that it was in a brown paper bag. *Is it some staff person's lunch?*

To make matters worse, my condition deteriorated steadily during the visitation. I became psychotic and delusional for the first time in my life, right before my poor wife's eyes. Beth performed some simple tests on me: she asked the president's name, what day and time it was, and made me try to focus on her eyes. I had great difficulty with all those tasks, and she soon left me alone with my sack dinner.

***

Beth's journal, May 20, 2011:

I called Pinecrest six times to speak with someone about Ken's treatment. I left messages each time, finally requesting to speak to an administrator. No one returned my calls. Later a social worker left a message on my answering machine requesting that I make an appointment with Dr. Alverez for 3:00 p.m. on Saturday, the twenty-first. When I returned her call, no mention was made of Ken's treatment plan.

Around 5:00 p.m., Ken called and asked to be picked up, stating that no one was doing anything to help him. I was very disturbed by the lack of communication from Pinecrest and appalled that no one was managing Ken's treatment, so I drove to Pinecrest to take him home. When I arrived, I asked the receptionist to get me someone who could release Ken to me. The social worker soon greeted me and asked to speak with me in private. We went into a meeting room to talk. She asked why I wanted to take Ken home. After a brief discussion, she left the room, locking me inside for several minutes. When she returned, she told me that if I attempted to take Ken home, the doctor would have him committed. When I asked on what grounds, she told me that he was a danger to himself. As evidence of that, she told me, "when I asked your husband what he would do when he got home, he told me that was irrelevant."

I was very upset and didn't know what our rights were. I didn't want to leave Ken there, but didn't have any alternative. It was just prior to visiting hours then, so they let me see Ken. His appearance and behavior shocked me. He had a shuffling gait and smiled blankly the whole time we visited. His skin was clammy, his hands had tremors, and he had nystagmus in both eyes. There was a strong fruity odor to his breath, and he could not focus on his watch to tell time, nor did he seem to know how. I asked him what date and day it was, and he had no idea. I asked him who the president was, and he replied, "Washington?" and grinned. His short-term memory was less than one minute. He kept asking when we were leaving. There were cuts on his face and hand. When I asked about them, he couldn't or wouldn't say anything. I learned that he hadn't eaten since breakfast, apparently as punishment for trying to escape.

Just before I left, a nurse handed me a sticky note with her name and the unit telephone number on it. I called her before I left the parking lot. She told me that Ken was taking Seroquel, Restoril and Ativan. When I asked how he hurt himself, she told me that he tried to walk through a wall.

Ken's changes terrified me. I expected that he was getting help with his sleep deprivation. When I got home, I researched the drugs given to him and was horrified to learn that Seroquel was an antipsychotic medication; Ken was hypomanic prior to admission, but now he was clearly altered cognitively: he had lost touch with reality. Many of the adverse side effects listed on the drug websites were evident in him.

I researched my rights and found an online attorney who informed me that the facility had no right to keep Ken and was, in fact, guilty of kidnapping. The attorney advised me on how to get Ken out of the facility. He also recommended that I program the local police number into my cell phone and have them assist me if Pinecrest refused to let him go.

Chapter 13

UTOPIA: FOUNDATION

That night I dreamed again of Utopia—or of things before Utopia. Much had to happen before Utopia could exist. I wondered how I was different from before. I knew there were things about me that I couldn't yet quantify, but I could tell that my emotions were different, so I started taking inventory. There are essentially six different core emotions: peaceful, powerful, joyful, sad, mad, and scared. There are, of course, infinite variations and combinations of those emotions that comprise all human emotion as we know it, but it was simpler to start with the basics. I was no longer sad, mad, or scared, nor had anything associated with those negative emotions. That may not seem like much, but it is half of all emotions. Negative emotions are the source of many of the evils of humankind, such as war and murder, and they are the source of many if not all dysfunctions. They are also the reason that we have to build walls around our homes, our workplaces, and our countries to protect ourselves. Besides being the source of physical barriers, they are also the source of societal barriers that separate instead of unite us as a human family. They are the single-handed impetus behind the design and manufacture of all machines of human destruction, all the bullets, and bombs of the world.

So there I was without negative emotions, experiencing life anew with only the brightest of human emotions, changed by the simple fact that what had once held me back was gone. Passion and energy filled me as well as a desire to help humankind finally achieve its destiny: ending war, poverty, hunger, and disease, even traveling to the stars. In short, whatever we were passionate about doing would be possible. Without negative emotions holding us back, and with a desire to seek out people who share our passions instead of building walls to protect ourselves from imagined enemies, we could do anything. Anything and everything would be possible.

That was the core of Utopia: a place only buildable by people not held back by negative emotions. Without that critical consideration, Utopia would be just another absurd social idea doomed to failure before it started. Located in a place of great beauty, Utopia would be one with nature and one with similar settlements around the world, uniquely networked to initiate and foster the most imaginative accomplishments of humankind, right from the comfort of citizens' homes.

Utopia would be the first of such places, the idea farm from which a new kind of humanity would branch out. Utopia would explore how humanity without negative emotions would interact, create, team build, raise families, educate children, and run businesses, then reach out and share those ideas with an evolving world—a world that, like it or not, was already changing.

The world was changing through no fault of my own; I was simply the vessel of change. With a touch, I could turn off negative emotions, release the demons that held us back, and bring forth our imprisoned passions. With a handshake, a smile, a kind word, I could create human life where there once was only human desert. I could do these things in that manner or simply by the fact of my existence. It was out of my hands, and I had no choice. I would infect people whether I liked it or not. Building a prototype, a Utopia, while not necessary for the change to happen, would give us an opportunity to prepare for how we would interact and make the most of it.

I awoke and rubbed my eyes. I felt an odd rush, goose bumps rippling over my body. Was it true or just a dream? Could I really turn off negative emotions in others? Could we really stop wars? My sleep was finished, and my mind spun wildly the rest of the night as I lay quietly in my bed imagining all the possibilities of a world without negative emotions.

Chapter 14

A NEW CARLOS

I felt rejuvenated as I awoke on May 21. Perhaps my brain flushed the Seroquel that previously clouded my mind and confused me. I made a mental note to refuse all medications from then on that I didn't feel were necessary. My thoughts were crisp and clear, and my energy boundless despite only having only a few hours of sleep. Not only did I have a grand vision for humanity, I saw opportunity everywhere: for an unhappy staff member to have a happier job doing something he was passionate about, for a schizophrenic to live a normal life—even better than normal. There were new things about me that were still fuzzy around the edges, senses or abilities that I could almost grasp or which were perhaps inappropriate for this wretched place. I decided to set those aside for now, having enough on my plate already.

On cue, Carlos entered our room, but he didn't shuffle; there seemed to be an uncharacteristic easiness to his gait. On our way to the cafeteria, I repeated the same joke about huevos rancheros and he grinned as always, but his eyes, no longer thin slits, sparkled with new life. We crowded through the small door and made our way into the food line.

Carlos cut in line, grabbed an apple, and headed off to pace. I remembered my milk and utensils, and finally—huevos rancheros. Not believing my eyes, I laughed aloud. *How outrageous.* The food worker filled my plate, I hastily made my way to Ray's table and set it down, and then I searched for Carlos. "Carlos, I finally got you some huevos rancheros!" I yelled. He grinned, an extra-large grin. I motioned to him to join us. He did so and took a seat. I pushed the tray to him and said, "Have at it." Then, after amazing myself yet again by automatically remembering my milk and utensils, I filled another tray and joined my friends to eat.

Carlos finished by the time I returned. "You really shoveled that in. Do you want more?" He nodded yes, so I gave him my plate and went back for another. We all had a splendid time with our huevos rancheros. I smiled and shook my head in disbelief throughout the meal. After all the joking about huevos rancheros, it seemed inconceivable that we were actually eating them.

As we ate, Carlos's subtle changes continued. His mouth relaxed and his characteristic grin vanished. Despite an abundance of clues to a miracle unfolding, I didn't manage to connect the dots: Carlos was rejoining the real world. When I finally noticed, I grew concerned. "Carlos, are you OK?" He stared at me for a few moments, nodded, and then smiled—a real smile. When he finally finished his meal, he leisurely pushed his chair away from the table, stood, looked directly at me, and offered his hand. "God bless you," he said. I hastily swallowed my food and stood to return his handshake. It may seem trivial, but Carlos said only one thing to me the entire time I knew him: his name. Overwhelmed by emotion, I grasped his hand firmly and followed his lead as he shook my hand with conviction.

Afterward I sat with Ray and finished my meal, all the time wondering if he would improve as well. A small voice in my head said, *everything happens in its own time, Ken.* It didn't seem odd at all to hear that voice. It delighted me to hear it because it meant that Ray still had an opportunity for a better life. After breakfast, I never saw Carlos again, but our parting moment couldn't have been more perfect. I was confident that he would continue to progress.

That day was my final day at Pinecrest with Carlos, Ray, my small gaggle of odd acquaintances, and the staff I had gotten to know, if only by name. After Beth saw me bloodied, confused, and barely able to function, she rightly concluded that Pinecrest was not the place for me. Had I continued my stay and adhered to the doctor's treatment plan, it's probable that within a few days I would effectively be a vegetable. Beth exhausted every potential lead to gain my release. Before long, she succeeded in obtaining all that was needed aside from one thing: Dr. Alverez's signature.

For that reason, Beth and I found ourselves sitting across a table from him in a small group room at Pinecrest. Watching Beth and him squabble for over half an hour was torture. Beth didn't buy his argument that it was better for me to be drugged into a stupor and abandoned in my room at Pinecrest than to be home with my family. I questioned his qualifications to make that kind of decision. That proved to be satisfyingly irritating but did little to resolve the conflict. The disagreement continued until everyone was exhausted. Then Beth did the only thing left to do: she slid the properly completed paperwork across the table and handed Dr. Alverez a pen.

"I'm taking him home. Period," she stated unequivocally.

The conversation ended. Doctor Alverez sighed heavily, took the pen from her reluctantly, and signed the papers.

"You're making a mistake" was the last thing he said.

Chapter 15

NINE HOURS AND A URINE TEST

We arrived home at 4PM. on May 21. Immediately, I noticed my dogs acting strangely toward me. We rescued Kobee, a small, tan-colored terrier mix, from an abusive home. It took years of love to gain her trust, and, sadly, she still scampered from us at times, her tail tucked tightly between her legs. She greeted me in an uncharacteristically accepting and frisky mood. Anna, a black-and-white Shih Tzu, who rarely wagged her tail and was the most reserved and aloof of the dogs, cocked her head curiously and wagged incessantly. Lastly, Washington, an almost pure-white Labrador retriever, seemed even more alert and attentive than ever. We raised Washington to be a guide dog, but after a year of training, he failed his first medical exam due to pinpoint cataracts. The blind couldn't lead the blind, so we adopted him and crossed our fingers that his vision wouldn't go completely.

All three of them followed me eagerly, maintaining an unusually tight pack around me wherever I went. When I paused, they sat and observed me inquisitively, turning their heads this way and that. I sensed an aura of calmness from them that I never noticed before. Then, it dawned on me: in my new mental state, I was living in the moment just as they did. For the first time, I seemed more doglike than human.

To pass the time, I decided to play with Washington. Washington loves to fetch the wood, a ten-inch scrap of two-by-four from one of my forgotten projects. He especially loves to retrieve it from the pool. I opened the sliding glass door to the backyard and yelled the magic words, "Washington, get the wood." Washington raced outside to the grass and froze in a pointer stance, his crazed eyes locked on mine, one paw in the air, and his tail perfectly parallel to the ground, eager for me to find the wood and throw it.

Washington was raised to follow orders but was bred to disobey constructively and protect his blind owner in the event of danger. He never had an opportunity to disobey constructively, however, having missed that part of his training. He steadfastly waited for a command before doing anything. I found the wood and tossed it in the pool. Washington rushed to the pool's edge, ground to a halt, and waited anxiously for the command to fetch, his entire body quivering in anticipation. "OK!" I yelled. Only then would he leap into the pool.

Initially at Pinecrest, I thought that I lost all of my emotions, not just negative ones. It made me wonder: what's left when you have no emotions? My conclusion: choice. Without emotions, people could still make choices. That was my explanation for people not changing, like Carlos did, after interacting with me. Otherwise, I just couldn't figure out why everyone didn't become like me. I tried something with Washington: I gave him a choice. The next time I threw the wood in the pool, I didn't give a command; I sat placidly and did nothing that could be interpreted as OK.

Washington struggled with his new freedom. It was hilarious watching the painful process of letting go of the old. I laughed like a madman at something so subtle that no one else could appreciate it—which didn't help my case. One thing I forgot to mention about losing your negative emotions: your inhibitions vanish and you laugh from the heart.

The more I played with Washington, the more emotionally connected we became. I tuned in to his language or, more appropriately, his body language for the first time. Previously imperceptible cues became as obvious as shouting. As Washington grew more comfortable with his new freedom, he taunted me. He brought the wood to me, held it within reach, and then pulled it away when I tried to grasp it. Eventually he let me have it, or he dropped it and backed away, wide eyed and panting. When I threw it into the pool, he occasionally pretended he would jump, and then gave me a silly look. I recognized for the first time that he was a clown. That realization led me to laugh even harder, to the point of bringing tears to my eyes.

Spent from playing with and laughing at Washington, I went upstairs to lie down. On the way, I clicked the thermostat down a few degrees. I took off my shoes, turned on the ceiling fan, and plopped down on a real bed. Our queen-sized bed is nothing fancy. We actually got it used from a neighbor who was upgrading. It was ten years old then, and that was ten years ago. Recently, however, Beth placed a three-inch slab of memory foam atop the mattress. That brought new life to the dying bed. After lying on a thin foam slab for several days, it felt like heaven. I doubted I could sleep, but I relished the cool breeze of the ceiling fan and the downdraft of the air conditioning working overtime to reach a perfect temperature. I closed my eyes and daydreamed of life's magnificent possibilities.

Sometime later, the unmistakable sound of a Cummins diesel-powered truck entering the neighborhood interrupted my contemplation. As it shifted through its gears, pistons clattered louder and louder until finally it seemed it must be right in front of my home. Then, with a hiss of air brakes, the engine slowed to an idle. Moments later, the front door opened and then closed, followed by the shuffling of many feet and the sound of men's voices trailing off. Curious, I arose from the bed, left the bedroom, and walked downstairs. I opened the front door to investigate and, to my surprise, a full-sized fire truck idled less than fifty feet away.

I immediately suspected that something happened to Beth. Not that long ago she threw her back out and couldn't move without excruciating pain. Paramedics came, lifted her onto a gurney, and whisked her to the emergency room. Another time she had a transient ischemic attack (TIA), collapsing into my arms as we left a movie theater. That time I literally carried her into the hospital myself. I quickly closed the door and rushed toward the family room in search of her.

I couldn't initially fathom what I saw next. Directly in front of me stood my sister-in-law, Kim; my best friend, Tim; Beth; and four firefighters. I skidded to a halt, as they all stared at me. It didn't take a genius to realize that this wasn't about Beth, it was about me. Worried about my odd behaviors, Beth called Tim. Tim recommended that if she was afraid, she should call the fire department. In our area, the big truck always responds first, and then the ambulance follows if necessary.

"What's going on?" I asked.

"You need to go to the emergency room for another blood test," Kim, explained.

"What are you talking about? I've had gallons of blood tested."

"We want you to go to Scottsdale Samaritan for more blood tests," said Beth.

In truth, Beth feared that my behaviors were the result of an infection, abscess, or abnormality of my brain. Besides recommending that she call the fire department, Tim suggested that she take me to Scottsdale Samaritan, where they have an excellent neurology department. For some reason they didn't think I would agree to see a neurologist, so they decided to convince me that I needed more blood work instead.

"I'm not getting any more blood work. I've asked people to test for adrenaline, and they won't do it. All the other blood tests showed that my blood is normal."

"You have to go," pleaded Kim. "There's something wrong with you."

"Aside from trouble sleeping, I feel fine. Unless someone is going to help with sleep, I don't see the point."

The debate went nowhere, so I spoke directly to the firefighters in an attempt to convince them that I was OK. They asked me typical paramedic questions, shined a penlight in my eyes, and conversed among themselves and with the others in my home. Soon, to my relief, they hefted their gear and walked single file out the front door and back to their rig.

After the firefighters left, the battle resumed. No one could give a sound reason for more blood work, but it became apparent that if I didn't agree, things would only worsen. I would end up taken by force to a hospital or a place like the one I left barely an hour earlier.

"OK," I finally said.

Kim and Tim came along to support Beth. They had no plan beyond showing up at Scottsdale Samaritan with crossed fingers that the perfect neurologist awaited. Not surprisingly, it didn't work out that way. At 6:00 p.m., I was admitted like any other patient, with the caveat that I was manic, released AMA (against medical advice) from Pinecrest less than two hours earlier. Beth begged for a neurological consult, but the ER doctor refused.

For the next nine hours, nearly all we did was wait. They did take my blood pressure: 166/93. Not only was that much higher than my healthy normal of 120/70, it's considered "stage two" hypertension (high blood pressure) and normally requires treatment or medication. No one batted an eye at the blood pressure reading. Beth recounted my entire story to anyone who would listen: every detail from admission to Desert Hope to my AMA release from Pinecrest, to no avail. I asked the ER doctor, a nurse, a nurse's aide, and even a phlebotomist, a specialist who draws blood for a living, if someone could test my blood for adrenaline. They ignored me. At 9:00 p.m. they requested the only test I would get: a standard urine test. We never received the results of that test.

***

In fact, there is a blood test for adrenaline. It's called a catecholamine test. It measures the amounts of the hormones epinephrine (adrenaline), norepinephrine, and dopamine in the blood. The adrenal glands produce large amounts of catecholamine in reaction to various forms of stress. Catecholamine increases heart rate, blood pressure, respiration, and mental alertness. They also reduce blood flow to the skin and increase it to major organs such as the heart, brain, and kidneys. There is also a twenty-four-hour urine test for catecholamine, which is more accurate than the blood test.

***

Over the next few hours, they shuttled me from one room to another. Few people questioned me and those who did were very uneasy. It was completely the opposite of my initial experiences at Desert Hope, where everyone was genuinely engaged in helping me. Here everyone seemed hostile and suspicious. As the evening progressed, Beth ran out of steam, exhausted from her desperate actions throughout the day on my behalf.

At 11:00 p.m. I turned to Tim. "Would you call a cab for the both of us?" I asked quietly so Beth wouldn't hear. "If we leave, Beth will follow. She's beat. She'll collapse any minute if she doesn't rest." Tim didn't respond. Puzzled, I spoke more loudly only six inches from his face and he still didn't respond. It appeared that he blocked me completely. Tim and I went back over twenty years. We worked side by side for long hours in foreign countries and started a business venture together; we played sports, shared hobbies, went to lunch, and talked on a regular basis. Now he was deaf to me. I wondered if he were possessed.

More and more it appeared that everyone around me acted the same way. Nothing I said or did registered. I had no ID, money, credit cards, or phone, having been released from Pinecrest only hours before, or I would get a cab on my own. At 11:30 p.m., we still needed to see one more person: the social worker.

"Beth, this is ridiculous. Why are we waiting for a social worker? Don't you remember the social worker at Pinecrest a few days ago? What are they going to tell us? You need to go home and rest. Let's get out of here. It's a waste of time," I pleaded.

Beth seemed irrational. "We have to see the social worker," she insisted. "They told me she'd be with us shortly, as soon as she's finished with her other patient."

Before long it was 12:30 a.m.—a new day, May 22: still no sign of the social worker. Beth was all but catatonic by then. I've never seen her so depleted. I, on the other hand, felt perfectly fine, though irritated by the entire situation.

"Beth, we have to get out of here. A social worker isn't going to do anything for us. It's twelve thirty. We've been here over six hours. Let's go home."

"No, we need to wait," Beth mumbled weakly.

"Come on, Beth, let's go. We can just walk out. No one will even notice." I tried to stand her from the chair she was sitting on. Shockingly, she grabbed onto the base with both hands and became rigid, with a look of fear in her eyes I'll never forget. I reconsidered that decision and instead coaxed her from the chair onto the bed so that she would rest. After helping her to lie down, I lifted her head to adjust the pillow, and she suddenly jerked.

Beth refers to that as a "startle reflex." She does it regularly and at the least provocation, but most frequently when I have to wake her for some reason when she's asleep. I've tried a dozen different ways to not startle her when waking her but ultimately could not avoid it. In her state of fatigue, it was no surprise for her to react that way.

***

Just after midnight on May 22, Scottsdale Samaritan RN Sharon Bell sat at her desk entering patient data into her computer. Hours earlier, a nurse escorted a psychiatric patient who became increasingly agitated while awaiting treatment to a special room, which by coincidence was in direct line of sight with her desk. Though she was not involved with the patient, the nurse asked her to keep an eye open and call for help immediately at the first sign of threatening behavior. Sharon frequently glanced from her computer monitor to the patient's room.

The last time she looked, he was standing and talking to his wife as she sat in a chair. Sharon sensed movement and glanced up. The light was now out, the wife was in bed, and the psych patient was leaning over her from the side of the bed doing something to her head. Suddenly, the wife's arms shot out to her side in a silent plea for help. It could only mean one thing…

"He's choking her!" she screamed.

The floor came alive. In moments, medical and security people converged on the room, coming to the hapless victim's aid.

***

"Stand back. Get away from her NOW," I heard as I finished positioning the pillow behind Beth's head. Stunned, I turned to see a security guard standing menacingly in the doorway. By instinct, I raised my hands to show that I was unarmed. I backed away from Beth, and the medical staff whisked her away while the guard stood threateningly between me and everyone else. As the last of the staff cleared the doorway, he backed out slowly himself, keeping a keen eye on me all the while. As he crossed the threshold, he pulled the door closed and then locked it from the outside.

When it finally seemed safe to do so, I walked toward the door and peered through its small window. The security guard standing nearby eyed me suspiciously as a small group of medical personnel gathered around my wife. They talked to Beth for quite a while, but I couldn't hear what they said.

After a time Beth, Kim, and Tim left, and everyone vanished except for a few of the nurses at their stations. Even the security guard disappeared. I had no way to contact anyone, and no one attempted to communicate with me. I felt as though I no longer existed. *Maybe someone will notice me at shift change in the morning.*

With nothing else to do, I took stock of my room. It was different than any hospital room I'd been in. There was nothing in the room except for the bed and the chair Beth sat in. The door, lockable from the outside, was steel and the window glass was reinforced with wire. Clearly, it wasn't a typical hospital room—it was more like a prison cell. *Why am I locked in? I haven't done anything wrong.*

Time crept by. I kept track of it by the clock on the other side of the nursing station. I paced for a while and then went to the bed and lay down thinking that I might sleep. I lay there wide-awake for half an hour, then stood and looked out the window again. Two nurses sat at their stations. I pounded briefly on the door to get their attention to no avail. In frustration, I pounded continuously until they finally turned and looked at me. I raised my hands and shoulders in a questioning way. "Why am I in here?" I yelled. Once again, Sharon responded, only this time she left the area to find the social worker. The other nurse resumed her work.

***

It was 1:30 a.m. As Sharon approached her, social worker Kathy Winfield, taking a break from patients and paperwork, sat at her desk sipping the hot coffee she'd just poured. "Kathy, you better get down to see your psych patient," Sharon said. "He tried to assault his wife a while ago. They've got him locked up in the ER. He just started pounding on the door, demanding to be let out."

"OK, I'll be right there." She grumbled. She gathered a pen and her clipboard, and took one more sip of coffee before reluctantly making her way to the ER.

***

At 2 a.m. I lay down on the bed again. A few minutes later, the door rattled. A portly woman around fifty years old with curly blonde hair opened the door, walked in, and locked it behind her. Eight hours after my admission, the social worker finally arrived.

I felt hatred radiate from her as she asked me questions and filled out paperwork. She never once looked me in the eye. When I asked her why I was there and what happened to Beth, she ignored me. Her only purpose for being there was to complete her required paperwork and get out as quickly as possible. She responded to nothing I asked. I felt invisible.

Noticing that she wore a wedding band, I asked her the one question that might garner a response: "If your husband were here suffering, would you try to help him? Would you get him into bed and make sure he was comfortable?" She grimaced and steeled herself even more. It was the rudest experience I've ever had in a hospital. Shortly, with only yes or no answers from me, she accomplished her objective. She left the room and locked me in once more.

At 3:00 a.m., the door rattled again, and to my surprise, Beth walked in. She looked worse than I'd ever seen her. I'm certain she had no rest between leaving here, driving thirty miles home, turning around a short time later, and driving thirty miles back.

"We can go now," was all she said.

"Can we stop at a McDonald's on the way home? I haven't eaten anything since lunch yesterday at Pinecrest. I'm starving."

"They're closed," she replied.

"Why?"

"It's after 3 a.m."

"I'm really hungry. Can we stop somewhere?"

"No. We're going home."

"Would you like me to drive?" I asked. She looked at me with glazed eyes and said nothing. Though I felt I in much better condition than her, there was no way she would let me put her life in further jeopardy.

***

Beth's journal, May 21, 2011:

We arrived at Scottsdale Samaritan around 6:00 p.m. The doctor in the ER diagnosed hypomania and suggested waiting for the social worker to discuss options. He would not listen to my pleas to have a neurological consult. They treated us like a crazy man and his stupid wife. At around 12:30 a.m., Ken insisted that we go home and tried to pull me off the chair I sat on. I held onto the base of the chair with my hands and wouldn't go. Somehow, after that I got onto the bed. Once I was in bed, Ken lifted my head. I didn't know what he was doing, and it frightened me. A nurse sitting at the nursing station observed everything. I can recall the look of complete shock on her face when we made eye contact during the time Ken frightened me. She called security and they separated us. They took me out of the room, and locked Ken in.

I knew that something was incredibly wrong with Ken and was so relieved when the doctor told me that he they would admit him to the hospital. He also told me that I might as well go home as nothing would happen for several hours. He recommended that I come back in the morning. We got as far as the Elliot Road exit when I received a call from the social worker, who informed me that I either had to file a petition that Ken was a danger to himself or persistently and acutely disabled, or I had to come take him home. I went to get him as soon as I could drop Tim and Kim off. Ken seemed very angry when I arrived. He asked to go to McDonald's but didn't seem to believe me when I said that they were all closed that late at night.

***

In that twenty-four-hour period, Beth did everything necessary to remove me from a psychiatric institution AMA, put together a small army of people—including firefighters—to coerce me to have more tests, and drove 160 miles—nearly four hours of city driving. She literally spent every waking minute of her day trying to help me. I, on the other hand, just wanted to play with my dogs and sleep in my big, comfortable bed. Our worlds couldn't be further apart. We got into the van and headed home without another word. When we arrived home at just after 3:30 a.m., Beth went straight to bed. I fixed a sandwich, poured a glass of milk, and went out to love seat on our patio to eat. Afterwards, too wound up from my ordeal to go to bed, I tried to piece together what happened.

I couldn't believe that perfectly qualified professionals who had dedicated years of their lives learning skills to help people with real medical problems would unilaterally turn their backs on me and lock me away. That was my introduction to the harsh stigma of mental illness. The entire experience convinced me to resist further testing even more. *No one is going to help me.* While I mulled things over, I unknowingly did something I managed to avoid since my first seizure: I chalked up a sleepless night. Strike one.

Chapter 16

UTOPIA: EXPERIMENTING

As the sun crept over the horizon, I still sat on the love seat, my pack surrounding me. Each dog stared intently at me, distracted only by the swoop of a mourning dove, a dog bark, or a hummingbird visiting the feeder suction-cupped to the kitchen window. Even then, their attention shifted only shortly. I knew it wasn't the case, but they appeared to be begging for food. I went inside, retrieved a sleeve of saltine crackers from a metal tin in the cupboard, and then returned to the love seat. I ate a few, and then threw one to each dog. Washington jumped and caught his; Annabelle ducked, the cracker hit her squarely on the head and slid down her right side to the ground; and Kobee cowered, turned to run, noticed the cracker, and changed her mind. I continued to eat and share crackers until we finished the whole sleeve. Parched from their dry snack, the dogs filed through the dog door into the house to drink from their water bowl.

Gradually the rest of the world awakened, and the sound of traffic filled the air. Though it was Sunday, in my timeless mindset, I imagined everyone going to work as I normally would. For some reason I no longer cared about work. I didn't worry about money, certain that the world would change soon and that money would either be easy for me to acquire or unnecessary. I also lost interest in material goods, and was eager to unload as much as possible at

Goodwill and simplify my life. I even considered donating my old Corvette to help disabled veterans. I also owned an antique Plymouth that ran, but needed much TLC. *That could help someone in need as well.*

After my experience with Carlos, helping others became a priority for me. Certain that I healed him, I thought of him often. Also important to me was my lack of negative emotions, which I believed I lost through my own efforts: freeing myself from them, as well as their associated baggage. It didn't escape me that I accomplished that on the supposed day of the Rapture: May 21, 2011, according to the media. I wondered if the Rapture indeed occurred and involved everyone losing their negative emotions, beginning with me.

I truly believed that losing negative emotions was contagious. Never mind that I lacked any evidence to support the theory aside from Carlos; I felt it to my core. Despite the lack of proof, I set about preparing for the new world. Since I rarely slept more than a few hours, if at all, I had plenty of time to ponder the possibilities. Since 4:30 a.m., that's what I'd done as I lounged on the love seat. In the process, Utopia evolved from curiosity into full-blown obsession.

I knew the end product, Utopia, but how would we get there? Where should we begin? What was the reason for Utopia? I found answers for all of those questions. First, we'd take baby steps: we needn't aim for the bulls-eye right away. Second, we should begin with me by trying to spread the gift in any way possible. Third, if everyone changed, then society would have to change. We'd need a new model for society and Utopia could be that model. As the world struggled through uncertainty, knowledge gleaned from Utopia could pave the way for a better future for all of humankind.

In the end, everyone would change anyway. Perhaps the new society would evolve just fine in its own time without intervention, but why not be proactive and potentially alter the course of history in the process. Why not drive the first stake now toward a healthier society and planet. Why would anyone in a position of advanced knowledge not want to accelerate the solving of man's age-old problems, and prevent needless suffering and death from continuing?

As far as baby steps, it would be prudent to experiment first. It could be done right here in my own community, the sleepy little suburb of Ahwatukee, which just happens to be ground zero for everyone changing. If I wanted someone on my team, all that I'd have to do is shake their hand, and wait for the change to claim them. In no time, there'd be enough changed people to get things rolling, all of them just as passionate about the venture as me. For tasks that couldn't be completed locally, we could employ satellites. Since everyone involved would be contagious, any one of us could travel to a potential satellite person or facility and evaluate them. If everything looked good, then, you guessed it: a handshake would be in order.

When it came to funding the venture, we could infect key employees at businesses who were already passionate about what they produced, then purchase stock in their company, and wait for their even more passionate efforts to pay off. As citizens in the community became infected and were willing to live in tighter quarters (because they all got along so well), they could sell their homes, move into smaller, more efficient ones, and donate their equity. Or, as they lost interest in accumulated material goods, they could sell their unwanted possessions on eBay, Craigslist, or other venues to generate cash. There were a myriad of ways to make money.

The most important and unknown variable of Utopia was the society. A society comprised of people without negative emotions has never existed in the history of humankind. There is no way to know how it would work or what would work best without taking a leap of faith to find out. Ahwatukee would be the proving ground. We'd create a mini Utopia (Utopia 1) there by modifying existing tract homes to study new ways of living together, and more space efficient, environmentally friendly, and reproducible furnishings could be developed. We could populate them with changed people of optimum character, expertise, and passion, and observe them living and working.

New means of communication would help to coordinate satellite design and distributed manufacturing. We'd contract with local vendors to address unique transportation and infrastructure needs. Finally, a team would locate Utopia 2, the real Utopia. After gaining sufficient knowledge from Utopia 1, we'd transfer all the personnel and knowledge to Utopia 2, shut down Utopia 1, convert the homes back to conventional standards, and sell them to help fund Utopia 2.

***

Later that morning I enthusiastically explained my plans to Beth. Though she feigned listening intently, her fear mounted with each word. She was more terrified than ever of my mental changes. It looked like Dr. Alverez was right after all: bringing me home was a mistake.

Chapter 17

THE LITTLE RED CAR

That's as far as I progressed on Utopia that day; I had other things I needed to address. For starters, the yard had gotten out of hand while I was away. I began by picking up after the dogs, which could have been worse. They don't like to get their feet wet in the grass, which is automatically watered twice a day, so they all relieve themselves in the same area of pea gravel behind a playhouse I built for the kids. Afterward, I plugged in my old Black and Decker electric mower and attacked "Easy Turf" so long it twisted itself into strands of rope.

I coaxed the underpowered mower through the dense grass, stopping frequently to clear it of jams. Washington heard the mower and pranced anxiously around the yard as he always does whenever I mow. For some reason, he associates mowing with fetching the wood. I stopped mowing repeatedly to throw the dripping piece of wood into the pool. When he finally tired, he jumped onto the love seat, kicked all the cushions off, and shook water everywhere. I continued mowing, and three bags of grass clippings later, finished the tiny plot of green. I skipped the leaf blower and the edger —it was enough work just mowing the lawn.

Next, I decided to treat myself to lunch at a Subway just down the road. I craved a tuna sandwich. Those reminded me of swimming: I used to order them for lunch on days I swam in an adult stroke class years earlier. I swam regularly ever since, and at least once a week, I ate a tuna sandwich afterward.

I ordered my tuna on nine-grain whole wheat (my surgeon said I needed to eat more fiber) with pepper jack cheese, jalapenos, spicy mustard (the hotter the better), lettuce, tomatoes, and—since I was feeling extra chipper—I got the better-tasting fried potato chips instead of the healthier baked ones. It wasn't a fancy lunch, but compared to the heavily processed food at Pinecrest, it was gourmet.

As I ate, one thought led to another, and before long I remembered several Hyundai Elantras I test-drove before my surgery. Beth even drove one. It occurred to me that a new Elantra would be a worthy reward for surviving my operation and related catastrophes. I was fifty-five, had a great credit rating, and no debt. What the heck. I finished my sandwich, chips, and drink and drove east to Phoenix Hyundai.

One thing I always wanted in my life was a perfect sale, one where I walked in, told the salesman exactly what I wanted, and after a perfect transaction, drove home in my dream car. OK, a Hyundai Elantra wasn't exactly be my dream car, that'd be more like a Nissan 370Z or even better a Porsche 911 Turbo, but it would be perfect for me to get around in. I was sick of my stick-shift Kia, not because it was a bad car but because I was weary of the stick shift—and the out-of-balance tire for that matter. I walked into the dealership and went to work with a salesman.

"Do you want to go for a test drive?"

"No, been on two of those, well, three including the one with my wife."

"What color do you want?"

"Red: I've never purchased a red car."

"What options do you want?"

"Everything but NAV, and no leather—it's too hot in Phoenix."

"What about financing?"

"You can finance it."

"Trade in?"

"No. Tell you what, you can keep that blue Kia out there and do whatever you want with it."

I was serious. I'll admit that it was drastic, but that's how I felt: I didn't worry about money anymore. I paid full price for the new car and abandoned the Kia, letting the dealer figure out what to do with it. The sale was perfect. There were no problems with financing, paperwork, nothing. The salesman brought me two small bottles of water. *Wouldn't it be great if, when the last paper was signed, I finished both of them?* As I signed the last paper, I glanced over at the bottles and noticed with satisfaction that they were both empty. I was on cloud nine as I drove off that lot.

In my entire life, I never did anything that impulsive. Usually Beth and I test drove vehicles for six months and discussed all the pluses and minuses in minute detail. We evaluated our financial situation, factoring in the kids, the dogs, and even the rats. After we scrutinized everything and decided on the vehicle, we haggled with the salesman for hours. By the time it was over, we often wondered if it was worth it.

Unbeknownst to me, the dealer called my brother Cole during the transaction. I put him down on the paperwork as a personal reference. I don't know how the conversation went between Cole and the dealer, but shortly after that, Cole was on the phone with my wife. Needless to say, Beth wasn't overjoyed with my spontaneous transaction. What upset her most (besides the fact that I did it without her consent) was the fact that I abandoned the Kia.

The whole thing was a bit of a stretch, even considering my state of mind, but I felt lucky to be alive and even luckier to be home with my family. So what if I bought a car ten minutes after conceiving the idea? So what if I left a $5,000 car sitting on the lot? "Screw it!" I yelled to myself as I drove away in my new car. I was elated and certain that Beth would be just as thrilled when I took her for a ride. When I turned into my driveway, I couldn't wait to show her. "Beth, I've got a surprise," I yelled upon entering the house.

"I heard. Cole called me. Apparently, you used him as a reference. How could you do this without talking to me? We always make these decisions together."

I was caught off guard by her response, but didn't miss a beat. "I bought it to celebrate. I could have died at Desert Hope or ended up a vegetable at Pinecrest. Besides, we have a great credit rating and no debt."

"We can't afford a new car right now. You're not even working."

"Everything will be OK; you wait and see. We don't ever have to worry again." That certainly seemed true in one respect: for the first time since I was a child, I didn't worry about anything.

"And what about the Kia? What were you thinking, leaving it there like that? You left a window down and everything in it. They had no idea what to do with it. You didn't even leave them the keys."

"I offered them the keys, but they wouldn't take them, probably because I didn't have the title." As far as the window, contents, or anything else having to do with the Kia, I really didn't care; none of it mattered to me.

The dispute continued but not for long. Though Beth was clearly upset, it was pointless trying to talk sense to me. Afterward I was optimistic that I'd be allowed to keep the car. Within the next twenty-four hours, however, I'd learn that my drive home in that little red car was both my first and last.

Late that night, as I lay in bed struggling to sleep, I reflected again on ending dysfunction and shutting down my negative emotions. All of a sudden, I realized that those things were a big deal. Not just anyone could pull them off. The knowledge that I had done it around the supposed date of the Rapture added even more to the miraculous nature of my accomplishments. The more I considered it, the more it occurred to me that I should receive some kind of prize for my deeds. *In fact*, a small voice said, *there is a prize*. The prize was that I got to design the future.

That was a huge responsibility for me, and I took it very seriously. I wanted to design a world that was perfect for everyone. After much contemplation, I finally arrived at the simplest design imaginable. It boiled down to five words: only good ideas will succeed. What that meant was that if an idea benefited humankind, it would succeed. An idea that was destructive or dangerous to humankind, a biological weapon, for example, would fail. Good ideas would percolate to the top, and bad ones would sink to oblivion. It was astonishing. It was flawless. I could no longer feign sleep. I got up, woke Washington, and whispered in his ear, "Let's go for a walk, Washie." Even though it was 2:00 a.m., he stood, shook, and was ready to go in an instant.

Washington and I walked many miles on that moonlit night in the neighborhood and on the nearby bicycle trails. In the dead quiet of the early morning, I couldn't help but notice the echoes of my laughter as one amusing "good" idea spawned another. I might talk to my dogs, or the rats, travel to Mars, be little kids with my brothers again. Any of those things were possible, assuming they *were* good ideas. That was something for a higher power to decide, I supposed. With plenty of changed people on the way, all of them as passionate and as eager to work together toward a better world as I was, ideas that would have taken lifetimes to come to fruition or that never would have been possible at all in the world of the past could be commonplace in a generation, or perhaps sooner. I vibrated with excitement as I contemplated a future beyond belief.

A faint glow began to spread across the eastern horizon, and I noticed that Washington's tongue dragged almost to the pavement. He never once complained, but he was exhausted and nearly dying of thirst. I put "only good ideas will succeed" on a mental sticky-note, placed it right next to the one that said "Utopia," and we headed back home. Once there I turned on the front faucet for Washington. He sat and looked at me. Instead of making him choose, I immediately said, "OK." So ended another night without sleep: strike two.

***

"When you're high, it's tremendous. The ideas and feelings are fast and frequent like shooting stars, and you follow them until you find better and brighter ones. Shyness goes, the right words and gestures are suddenly there, the power to captivate others a felt certainty. There are interests found in uninteresting people. Sensuality is pervasive and the desire to seduce and be seduced irresistible. Feelings of ease, intensity, power, well-being, financial omnipotence, and euphoria pervade one's marrow."—Dr. Kay Redfield Jamison, describing mania.

Chapter 18

A FLAWLESS NIGHT

As the next day, May 23, dawned, nothing seemed out of the ordinary. I hadn't seen much of the kids but didn't realize that it was because Beth was shielding them from me. She didn't want them to hear their dad babble about Utopia, about talking with dogs and rats, traveling to Mars, and being little kids with his brothers. I was perfectly content to discuss any of that with anyone who would listen. For me, they weren't realities; they were inevitable possibilities.

My older brother, Dana, arrived that day. Dana is less than a year older than me, 360 days. Growing up, Dana and I were inseparable. In the brick, row-house neighborhoods of Baltimore where we spent our youth, we roamed wild. We were rarely home; instead we built tree forts from scavenged lumber, explored the nearby woods, or played baseball or some other pickup game with the many other children in the neighborhood. As we grew older, we remained close. We were on the high school gymnastics team together; moved into an apartment together; worked together; and attended the same community college and later the same university, where we received the same undergraduate degree. We were a regular part of each other's lives until I moved across the country a few years after graduating. We hadn't seen each other much lately but still kept in touch. Dana's youngest daughter moved to Phoenix several years ago to attend Arizona State University (ASU). She stuck around, got married, became pregnant, and her due date was fast approaching. So Dana had additional incentive to visit the area.

It wasn't a surprise that Dana came. He is the quintessential big brother, the kind of guy you want watching your back. He is cool, calm, and analytical, and always takes time to understand the situation before making decisions. He's the first guy I call if I'm in a bind, and as far as Beth was concerned, I was well beyond a bind. She made the call. The doorbell rang and I answered it. When I opened the front door, there he was with his unmistakable mountain-man looks, well-worn running shoes, baggy shorts, and hunting-themed T-shirt.

"You're looking good," I said, reaching out to shake his hand. "I haven't seen you since Desert Hope."

"Yeah, that was sure a lot of fun. Let's don't do that again," he said with a grin.

"What brings you here?"

"I was just out here visiting my daughter. The baby's almost ready to pop, you know."

"Yeah, she must be pretty big. I haven't seen her in a while with everything going on."

"She's OK, just has a little basketball. Doesn't seem like a very big baby."

"Well, that's good. Come on in out of the heat." I opened the door the rest of the way for him.

Dana acted normally, but I knew the real reason he was here: he was part of the ever-growing "Army for Ken." That's how I viewed everyone who banded together to help me. No one in the growing army had any experience with my particular issues, nor had they done any appreciable research, so to me they were a bunch of vigilantes united behind a cause but clueless how to win the battle. I didn't mind. If I wanted anyone on my side, it was Dana. We didn't always see eye to eye, but when push came to shove, I knew I could count on him.

Like everyone else, Dana didn't have a plan; he just wanted to assess the situation and wing it from there. Things looked grim to him right from the get-go. We sat down and started talking, and it wasn't long before he realized that his brother was AWOL. Some freak with relentless ideas and nonstop energy had overtaken his body.

Once he finished the assessment, it was time to get to work. First thing on the agenda: the red car had to go. The story was that the dealer was going to hold it for thirty days. I know I should have thought, *Yeah, right.* Normally I would have, but one odd thing about being manic is that I trusted the ones I loved even when they lied outright. It was easy for loved ones to trick me. Beth returned the car with less than ten miles on the odometer and got our money back, end of story. A while later the little blue Kia I abandoned returned to the driveway.

***

Beth's journal, May 23, 2011:
Dana arrived just after the girls left for school. He spent much of the day with Ken. I went to the car dealer to see about returning the car. I had no choice. I could not afford a car payment on my part-time salary, and if Ken was unable or unwilling to work, I didn't know how I would support the family. The dealer was reluctant to take it back and kept trying to make a deal with me. When I told them that I was leaving to consult with my attorney, they rapidly agreed to take it back. The salesman admitted that Ken behaved very strangely during the sale, and there was no way that they would win if a lawyer heard what happened. I spent much of the rest of the day freezing our bank accounts, credit cards, and investments. I didn't know what Ken would do next. He could easily spend all of our money.

***

I spent all morning with Dana and then ate lunch with him. In the afternoon, we went to see a movie, but at the last minute decided against it because I wasn't feeling very well. We went home, but rather than lie down, I took the blue Kia for a drive to clear my head. While driving, I wondered if the Elantra might still be sitting at the dealership, waiting to go into "storage." If so, perhaps they'd let me take it for one more drive. That raised my spirits, and I set a course for Phoenix Hyundai. As I turned into the dealership, I grew excited at the sight of a red car out front. Unfortunately, it was someone else's Sonata. My Elantra was nowhere to be seen, so I walked into the dealership and asked for the salesman who'd sold me the car, then waited. As the minutes passed, I felt increasingly uneasy. Eventually I decided the whole thing was a bad idea and left. The dealer, aware by then that I had psychiatric issues, called Cole again. Word made it back to Beth, and that few minutes at the dealer transformed like a fish story into "he's trying to buy another dream car."

I desperately needed some quality sleep, so I came up with a plan. I drove a short distance from the dealership to a hotel. I asked the desk clerk for a dark and quiet room, one shielded from road noise and the morning sun so I might finally get some decent sleep. They found a perfect room for me. It was cool, quiet, and pitch-black with the lights off. Beth's credit card cancellations had not yet gone through, and they accepted my card. After getting the room, I realized that I hadn't thought ahead enough to pack a bag. I drove home to collect some things.

In the short time I was away, the Army for Ken grew and planted a trap for me. My first clue of something amiss was the large number of cars parked near my home and in my driveway. I was wary, but not seeing a fire truck, I entered my home anyway.

As soon as I entered, they surrounded me: people were on the stairs, in the living room, and in the hallway, some family, others friends, and a few I never saw before. It appeared that I walked straight into my own intervention.

Everyone spoke at once. One woman I never met explained that she had an adverse drug reaction once. My interest spiked, when it appeared she might have a solution to my sleep problem, but waned when her story offered me nothing. Others professed that I needed help but neglected to elaborate on what kind of help. Still others seemed to favor a "shock and awe" approach, hoping that if they repeated things loud and long enough, something in my brain would switch and I would snap back into reality.

Regardless of what people tried to tell me, I *felt* perfectly fine, and I didn't want to be told what to do by a truckload of people, especially with memories of Pinecrest and Scottsdale Samaritan still fresh in my mind. I had no desire whatsoever for any more testing or treatment. As I glanced around at the jabbering crowd, I noticed my haggard wife standing quietly in the background. My heart sank. It was clear to me that of the two of us, she was the one who needed help the most at that particular moment. She looked more beaten down with each passing day and now looked worse than ever. I tried to convince everyone that Beth needed help. I emphasized how run down and gaunt she looked, but they wouldn't listen, believing I was trying to deceive them. The more I begged them to help her, the more I enraged them.

I was simply throwing gasoline on fire. It infuriated them that I wouldn't see the light. In the movies or on television, when someone loses his mind, a slap in the face brings him right out of it. In real life, if someone is mentally ill and you slap him, he'll most likely remain mentally ill. The verbal battle continued until finally, the gal who suffered the adverse drug reaction agreed to help Beth.

That was a big turning point for me. I was overjoyed at the possibility that Beth might stop her downward spiral and return to her normal self. Everyone settled down after that. They convinced me to stay home instead of returning to the hotel and said they'd take Beth to her friend Caroline's home, which was just around the block, so that I could get some decent sleep. In the morning, they'd take her to get help.

My brother then drove with me to the hotel. He asked me to stay in the car while he worked on getting my money back for the room. I didn't know what his plan was, but I imagined he tried to convince the desk clerk that I was mentally ill and that he should give me a refund. When he came out, to my amazement, he claimed he took care of it.

Dana then took me home. Just after arriving, I asked him if I could see Beth so I could show my support and wish her luck the next morning. He walked with me around the block to my neighbor Caroline's home, rang the doorbell, then turned and asked me to wait outside while he talked with everyone. The door opened and Dana walked in. He remained inside a long time. When he finally came out, he said it wouldn't be a good idea for me to see Beth just then, so we turned around and walked back home. Dana and I talked briefly in the quiet house after that, and then he went to bed early.

On a whim I decided to give my close-knit dog pack a test by taking them for a walk without leashes, something I never did before. I wanted to see if their "stick tight" attitudes were for real. Sure enough, as we walked they kept a close eye on me and never strayed more than a few feet away. We walked like that for a quarter of a mile before I felt concern for their safety. They never behaved that way before. The whole arrangement seemed destined to self-destruct at any moment if I continued, and one of my friends would separate from the pack and be hit by a car, or they'd all disperse and I'd be unable to round them up. That was the only time the dogs strayed a little farther—when I turned around to walk home. Their look said, "You've got to be kidding." Annabelle cocked her head, Kobee perked her ears, and Washington looked over his shoulder; then they fell back in around me, and we walked as a unit back home. Once there, I opened the door and the dogs filed in one by one and sat, calmly waiting for me in the entryway. I followed them in, shut the door, and locked it.

***

If I had known better, I would have recognized the warning flags that popped up that evening. My two days without sleep approached three, and my mind reached the point where it could no longer compensate. It narrowed my brain function and heightened my senses even more. My mind was so narrow and my senses so heightened that the world was on the edge of looking magical.

After locking the door, the family portrait on the wall by the stairs caught my eye—there was something odd about it. I approached and studied it. It seemed more vivid than I remembered, but there was something else. Upon scrutiny, I noticed that the kids looked no different, but both Beth and I looked younger, and in particular I was thinner and my hair was darker. There was another portrait below it from a few years earlier. The natural desert backdrop of that portrait was lusher, and Beth and I looked the picture of health and years younger. Not believing what I was seeing, I removed the portraits from the wall and took them into the nearby laundry room where the light was brighter. In that light Beth and I looked as we did when we first met. In disbelief, I lay the portraits down on top of the washer and dryer and began examining other objects in the house.

I walked to the family room and picked up a photo of Beth's parents from the entertainment center. Their wrinkles were gone and her father had more hair. As I continued my investigation, it became more and more apparent that everything in my home, to one extent or another, was now a perfected version of its former self. The things I saw brought tears to my eyes. *How am I seeing this*? It was as if I was awake but dreaming at the same time. Everything was where it should be, but all of it was different in unexpected ways. I removed an antique saltshaker from a cupboard and examined it closely. The previously random scratches in its finish were even and symmetric, and the formerly blotched and faded paint uniformly aged.

I walked into my garage, turned on the outside light, and then continued through the side door. There, on a concrete pad, sat my unrestored 1954 Plymouth Belvedere. The car lay under a nylon cover and a large tarp. When I purchased it, it hadn't run in thirty years. It was all original, complete with scratched, dull paint and a stained, torn, and faded interior. I opened the gate to my yard, removed the cover and tarp, and threw them through the gate. The paint had the same symmetric scratches as the saltshaker, but they seemed prismatic and suspended in a thick layer of clear gloss that protected the like-new color of what until then had been a fifty-six-year-old factory paint job. When I peered through the driver's window, there was still a hole in the driver's seat, but instead of a jagged and frayed tear with chunks of discolored foam missing, the tear was smooth and beautifully shaped, encircling fresh foam, and the stains in the fabric were nonexistent. In addition, the once aged gray headliner was its original pastel blue. In excited anticipation, I attempted to raise the hood to see what wonders might await in the untouched, original engine compartment, but oddly, the hood latch, which had worked perfectly until then, refused to budge. I wondered if perhaps, unlike the objects inside my home, it was not finished perfecting.

I continued to the pool, uncertain what to expect. I turned on the pool light and pump, and waited for the sheer-descent waterfall to pour out its thin sheet of water, believing that somehow it was going to be "the big show." As I waited for the pump to fill the plumbing, I casually observed the water jets along the side of the pool about a foot below the water surface streaming bubbles as the plumbing filled with water. In stark contrast to the blur I expected, I could see each individual bubble slowly dance and undulate on its way to the surface as if it moved through mineral oil. Some of the smaller bubbles merging on the underside of the water surface formed flat, pancake-like bubbles. I didn't know why they looked so peculiar at first, but then noticed they weren't dome shaped like other bubbles; they were upside down. Apparently, the surface tension of the water trapped the air below the water surface. Those bubbles must have always been present, but were so short lived and lost in the blur that I couldn't see them before. As I puzzled over why I was able to see them, I realized that my brain was apparently processing things much faster. It was like watching a slowed-down, high-speed video—only it was real time.

***

I've since re-created this event and photographed these unique bubbles with a high-speed digital SLR camera. The bubbles formed by the jets are indeed different than those of the sheer descent or any other bubbles we typically see. Amazingly, though most of the other experiences of that evening remain a mystery, the unusual bubbles were, in fact, real.

***

I shut the pump off to save what air remained in the plumbing and ran to get Dana, unsure if he would see anything or not. Surprisingly, he'd locked his door. No light showed from under it, and I detected snoring from inside. With nothing else to do, I decided to explore my neighborhood. When I stepped out the front door, the miracles continued. A warm, inviting glow from the streetlamps showed the world in a new light. The street looked the same from a distance, but when I approached it, the jagged cracks were gone and the asphalt appeared freshly laid. I could almost smell the smoking tar and feel the heat rising from it. The sky was black as coal on a moonless night. Each star was the brightest of bright, and there seemed a billion more than usual. The temperature felt neutral, neither too hot nor too cold, and a steady breeze blew. The fronds of a nearby date palm rustled in the breeze, its majestic trunk lit in its entirety by a single ornamental spotlight at its base. When I gazed up the trunk, I saw the shadows of cut marks from years of trimming. The cuts were so uniform that the tree looked turned on a lathe.

A car glided by at an ideal speed, its engine purring like a newborn kitten and tires completely silent on the new blacktop. Every object I encountered displayed its own magic, and the surprises seemed never-ending. My walk took me by my neighbor's home where Beth was staying. I rang the doorbell, hoping to see her. No one answered, so I rang again. The house remained silent. I noticed that all the lights were off. I left and continued to explore the neighborhood.

***

Beth's journal, May 23, 2011 (continued):

Ken was increasingly intent on the idea that I needed help today. He also kept stating that he just wanted to get some sleep (and rightly so). At one point, he admitted that he might sleep better in his own bed than in a hotel bed, so I agreed to leave the house. I was afraid to be alone with him anyway because he seemed so agitated. His behavior was very strange and unfamiliar. I didn't know what to expect from moment to moment. Dana took him out for a little while to go back and check out of the hotel, and Kim helped me pack bags for the girls and myself. I arranged for Kaitlin to stay at a neighbor's house and for Hailey to stay with a friend. I didn't want the girls to see their father in such a compromised state. I think Ken thought I was going to the neighbor's house as well, but I went to a hotel instead. I didn't tell anyone where I was for fear that Ken would find me. It was a terrible night. I've never been afraid of anyone before in my life, and to be afraid of my own husband broke my heart. I spent most of the night awake—the slightest noise frightened me.

***

After a time I returned home and tried to sleep but only tossed and turned as memories of the wonders I saw replayed in my mind. After an hour or so, I went back downstairs and logged onto my computer to investigate how the Internet might have changed. I couldn't help but notice that it had become blazing fast: videos streamed without progress bars, and downloads were instantaneous. As I navigated from site to site, I was amazed at how uncluttered and intuitive everything had become, and at the extraordinary quality of images, video, and sound. It was as if the entire internet had upgraded to HD. The Internet itself appeared to learn about me with each mouse click or search, catering to and even anticipating my desires as time passed. There seemed to be an underlying intelligence trying its best to please me.

I spent hours on the Internet until my head ached from media overload. I finally stood and stretched, then noticed some tufts of dog hair on the tile from Washington. The downstairs of our home is nearly all tile, and Washington's white hair readily stood out against the earthy-colored flooring. I reached down and collected some. Not surprisingly, each hair was a tiny work of art. I felt compelled to clean the hair up, but not wanting to wake my brother by running a vacuum cleaner, I retrieved a broom from the back patio to sweep it. The broom bristles caught my attention as I walked back into the house. They weren't split, bent, and dirty as they had been previously. I paused and examined them more closely. Each black plastic bristle was the optimum length, straight as an arrow, and shined as if recently extruded. I turned the broom admiringly at arm's length. I couldn't remember ever seeing a more beautiful broom.

As I swept the tile, expecting the hair to accumulate into a pile, it vanished. Puzzled, I swept a small amount of hair more slowly to discover where it went. By the third sweep, all the hair was gone. The broom bristles somehow absorbed it. I loved it and beamed as I swept the entire downstairs.

I finished in the laundry room. Not wishing to end the fun, I opened the door to the garage, intending to experiment on dirt, twigs, or bolts. It was fast becoming morning, and when I opened the door to the garage, light from the garage door windows shone on the tile and turned it ordinary. I swung the door open and closed: when closed, the perfection of the tile was everywhere. When opened, the perfection retreated from the light.

About then, my brother walked down the stairs. I turned and watched the perfection recede from him as if it were trying to escape his view. It flowed like liquid across the wall and down the banister leaving plainness in its wake. Dana was too busy texting on his BlackBerry to notice. Everywhere he walked in the house, he banished perfection. It was a marvelous effect. Soon all the perfection vanished and everything returned to normal.

***

When you are extremely sleep deprived or under high stress, you may have hypnagogic dreams. Essentially, you can dream while you are awake. These dreams can be interactive, like the broom absorbing the dog hair or the wonders I saw as I walked. Real objects and dream objects can coexist so seamlessly that you cannot tell where reality ends and dream begins.

***

As the morning of May 24 began, a feeling of dread filled me and I could think of nothing but Beth. I didn't know if I needed her or she needed me, but I wanted more than anything to be with her. Dana interrupted my troubled thoughts and asked if we could get some breakfast. I suggested we go to IHOP, and he offered to drive. He drove us there in a white Camry he borrowed from my brother Cole, and I directed him. It was fortunate that Dana drove; I just had my third strike—three days without sleep. I didn't realize it, but my hours were numbered.

We had a nice breakfast at IHOP, but my mind was on Beth the entire time. There had to be a reason. Did I need her protection? I asked Dana if I could see her.

"We'll see," he replied with no intention of letting me see her. I ate my breakfast, trying to ignore my troubled thoughts. When we finally left, I asked again to see her. "In a while," he responded. When we got home, we took Washington out back and I threw the wood in the pool for him. While doing so, I asked Dana once more if I could see Beth. "I'll find out," he replied as he hammered away on his BlackBerry. After playing with Washington, we went for a walk through the neighborhood. It was unusually quiet. I didn't feel right, and was more anxious than ever. Something was wrong—I could sense it.

Something was indeed wrong, but I no longer knew how to interpret the cues my intuition sent me. My new level of mania changed me. It took away parts of my mind that knew fear. It hid useful memories: memories of the monster. The monster stalked me now, taking two steps for each of my one as my brother and I walked down the edge of the street. I sniffed the air like a wild dog and glanced nervously behind me. *What is it?* There was something, I was certain.

I started to ask Dana once more if I could see Beth when the monster surprised me from behind. He grabbed my throat and choked off my words, at first slurring them and then stopping them completely. Then, he leapt heavily onto my back, snarling, and hissing as he silenced me. My sleep-deprived body could not support his immense mass. I stumbled forward and then crumpled like a drunk as he took from me what he wanted without resistance.

As I collapsed, Dana reached out and caught me by my shirt collar, saving my head from striking the pavement. He shouted to me. I saw and heard him but could do nothing to respond. He reached under my arms and dragged me like a sack of potatoes from the street and across the sidewalk to a grass lawn. He laid me down gently and disappeared. I watched the sky for a long while; gazing unblinkingly at one solitary patch of the endless blue. Then I felt it: the bees, the bees stinging my arms and legs—a thousand bees.

My voice returned and I cried out, but it was weak, like a puppy's whimper. I remembered then. I remembered that pain. It was the only thing remembered of what was happening. My strength started to return and I turned my head to the side to see Dana screech to a halt in the white Camry. He jumped out, ran around the car, opened the passenger door, and rushed to me. He reached under my armpits and dragged me toward the car. I tried to help, but I was too weak even to hold my head up. We somehow made it to the car. He shoehorned me into the passenger seat and shut the door.

We drove after that. It seemed a pointless drive. I knew all the mountain views and road signs that I saw from my vantage point and it was clear that we weren't going anywhere; we were just killing time. The bees were gone, and I felt stronger by the minute, but I also felt sick, disoriented or—what? I couldn't put my finger on it. I was beyond anywhere I'd ever been before, and wasn't sure what anything meant.

I felt hot and in need of fresh air. I struggled up in the seat and reached for the window button. I powered the window down and rested my chin on the windowsill like a dog. I watched lethargically as we passed Foothills Drive. Shortly after that, we turned around, driving back toward my home. I took deep breaths of the warm air as the white lane lines on the road and the street signs ticked past, feeling worse as we went. It wasn't long before we turned into my neighborhood.

I closed my eyes and lost memory. The next thing I remember is being on a gurney in an ambulance. I braced myself up with my elbows just in time to catch a glimpse of my neighborhood racing away through the two small windows of the back doors. Each time I braced myself, I saw another familiar landmark disappearing behind us. The distance from my home grew rapidly: ten miles…fifteen miles. I moaned in despair with every new view.

I wanted to go home, not away from it. I wanted Beth, but Beth was already beside me. She was right next to me and I didn't even know. I have no recollection of her or anyone being with me, just everything I knew shrinking to a pinpoint, to nothing, so far away.

Chapter 19

PHOENIX MERCY

When we arrived at Phoenix Mercy hospital, paramedics helped me out of the ambulance. I could walk but not for long. They decided to place me back on the gurney. It's a good thing they did because the monster was only resting: he'd be back for me shortly. Beth was there, but when I looked at her, she looked like a paper cutout with a sad, pasted-on frown, not like the Beth that I knew. I held her hand as they wheeled me in, but it was a lifeless prop made of cardboard. My real wife was gone, frightened away by the stranger who now inhabited my body. She went through the motions to save my body, in hopes that the man she really loved would return to it.

Before I knew it, the monster attacked again, more frequently and viciously than ever. That day is the most unclear of my life as we struggled together in a strange hospital: Beth, Dana, the monster, and I, from seizure to seizure, between reality and dream, from pain to suffering to pain again. I could not distinguish what was real and what was not. In the end, when I had nothing left with which to fight, I felt a prick. A bump on my arm marked the injection site of whatever they gave me. "Don't worry, it's just Ativan. It will help you to sleep," I heard a nurse say. "It's thick and gooey, that's why it made an anthill like that on your arm. I'll massage it a bit to work it in." Then it was over. The seizures ended and left me at peace. The monster was gone.

***

Beth's journal, May 24, 2011:

Today was terrible. Around 8:45 a.m., Dana called and informed me that Ken collapsed in the street near our home and that he called 911. I rushed home as quickly as possible. When I arrived, the paramedics were there and Ken was half-sitting, half-lying on the passenger seat of Dana's car, his face wet with tears. He could not speak, and shook uncontrollably. I was frightened for him and held onto him for several minutes. When I asked if he would go to Phoenix Mercy, he barely nodded "yes." During the ambulance ride, he kept trying to get up off the gurney and cried out each time he failed. He was very emotional. Tears streamed down his face the entire trip to the hospital.

The hours passed slowly, and Ken's condition continued to worsen. Eventually he alternated between bouts of dry heaves and grimaces of pain. No one could tell me what was happening to him, and I was terrified that the man I loved was gone and that nothing would bring him back to me. I felt certain he would die. Never in my wildest dreams could I have imagined the events of the past few days.

Eventually Ken went for a CT scan. When he returned, his nurse produced a large needle. He injected Ken on the arm with it, and a lump appeared at the injection site. Mercifully, Ken fell asleep. It was wonderful to see him resting peacefully, and for once, his snores seemed the most beautiful music imaginable. He slept for a few hours after that. When he awoke, he looked at me with recognition and reached for my hand. He seemed very weak but managed to say, "I'm so sorry for all that I've put you through." At that point, it seemed as if a miracle had occurred and my Ken had returned to me. I was so thankful that I cried tears of relief. It seemed the ordeal of the past few days was finally over. Unfortunately, it wasn't very long before he was gone once more.

***

A few hours later, I awakened. Then, for a brief moment, the real Ken returned to my body—or at least that's how my brother and wife describe it. They say I was me again for a few minutes, that I said I was sorry and held Beth's hand. I can't tell you if that is true or not. My next clear recollection was just past midnight on May 25. They released me from my room under Dana's care. I believed that I was getting out of there and that all I had to do was sign a few papers. I followed Dana to a waiting area that seemed like the waiting room from hell. Even though there were only a few people there, they processed just one per hour. After a while, it was comical. The same people remained in the same places and positions for hours on end. I wondered if Dana somehow staged it. I laughed. I must have sounded insane, but the entire situation was insane. Who sits motionless for hours on end waiting for something? At some point, you have to get up and ask, "What's going on? Am I next or what?" I could deal with time any way it came at me, but it had to be painful for my poor brother. By then it was nearly 4:00 a.m. He must have been cross-eyed from lack of sleep.

Finally, they called my name and Dana led me back to a small room where we met a social worker. *That explains the long wait.* Once Dana and I sat, the woman read a familiar list of psychiatric profile questions from her monitor. I answered them succinctly, careful not to provide too much detail and have her cherry pick for facts. I finally finished, and what happened after that doesn't exist in my memory. They must have taken me to a bed where I somehow managed to sleep again.

***

Sometime during the evening of May 24 or early morning of May 25, my mind reorganized to a completely new level of mania. Stripped of anything superficial, my mind operated in its narrowest, fastest, and most efficient mode. I sensed things I never before sensed and quickly learned to interpret information from my senses intuitively. From the outside world's perspective, I was a mere shell of my previous self, much like a child living in a world of new sights, sounds, and experiences, free from fear or worry, fascinated by everything, and living entirely in the moment. From my own perspective, it was a mystical world I never imagined. In my new environment filled with the extremes of society, I quickly noticed that people were no longer just people—they each had auras of emotion, strange abilities to block each other, and, though I could easily manipulate them when alone, their prejudices proved impregnable when they banded together.

***

The next thing I remember is waking up in an unfamiliar place. Groggily, I slipped from a bed and walked out of my new room. I soon found myself in a relatively large open area with dark brown industrial carpeting; low-backed, brown fabric-covered armchairs; a small eating area; and a smoking area outside visible through glass doors. People roamed around, shouting, cursing, and swinging punches at imaginary foes. It all clicked at once: It was another psych ward.

It was one of Phoenix Mercy's many psychiatric units, and I immediately sensed that it was far worse than Pinecrest. Just then, something distracted me from my exploration. I saw something—or, more accurately, I sensed the presence of it: a sort of invisible shield between each patient and between patients and staff. I never sensed anything like that before. I didn't know what it was, but it was everywhere. My intuition told me it was a defense mechanism. I sat next to one of the patients to test the hypothesis. "Hello, how are you today?" I asked. The female patient scowled, but was intrigued. As I chatted with her, the shield flickered. It indeed appeared to be defensive. In no time, it vanished, replaced by an aura of trust. *She let me in. She let the shield down and let me in.* I was fascinated.

Another patient who sounded threatening only minutes before approached, and snap—his shield disappeared, too. The three of us chatted like good friends. At that point, I stood and stepped back. I suspected the effect was contagious, and wanted to watch it happen. Sure enough, other patients migrated toward the crowd gathering near the chairs, and one by one, their shields dropped. Before long, almost all of them joined in. They were loud, boisterous, and at one point, started to play hangman on a large whiteboard. It was surreal watching a collection of mentally ill patients, who acted out and wandering aimlessly only moments before, pull together and problem solve as a team.

It brought me joy to witness the camaraderie I initiated, but I noticed that the staff was, for perhaps the first time, reacting to the patients as well. They looked terrified. I doubt they'd ever seen anything like it. In no time, every patient's behavior had altered from bad to good. *They should be ecstatic.* I moved closer to hear what they said. Surprisingly, they wanted to call security. Fixing mentally ill people was fun, but in a twisted way, breaking normal people was even more fun. I took a seat in a chair by a wall to watch the mayhem.

A short time later, a PA announced it was time to smoke. All the patients, now friends, lined up for a smoke. Just as in Pinecrest, I was the only nonsmoker. They walked single file onto a balcony enclosed by white painted steel bars, and proceeded to generate the biggest cloud of smoke I've seen in a long while. They were very animated, telling stories, laughing, slapping each other on the backs. Mortified, the staff wondered what was going on. Once everyone got their fix, it ended. Rather than return to playing hangman or talking together, they took up their independent wandering again, as if the spell had broken. It was sad to see it end, but the staff breathed a sigh of relief.

After that, I decided to explore what little there was to explore and better understand my prison. I didn't get very far before a loud voice distracted me. "You fat bitch! Why don't you get a fucking life? I bet your husband is fat and ugly just like you. Your fucking kids are probably fat, too, aren't they? Are you listening to me? I'm talking to you, bitch!"

I walked toward the voice and found a scrawny, longhaired, bearded man berating a plump nurse. While he insulted and cursed at her, she merrily worked away on her computer, oblivious to him. I sensed that she had her shield up. *How can she block something so invasive? This shield phenomenon is obviously a lot more effective than I imagined.* I never saw anything like it. Curious, I approached the counter, rested my elbows on it right next to Rude Guy, my nickname for him, and studied everyone's reaction. Not only did the nurse not react, no other patients or staff reacted.

Then I performed an experiment. "Excuse me? Could you please get a cup of water for my friend and me?" I asked. I winked at Rude Guy, and he growled at me for interrupting his fun.

"Of course," the nurse replied in a cheery voice. She stood immediately, poured two cups of water, brought them back, and with a beaming smile, offered one to me and one to Rude Guy. *I broke through in an instant. I broke through her most powerful shield by being courteous to her.* It astonished me, and Rude Guy, too. He wanted to know how I did it. I shrugged, but probably should have told him. The staff might appreciate him being nice to them. Rude Guy decided I was some kind of wizard after that and followed me around for a while with his cup of water, hoping to con me out of my secret.

We ended up leaning against a wall by the entrance sipping from our cups. While we stood there, a pretty, young woman with brown hair and a shapely figure and another woman unlocked the doors to the unit and walked in. With no idea what they were in for, they stopped right in front of us and began a conversation. Rude Guy smiled slyly.

"Man, I'd sure like to get a piece of that fine ass," he said, loud enough that anyone within fifty feet could hear.

It embarrassed me at first. *I wish he'd shut up. She's only six feet from us.* Then, I realized it was a perfect opportunity to see the shield in action again. I encouraged him, and before long he said such nasty things that I can't bear to repeat them. The pretty woman and her friend calmly continued as if we didn't exist. They heard each other just fine but didn't hear a word he said. It was wickedly hilarious. Further experiments showed that I could easily penetrate people's shields when they were alone, but it was nearly impossible to break through when they were in a group.

Within hours of waking up in that unit, I wanted to go home. Around ten o'clock, I decided to capitalize on what I'd learned. I knew that I'd be ignored if I spoke to a group of staff, or that they'd be more apt to follow the rules to a T, so I politely approached nurses and PAs one at a time to determine what I needed to do to be released. I spoke courteously in a clear, calm voice, informing them that I came to the hospital the day before and didn't know why they put me in the psych unit. I adjusted my wording, tone, and choice of words on the fly based on their reaction. Before long, I knew everything I needed to know: who I needed to talk to, where to go, what forms were required, and who needed to sign each one. I made it my mission not only to take care of everything, but also to push things along, in a nice way, to expedite my release. In short order, I was done except for one signature: that of the staff psychiatrist. I waited by his office door until he finished with another patient and then lightly knocked on the doorframe.

"Excuse me, Dr. Bailey, I was told you could help me with these papers." Though it was early, Dr. Bailey was already in a sour mood from dealing with patients, that and his office was right across from where Rude Guy berated the nurse just a short time before. Perhaps he heard more of what Rude Guy said than others did. I promptly put him at ease by communicating in ways that I noticed gained his trust and improved his mood. When I left his office, he wore a smile on his face, and I had my final stamp of approval.

By noon on my first day, I was ready for release. Though I was at the highest level of mania I ever reached, I convinced everyone that I was normal and was there by accident. About that time, Beth called to find out when she could visit me. To her surprise, she learned that I was ready for discharge and that she could come pick me up.

With nothing better to do, I asked a nurse at the front desk near the entrance if I could wait in the lobby for my wife to pick me up. It was obvious that I was pushing the limits with her—she was visibly nervous. Normally, patients must wait in the unit for their responsible party. I was so calm and courteous that she did the unimaginable: broke a rule, the most sacred of directives. She released me on the sly when no one was looking. We walked together to the entrance of the facility, she placed the key in the lock, turned it with a smile, and shooed me through the doorway.

Once released, I had no idea where I was. I politely asked the first hospital employee I encountered where the lobby was, and he happily escorted me there. *Nothing like the red-carpet treatment.* Once in the lobby, I plopped down in a chair, laced my hands behind my head, and watched CNN on a flat screen TV.

Unbeknownst to me, Beth called the charge nurse moments after my release, trying to find out how it happened. The charge nurse knew nothing and worse yet, couldn't find me in the unit. It took a while to discover that a nurse let me out. Within minutes of getting comfortable in the lobby, I noticed two PAs headed my way.

"Sir, you need to come with us," one said.

"OK, I'm just waiting for my wife."

Rats! I remained calm and courteous. They took me back to the unit, locked the doors, and then stood guard over them so I wouldn't slip out again. Later, Beth took me home.

That afternoon, despite everything that happened, we made love for the first time since before April 10 when I unknowingly injured myself swinging that pick into the hard caliche of my backyard. Nearly a month and a half had passed since then. It turned out to be the most momentous lovemaking of my life. With my heightened senses, I detected things I never could before; where previously there were mysterious and finicky erogenous zones, there now were precise erogenous buttons. Just as I could read everyone's emotions in the Phoenix Mercy psych unit with my heightened senses, I could read everything about my wife. I pushed every button I could push until Beth could take no more. My own body was like that of a teenager. With no fear or worries and an endless supply of adrenaline, it was perhaps even better than when I was young. With my mind so clear and with an open freeway in my brain to allow all the physical sensations full priority, I felt things I never imagined possible. It was an experience beyond human experience, and I wished it would never end, but Beth grew exhausted. I pulled her close and whispered, "We should rest."

"What about you?" she asked breathlessly.

"I'm OK. Maybe we can do something again later."

After that we lay quietly for a time, Beth nearly asleep while I remained wide awake marveling at what I'd just experienced. The kids were away, and it was just us at home with nothing but time. It felt like everything was finally going to be all right. Unfortunately, things were not going to be all right and that was the last time I would even share a bed with my wife for a long time.

Chapter 20

A DANGER TO MYSELF AND OTHERS

I wasn't home long before people started trickling in. Among those people were Dana and Tim. I was happy to be around both of them but there was an ominous aura surrounding the other people. Around 5:00 p.m., the doorbell rang and Beth answered it. She welcomed two people and began talking with them in the entryway. Shortly thereafter, she escorted a slim blonde woman and another woman, who seemed to be shadowing her, into the family room. She introduced the blonde woman as Shirley Steinfeld from Family Crisis. I had no idea what that was, but it sounded like another place to confine me. I politely shook her hand, and introduced myself in return. As our hands connected, I immediately sensed animosity, as if she had formed a dislike before even meeting me, something I'd experienced often recently.

As Shirley and her companion made themselves comfortable in the family room, Beth recounted the entire story of what happened to me from the beginning. I'd heard the story many times, and I didn't want to be around Shirley, so I made my way toward the backyard sliding door, anxious to escape whatever was happening. Dana and Tim followed close behind me.

Soon I had an animated discussion with them in the backyard regarding the bubbles in the pool. I turned on the pump and showed them the undulating and pancake bubbles. To my surprise, they didn't dispute my claims. *Maybe they are like me.* I played with Washington and explained my theory about choice to Tim. He seemed to understand. *Finally, I'm no longer alone in the world, the only person who can see the bubbles, the only person without negative emotions. I've been around them both; could it actually have rubbed off?* Soon we were laughing at ideas for the new world. We even came up with a term for ourselves: "new thinkers." The rest of the people in the world were "old thinkers."

Whenever I went into the house to get a drink or to get something from the garage to show Tim and Dana, I felt uncomfortable around the group of people somberly talking in the family room. Whatever was going on, it was a very serious matter, but I was enjoying myself too much with my brother and friend to get involved. The crisis team eventually left, and Dana, Tim, and I decided to get some dinner. I suggested the Chinese restaurant run by my daughter's boyfriend's parents, and that's where we ended up.

I expected that people without negative emotions would be just like me: bubbly, caring, full of energy and ideas. It never occurred to me that it could be otherwise. Dinner with Tim and Dana was a real revelation.

Everything seemed fine as the waiter took our order. I was disappointed that he wasn't Kaitlin's boyfriend. He frequently helped his parents there. Then it grew quiet except for Dana's occasional finger tapping on his BlackBerry. The quiet was very unsettling, so I started making small talk. No one responded. It appeared that when people were new thinkers, they weren't worried about offending anyone. If they weren't interested or didn't have anything to say, they sat quietly. Things like common courtesy went out the window. My impression of those particular new thinkers was that they were emotionally flat and uncaring. Something was wrong, but I couldn't place my finger on it.

During my discussion, I brought up one of my ideas for funding Utopia that would only be possible if we were contagious. First, we could infect our immediate places of employment so that everyone would get along superbly. Though we might lose a few people who chose to pursue other passions, the remaining workforce would be such a passionate, cohesive team that they would produce a quantity and quality of work previously unheard of. We could then immediately buy enormous amounts of stock in the companies. Secondly, why stop there? Every company was going to experience the same thing as the change spread. The entire stock market would take a big jump. Eventually, it would equalize at a new standard, but in the meantime, we could make a killing. My brother got the bright idea to take advantage of that to crush the federal government. He tapped on his BlackBerry for a bit and then announced, "Done." He had created a one-man company called "Freedom.com" or some such thing that would grow so fast it would crush the government financially in no time. I laughed uproariously over that. It sounded far-fetched, but it was right up my brother's alley, and I believed he could really pull it off. Later I felt guilty about the impact that would have on the common person. I convinced him to shut the company down and instead start another just to make money for himself. Tap, tap, tap...

"Done," he exclaimed.

During dinner, my brother was on his BlackBerry frequently. He even got up a few times and went outside to talk to someone. It seemed that work was running his life. What I didn't realize was that all the text messages and phone conversations were about me. A meeting was taking place right before my eyes to determine what to do with me, and, by the end of dinner, the decision was made. My brother put his BlackBerry in his pocket and didn't use it again until we headed home.

We decided to go to Baskin-Robbins after dinner, which was just across the street. As we walked in, Tim and Dana walked ahead of me. It surprised me when neither of them held the door and it literally swung closed in front of me. I ordered my ice cream and waited to sit until Tim and Dana got theirs, Dana turned to me and asked, "Why aren't you already sitting down?" I felt like an idiot, stuck in my old ways of being courteous. Why should I worry if I hurt someone's feelings? For one, I didn't worry; for another, they didn't care. I hustled to a table. We sat quietly and ate until the cones were gone.

I watched Dana and Tim in amazement. It was so strange for no one to talk. I hoped the future of changed people wouldn't be like that. It wasn't the way I imagined people without negative emotions would be at all, but it did make me wonder if it was true. So many of the things we do are to prevent hurting others' feelings or to make them feel better. All those needs might disappear. It might be a very strange world.

As we left, unable to help myself, I made a point to hold the door for Tim and Dana. As we walked to the car, Dana fished his BlackBerry out of his pocket and texted again. If I were able to see it, I would have seen, "on our way."

When we got home, Tim said good-bye before we went in and he left. While we were gone, my youngest brother, Cole, and his wife, Andrea, arrived. They had yet to be involved due to heavy family commitments of their own. They have four children, two in college, and on top of that, finances were tight with Andrea's recent layoff. As we all conversed in the family room, I noticed that Cole and Andrea were immensely uncomfortable. I wondered if they were mad at each other. *That's OK; they'll soon feel much better. They'll have a better relationship than they've ever had.* Dana and I made jokes about new thinkers and old thinkers, knowing that no one else had a clue what we were talking about. I laughed genuinely, but everyone besides Dana rolled their eyes and showed concern.

After a while, Beth asked, "Ken, would you go for a walk with me around the block?"

"Sure," I replied. I got up from the rocker in the corner of the family room I was sitting in, and the two of us went out the front door. Once outside I took Beth's hand, laced my fingers through hers as I have countless times, and held her hand as we walked. She was strangely quiet and sad, but I didn't dare ask why—she had plenty going on in her mind lately, and all of it had to do with me. Instead of talking, we walked quietly around the neighborhood in the glow of the streetlamps.

It was well after eleven o'clock by then. The temperature rose to 111 degrees that day and was still over 105, but a dry, steady breeze blew from the west as it often does this time of year, which at least prevented us from sweating. As we passed the halfway mark around the block, I heard the rustling of the fronds of the date palm that I'd heard just a few evenings earlier during that flawless night. As we passed it, I looked up at the grand tree glowing in the beam of the spotlight at its base, but it no longer seemed special. I loved the sound just the same.

A hundred yards from my home, I noticed a police SUV parked across the street and an officer speaking with my brothers in the middle of the road. It seemed very odd, so as we got closer, I released Beth's hand and went to see what was going on. As I approached the officer, Dana took Beth into the house.

"Hi, officer, can I help you? I live here," I said, pointing to my house.

"Are you Mr. Dickson? Mr. Kenneth Dickson?"

"Yes. Is there a problem?"

"Mr. Dickson, I need you to take a seat in my vehicle, please."

"What's wrong?"

"Just take a seat."

The officer opened the rear door of the SUV and motioned for me to get in. "Watch your head," he said and put his hand against the doorframe to protect my head as I got in. Once inside, the officer closed the door. He spoke briefly with my brothers again, but I couldn't hear what they said. Then they both turned and walked toward my home, never looking back.

***

Beth's journal, May 25, 2011:

I invited Ken to go for a walk with me. We walked down the street holding hands. It was so wonderful to have my gentle, loving Ken back who would walk quietly with me. The police arrived sometime before midnight when we were returning from our walk. Dana sent me directly into the house so I wouldn't have to watch whatever happened. I cried for hours on the rocking chair in the family room. I don't ever recall feeling so desolate and hopeless. At some point, I went upstairs to lie down in bed. I don't remember if I actually slept.

Chapter 21

THE PDC

I was sure my brothers would return to rescue me from the police SUV. I begged the officer to wait for them. I begged until it was beyond doubt that they weren't coming back. After patiently obliging me for considerable time, the officer turned to me and said, "I'm sorry, sir, we have to go."

I had no idea why I was in a police vehicle or where he was taking me. The SUV was hot and stuffy. There were several air-conditioning vents in the dash of the vehicle but none in the back. I noticed that all but one of the dash vents pointed at the officer and none pointed at the few small holes in the clear Lexan panel that separated us. Precious little cool air made it through those holes to me. I reached out to them and was only able to cool the palms of my hands. As we drove to our destination, I dripped sweat onto the smooth, black leather upholstery of the seat. I couldn't help but wonder how many others' sweat had soaked that leather.

It seemed an eternally long ride in the sweltering SUV. I could see very little through the bars and limo tint blocking the view of the night through the vehicle windows—mostly just headlights and streetlamps. I could see no landmarks to give me any idea of where we might be; the route we took was a mystery.

Eventually we arrived at an imposing, single-story, mud-colored brick building. Along the side of the building about six feet from the ground, a row of long, squat, tinted windows glowed ominously in the night. They gave the impression that the building was a prison. We turned off the street and drove behind the building to a lit area. There, a single primer-red canopy protected a gray steel door beneath it. On the door was a white sign with the words EMERGENCY ENTRANCE in red. Right below the sign, a hastily spray-painted patch highlighted what appeared to be a dent from a small caliber bullet. The officer parked the SUV next to the entrance. He radioed his status and then exited the vehicle. Moments later, he returned with two men in scrubs. He opened my door and let me out of the SUV.

"You have a good evening, sir," he said to me.

"You too, officer," I said automatically. I couldn't bring myself to thank him, but I also couldn't help but notice that he was the kindest to me of any professional in a long while. It occurred to me that I was probably the easiest "criminal" he ever dealt with—I gave him no trouble whatsoever.

As the officer reentered his vehicle and again radioed in, the two men asked me to follow them. I didn't notice much about them through the poor visibility of the SUV windows, but now, standing beside them, I was truly intimidated. Each of them was over six feet tall and built like a football player. One pressed a button on the right side of the door and spoke into an intercom just above it. Moments later, the door buzzed. He opened it and motioned for me to enter while the other followed close behind me.

Once inside, the men escorted me through the facility to a small room packed with recliners. There were twenty seven of the dirty-beige leather recliners arranged in three rows of nine each, all facing a large pane of glass at the front of the room. The two rows in the front were so close to each other that when reclined, I didn't think it was possible to walk between them. The third row was a ways back from the front two near the back wall of the room. Each recliner in a row sat so close to the next that there was barely enough space to access the levers to recline them. The room was apparently co-ed, with a mix of men and women curled up on the recliners under ratty, threadbare blankets. It was just after midnight by then, and most of them were asleep.

The first man directed me to a recliner at the far end of the front row. "This is yours. You'll be here until you're moved to another facility. You can walk around whenever you want, but I suggest that you stay in the recliner as much as possible. Things can get out of hand quickly here. The bathroom is over there if you need to use it." He pointed back in the direction from which we had come. "If you want to call someone, there's a portable phone at the nurse's desk by the bathroom. Just ask the nurse for it. You have to dial nine to get out. There's a blanket on your recliner if you need it." I looked and saw a thin, discolored, and well-worn blanket folded on the recliner seat. "If you have any personal items on you, we'll need to take those now. You can get them back later."

"No." I pulled my empty pants pockets inside out, then turned and patted my empty rear pocket. It occurred to me that I had nothing on me to identify who I was.

"Do you have any questions?"

"Yes, where am I and why am I here?"

"You're at the PDC. I don't know exactly why you were brought here, but you'll be here for anywhere from a few hours to as much as a week until a bed opens up at another facility."

"What kind of facility?"

"From here you'll be placed in a high-security psychiatric unit where they will evaluate you for a minimum of seventy-two hours. That's all I can tell you. Any other questions?"

"No."

"If you need anything, you can ask us or any other PAs in scrubs." With that, the two men returned to their business.

Not knowing what to expect, I was numb. I picked up the folded blanket and sat down. I looked at the large glass pane a few feet in front of my recliner. Its length was slightly more than the length of the row of recliners. It ran from three feet above the floor to three feet below the ceiling. There was a clock mounted in the center of the wall above the window. Through the glass, I noticed another glass pane at right angles to it. Behind that pane was another smaller area with about fifteen recliners.

Scattered desks, with stacks of paperwork, office supplies, and computer monitors were visible through the glass directly in front of me, all of them facing the glass. A dozen eyes could watch us at any given moment, but everyone sitting behind them seemed too busy to care about us.

From my vantage point near the corner of the room, I could see nearly everything. I swiveled my head and took stock of my new surroundings. I noticed that a separation between the back and front rows of recliners created a walkway between them. At the farthest end of the room from me, the nurse's desk faced the recliners. On the opposite side of the room, next to a small open area, stood another desk at an angle, which also faced the recliners. PAs sometimes used that desk, but it was frequently vacant. A short way from my recliner, built into the wall near the large glass pane, was a glass door to the office area.

It was after midnight and another day had begun, May 26. I decided to recline my recliner and attempt to sleep. I searched for a lever on the right side and instead found an unfamiliar mechanical assembly. It was only capable of rotating up, so I rotated it. Once all the way up, a small table fell with a clunk across my recliner above my lap. *I guess that's where I eat.* I folded the table and rotated it back down, then tried my luck on the other side with a thin wooden lever. I pulled and then pushed to no avail. I rocked forward and backward while doing the same and still nothing happened. I tried again, harder. With an audible creak, the footrest sprang up, and the back of the recliner slammed full force to the most reclined position. I tucked my still-folded blanket behind my head as a pillow and lay in triumph.

Only twelve hours earlier, they released me from Phoenix Mercy where I managed only a few hours of drugged sleep after suffering the worst seizures imaginable. Prior to that, I went three days straight without sleep. I knew I was a ticking time bomb. I tossed and turned fitfully in the recliner, unable to sleep. Besides the discomfort of the recliner, I couldn't shut out the sounds of people with psychiatric and addiction problems: unpredictable outbursts of screaming, frequent cursing, and fights followed by a stampede of PAs rushing to regain control.

Some sounds were particularly difficult to ignore. As I lay with my eyes closed, trying my best to sleep, I heard faint wailing. It ceased, and then began anew. From its frail beginning, the wailing grew into nearly a scream before sobbing punctuated it. I rose onto my elbows and scanned the room for its source. Near the opposite end of the row behind me, a woman sat sobbing with her face buried in her hands. Her long, caramel hair flowed over her arms, hiding her features. Spotting an empty recliner next to her, I slid from my own, walked over, and sat beside her. Though intending to calm her so that I might sleep, I also felt genuine compassion for her.

"Hi," I said. "I'm Ken. What's your name?" Her face remained buried in her hands, and she continued to sob. "Everything's going to be OK," I said, trying to relieve her pain. She raised her head and turned toward me, her face, wet with tears and snot. She squinted at me through eyes so red and swollen I couldn't tell what color they were. Her lips quivered, and she could barely catch her breath. She swept her long hair away from her face with her hand and it fell heavily behind her shoulder.

"Are you Caspian?" she inquired.

It was the oddest question anyone ever asked me. It took a moment to formulate an appropriate response. "No, but you will meet him some day. When you do, your life will be perfect." That struck a chord. She slowly straightened, wiped her face with her hands, and studied me curiously for a moment. Then she smiled— not much of a smile but enough to notice. My heart soared and I returned the smile. *I made a difference in her life.* Afterward she turned away, and her hair slid back over her shoulder and swept across her face, hiding it once more. It reminded me of a stage curtain closing, and I wondered if she had somehow left the stage. She remained quiet for a time, and then unexpectedly from behind the hair said, "Jessie. My name is Jessie."

I comforted her a bit longer, and then returned to my recliner to continue my pursuit of sleep. Less than thirty minutes later, another commotion at the opposite end of my row caught my attention. Two PAs dragged an older man toward the last recliner. The man, apparently heavily inebriated, stumbled and cursed. They hefted him into the recliner and left him.

"Where's my fucking phone? I want my fucking phone. Don't I get to make a phone call?" bellowed the drunk. He tried to leave his recliner but thankfully could not. He continued ranting, so I left my recliner and took a seat in the empty one next to him to try to calm him.

"Hi, I'm Ken. How are you doing?" I asked. He pushed his disheveled white hair away to get a better look at me, his blue eyes jittering slightly behind heavily fingerprinted glasses. "Whaddya want?" he asked.

"Hey, I'm locked up in here just like you. I just came over to see if I could help you." "Yeah, you can help. Get the fuck outta my face. God damn it, where's my fucking phone?"

"Look, everything will seem a lot better in the morning. Why don't you lay back in your nice, comfortable recliner and get some rest, OK?"

"Fuck you," he cursed, but part of his mind registered my recommendation. He glared at me and then relaxed. I showed him how to recline his recliner, then left him. He remained quiet after that and eventually fell asleep, snoring like a buzz saw. Back in my own recliner once again, I felt pride for helping yet another troubled inmate.

Before long, a tall, lanky, black man with lengthy dreadlocks shattered the relative peace and quiet again. He wore colorful clothes that looked straight from Africa, but what spewed from his mouth was not an African dialect, it was the incoherent ramblings of a homeless American schizophrenic. I wondered if I could make a difference in his life as I did with Carlos. I rose and walked slowly toward the back row of recliners, smelling him before I was even close: he reeked of the street. I stayed close by for a while and then continued down the walkway separating the second row of recliners from those in back. I'll never know if I made a long-term difference, but he did settle after that.

I walked around the rows of recliners a bit longer and then crawled back into my own. I closed my eyes and, before I knew it, thought of Utopia. It was a part of me, a part of my heart and soul, and it comforted me to have that place to go to. *Now, where did I leave off? Ah yes.*

Chapter 22

UTOPIA: MY PROBLEM SOLVER

One thing I wondered about Utopia is if we should design it in secret. Should we encode our communications and hide our activities, or was it OK to go about our business without a care? I scrutinized every possible scenario and couldn't arrive at an answer. The concern eventually slipped from conscious thought as I moved on to other dilemmas.

I pondered for a time the optimal size of the community of Utopia, but that didn't lead anywhere either. Next, I considered managing people who all were passionate, got along with each other, and perhaps noticed that all their good ideas succeeded. Once things were underway, it wouldn't take much effort to manage them, possibly none at all. It seemed prudent, however, to have someone with vision lead the project and to have some kind of structure.

I envisioned a wagon wheel with me at its hub, coordinating communication among the spokes, each representing a department such as water, sewer, power, etc. To get the wheel rolling, I'd simply plant a seed concept in each spoke, then let people brainstorm solutions from there, consulting with me as necessary to synchronize with the activities of the other spokes. Eventually, my head ached from thinking. I couldn't sleep but needed to put my spinning mind on pause. I cleared it of thought and tried to relax. Time slipped by.

***

Hours after I wondered whether to design Utopia in secret, a kind of "bing" went off in my mind. *The smallest possible community for people without negative emotions is two.* That was odd. I remembered my concern about Utopia being planned and designed in secret, but *oh yeah, I wondered about the size of the community as well.* It was a wonderful coincidence that my mind was perfectly clear when the solution returned; the notification was impossible to ignore.

I suddenly realized that must be how the subconscious worked. It took ownership of problems that the conscious mind abandoned and continued trying to solve them in the background. If it found an answer, it presented it, whether it was minutes, hours, or days later. I glanced at the clock and it was four hours since I last thought about the size of the community. I'd just learned how "eureka" moments came about.

I reveled in that knowledge for a time, then realized that the big machine from days earlier returned an answer as well about negative emotions being the source of dysfunction. The big machine was no miracle after all; it was my subconscious, my problem solver. I wondered about other things I experienced back then, and it occurred to me that my subconscious also guided me through my loss of negative emotions in its own creative way, by slowing or speeding the big engine in reaction to my emotional responses. I needed only to persevere and follow its lead.

I considered my recent answer regarding the size of a community. *What use would a community of two be?* Perhaps people without negative emotions don't fare well alone; they need other people, but in a pinch they'd be happy with only one other person, because the things that made it difficult for people to coexist no longer were a factor.

As far as keeping the development of Utopia secret, my problem solver never provided an answer. Perhaps it was unsolvable given the few known facts.

Chapter 23

THE CRASH

Thoughts about Utopia, and how my subconscious worked, carried me through until breakfast. Not surprisingly, meals weren't fancy at the PDC with zero prep time the guiding rule: premade sandwiches, cardboard boxes of cereal, fruit, and anything that could be torn from a wrapper. Breakfast that morning consisted of a banana, orange juice in a sealed plastic container, a small carton of milk, Frosted Flakes, and a muffin wrapped in plastic. I lined up with everyone else in the open space ahead of the back row of recliners and received a tray already filled.

After returning to my recliner, I set the tray on the floor, yanked firmly on the lever and the back of the recliner at the same time to raise it. It creaked and groaned in protest but ultimately sprang upright sending the footrest back into storage as well. I sat, flipped the tray arm up and over from the side of the chair, rested the tray on it, and set about eating my meal. The milk was whole, not the fat free I typically drank at home. I poured a little on the cereal and drank the rest. The rich, satisfying taste provided a small comfort. After I finished, I realized that Beth was probably awake by then. I felt I should call her and tell her as much as I could about where I was. I walked over to the nurse's desk.

"Can I use the phone, please?" I asked.

"Yes, but you'll have to wait your turn," the nurse replied crankily, motioning with a pencil toward a man a few yards away vigorously berating someone on the receiving end of the portable phone. I paced anxiously. A few minutes later, he swore one final time, disconnected, and slammed the phone down on the desk. I reached for it and dialed home, but nothing happened.

"You have to dial nine first," the nurse grumbled without looking up.

"Oh yeah, I forgot."

I dialed again and put the phone to my ear. It was so hot it seemed it would burn my skin. I wasn't sure if it was defective or if it was the heat of anger from the previous user. The line connected and the phone rang until the answering machine picked up.

"Beth? Beth? Are you there? If you are, can you pick up? I'm somewhere called the PDC. It's a horrible place filled with street people, drunks, psychos, and addicts. It's really loud, and there are fights all the time. I haven't gotten a lick of sleep since I've been here. Please pick up if you're there..." I waited until the beep signaled the end of the recording. Then I called Beth's cell phone, but she didn't answer that either.

Twelve hours after arriving at the PDC, I sensed the monster stirring. After my most recent encounter, I remembered him instantly and bolted upright in my recliner. Fresh memories of him played out in my crystal-clear, manic brain. I stood and tried to figure out what to do. I asked to use the phone again; this time there was no waiting. I called Beth at home, and the answering machine picked up once more. When I could record, I pleaded into the phone, "I'm going to have a seizure. It's coming. I can feel it. I don't know if anyone here can help me. Beth, if you're there, pick up, please..." There was nothing, just a long silence and a familiar beep.

***

Beth's journal, May 26, 2011:

The crisis counselor recommended that I turn the ringers off on the telephones. I did that to the one near our bed and my cell phone, but I forgot to turn it off on the phone downstairs. As I lay in bed upstairs, I heard it ring, then Ken's voice on the answering machine. He sounded frightened and desperate. I wanted so much to answer his calls and come to his aid, but I couldn't do anything. Everything I tried to get my Ken back utterly failed. The entire medical system let me down. Now, events were out of my control.

I never had a worse night in my life. No one that I knew could begin to comprehend what was happening to me. Completely torn apart in just a few weeks, my family seemed to have no hope of ever being back together. I don't know if I will ever be able to forgive myself for not answering that night. Maybe someday he'll think of me as his "angel" rather than someone trying to hurt him. I was only trying to help bring him back to me.

***

I walked to the desk and returned the phone. "Can you help me? I'm going to have a seizure," I informed the nurse matter-of-factly.

"OK," she responded, scanning the room to see where the PAs were.

"I'm serious. I can feel when they're coming. I've probably got less than fifteen minutes."

"Uh-huh." She didn't look up.

"Please."

"Mike, can you get this man out of my face?" she shouted to the most intimidating of the PAs. I backed away from the desk as he approached.

"Is there a problem here?" he inquired.

"No, uh, I just need a pencil and some sticky notes to write some things down," I said, thinking quickly and noticing that both those items were within my reach. The nurse pushed a pad of sticky

161

notes and a pencil toward me, and the PA watched as I hurriedly tore off several of the yellow squares. I filled out a sticky note with "KEN DICKSON NEEDS HELP CALL 911." Then I filled out another, then a third written on the sticky side of the note. My writing became more and more labored as I progressed. The monster was close: I was running out of time.

Gritting my teeth, I slapped one note on the desk in front of me, directly in the nurse's view, then, I turned and weaved toward the other desk and slapped another note there. Finally, I staggered toward the large glass window separating patients from observers. I took the last note and stuck it on the glass with the text facing everyone on the other side. I turned and stumbled the last six feet to my recliner and collapsed into it, praying that someone, anyone, would heed my desperate pleas.

With only seconds left, my mind searched for anything I might have missed that could save me. I suddenly knew what I must do. No one on my side of the glass was going to help me. I needed to make an unmistakable appeal to those on the other side. I consumed my last remaining strength to throw my failing body toward the glass door that separated the two rooms. My hope was that someone on the other side would recognize that I was in jeopardy and swiftly open the door to rescue me. The monster overtook me and my body melted halfway to the door. My face hit the glass and left a trail of spit on it as I slid to the floor.

At that point, I was at the mercy of fate. PAs leapt on me like vultures on carrion. Hands pulled at me from all different directions. At first, there was concern over my escape attempt. Then, they laughed, finding it hilarious that I feigned paralysis to try to escape. They didn't appreciate me manipulating them, however, and they quickly turned mean.

I didn't know who they were or how many there were. They grabbed me by the fabric of my shirt, pulling it over my head in an effort to make me stand. Then, they dragged me across the floor when that didn't work. My limp head flopped uncontrollably from side to side inside the cotton T-shirt and I could see nothing but the gray fabric.

"Stand up...stand up...," they yelled as they mopped the filthy floor with my flaccid body. I couldn't say, feel or do anything. Abruptly they threw me onto something soft. Then, I lay face down in a world of gray, waiting for the paralysis to end.

Mercifully, there were no stinging bees, pain, or vomiting. Instead, I felt only pins and needles as my body returned to me. I pulled my shirt down and found that I was back in my recliner. It seemed like they dragged me twenty feet, but in fact it was only the few feet from the door back to my recliner. I took stock of my surroundings. No one came to my rescue, and nothing changed except that all the PAs eyed me suspiciously. They needn't have worried: I was so weak I could do nothing but stay put.

Not long after that, it was lunchtime. I wondered if food would help to stabilize me. Another inmate who'd just been assigned the recliner next to me had just gotten his lunch.

"Excuse me, I'm not feeling very well and don't think I can make it to the food line. Could I have your lunch and could you get another, please?"

The unkempt, longhaired man looked at me with bloodshot eyes and said, "Fuck you, asshole. Get your own fucking lunch."

After resting a few minutes, I decided to try his suggestion. I stood like a drunk and walked slowly, shakily to the food line. I barely made it back before the monster set his sights on me once more. With only moments to spare, I sat in the recliner and placed the tray on the floor next to it. This time the monster had a new trick. He snatched my puppet strings and shook them with glee. In response, I flailed uncontrollably in the recliner.

"What the fuck...what's the matter with you, man?" I heard from the recliner next to me. Instantly I attracted the full attention of all the staff. Just as suddenly as the flailing began, it ceased. The monster dropped my strings and watched in satisfaction as my head fell limply to the side and my body slid to the floor. Hands pulled at me again, and the yelling and laughter began anew. Arms dug painfully under my armpits as PAs tried forcing me to stand. *Why are they hurting me? Why are they laughing at me? I need help. I tried to tell them. Why will no one listen?*

The pain in my armpits was excruciating. Using all of my willpower, I managed to persuade my legs to swing a bit as they held me in the air, making it look like I was trying to walk so they would stop hurting me. It only made them laugh harder.

Just when it seemed that it could get no worse, the pain subsided as the arms digging into my armpits relented. I heard a muffled conversation far away, and then more laughter. From the edge of my field of vision, I barely made out a PA talking to two paramedics with a gurney. My heart leapt for joy. *Someone is going to help me.* I was incredulous. Someone answered my pleas. I was going to be all right.

With my head hanging down and my legs swinging loosely, the PAs carried me by my armpits and hefted my limp body onto the gurney, then two paramedics restrained my hands and feet to it. I was so thankful that tears of joy streamed down the sides of my face as I lay there. They rolled me into the bright sunlight of midday and lifted me into an awaiting ambulance. Though I'd grown to dislike ambulances, this one was a blessing; it saved me from the PDC and would take me to salvation.

As the ambulance drove away, the monster remained right by my side. This time, he wasn't freeing me any time soon. I remained paralyzed and unable to talk longer than ever before. I wondered if it was over for me—if this was how my life was going to be from then on.

Told that I was faking the paralysis, the paramedics made a game of filling out my medical information. While we drove, the paramedic riding with me asked questions, and the driver, pretending to be me, yelled back ridiculous responses. Then, they both laughed hysterically. During moments of silence, the paramedic next to me checked off boxes and filled in information as if I had given it to him. I never before experienced anything like it. I couldn't believe that anyone could be so cruel to a person in my condition.

Before long, I arrived at my next stop where RN Raul awaited. The paramedics wheeled me into a small, white room with a thin mattress covered only with a fitted sheet on a steel frame bolted to the floor. There was nothing in the room aside from a convex security mirror in one corner, and there were no windows. After the paramedics removed my restraints and rolled the gurney next to the bed, Raul ordered me to get onto it. When I didn't respond, the paramedics rolled me from the gurney face down onto the bed and laughed as they walked out. Raul rattled through a list of questions and checked off boxes on his forms as if I had answered, sometimes making up his own answers, and laughing as well. Eventually, he stuck his pen in his clipboard and said, "Welcome to Gracewood." Then he abandoned me in the room. Having made me suffer enough, the monster finally released me and left me alone with my pain as my body returned.

Part 3

RESOLUTION

Chapter 24

MAKING LEMONADE FROM LEMONS

Gracewood was indeed a hospital but not one where I would receive any medical attention. It was a psychiatric hospital, perhaps the highest security of its kind in the Phoenix area. The unit I was in was for patients under court-ordered treatment considered a danger to themselves and others, or persistently or acutely disabled. Unknown to me at that time, I was considered "all of the above." When you enter Gracewood, much like the other places I was in, you don't get a tour. You aren't greeted by the staff or introduced to other patients. No one explains the schedule; how to get your clothes washed; where the showers are, or when to eat. You don't get a toothbrush, toothpaste, or soap to wash your hands. The only thing they do is show you your room. You have to figure out the rest on your own.

As far as treatment goes, I can tell you the sum total of my treatment in a paragraph. If there was a treatment plan for me, no one bothered to inform me of it. The psychiatrist did talk to me a few times, but he was only interested in how I felt, which was always "fine." There were group meetings at Gracewood—most of them involved substance abuse. I went to two of those before deciding that they were a waste of time. Because of my recent history with medications, I was already saying "no to drugs" twice a day (specifically Haldol and Depakote) when the medication cart arrived at 9:00 a.m. and 9:00 p.m. The only medication I accepted was an occasional Ativan to help me sleep. I went to a few other group meetings: one for a movie, two for yoga, and another to play bingo. I won at bingo twice in a row. Everyone complained that the game was rigged. In reality, I was probably the only one paying attention. I also participated in the community meeting at the end of every day and tried to establish a worthwhile goal for the next day. That was it. That's what you get for the bargain basement price of just over $2,000 a day.

One thing I have to admit is that meals at Gracewood were excellent. The food was always fresh or freshly cooked. Since we were already dangerous, perhaps they didn't want to complicate things further by adding more chemicals or preservatives to the mix.

My unit wasn't large, perhaps eighty feet long by forty feet wide. Twenty-five feet or so on the east end included the men's rooms (four double-occupancy and one that housed four patients), two single-stall showers, two seclusion rooms referred to as "quiet rooms," and the nurses' station. There was a U-shaped hallway through that section with the patient and quiet rooms around the outside perimeter.

The women's rooms were in twenty-five feet or so of the opposite side. The women's side was a mystery to me since it was off limits to men, but was most likely a mirror image of the men's side. Word had it that each room had its own shower though. The women's side also housed the snack room with a roll-up steel security window facing the main area. The window only opened at snack time. If you weren't fast enough getting in line, the snacks often ran out before you got yours. The linen and medical supply rooms took up part of the remaining area. That left an area of roughly thirty by thirty-five feet in which the twenty-some patients spent nearly all their time.

In that area were six oak tables with four oak chairs around each and several rows of low-backed armchairs facing the television mounted on the west wall. The television hung from the ceiling in a white painted wooden case with an unbreakable sheet of Lexan screwed to the face to protect it from rogue patients.

On the north wall was a row of windows with steel security mesh in front of them. Through the mesh, the view of the outside world was a parking lot. The unit was at ground level, so that's all you could see. Along that wall were several armchairs and a few matching sofas. On the east wall of the area was a long table with a few tattered magazines. Just above that were two well-worn, tan-colored, touch-tone, corded telephones. Next to the table was another sofa and above that sofa was a large chicken wire-reinforced window through which the nursing staff could monitor the area.

The nurses' station remained locked. If you needed a nurse, you knocked on the door to the office and waited for someone to unlock it. Across from the nurses' station on the south side were the double doors of the main entrance. On the south wall, adjacent to the snack room, were the double doors to the outside recreation yard and the group room. On the southwest wall of the main area was a whiteboard with the schedule for the week, and just left of the roll-up window for the snack room was another whiteboard with all the patients' names and their daily goals (if they had any).

PAs and nurses were always in the room and had a small table and chairs along the south wall where they congregated to keep a constant eye on everyone. There were always at least two PAs on duty, and frequently a nurse or two as well.

Some patients elected to spend much of their time in their rooms, and I rarely saw them. Others spent time in quiet rooms for misbehaving or because they posed a danger to the rest of us. Since there was little to do but socialize, watch TV, and eat, I couldn't help but get to know the rest of the patients to some extent. I spent nearly all of my confinement with those people in that small room. As a consequence, the biggest thing I took away from Gracewood was our stories—some left me in stitches, others were horrible but had silver linings, and a few were just plain inspirational.

In the end, life is what you make of it. Though many people would be horrified in my situation, like everyone else at Gracewood,

I was there for the duration, so I made the most of my time, making lemonade from the lemons life handed me.

One thing about mania, particularly when you're in a psych unit, is that what day, month, or year it is loses its importance. I was living in the moment. The only day that really mattered to me was the day of my release. As soon as I knew that day, I paid attention to how close it was. I wouldn't have cared about time if meals, breaks, going outside, and visiting hours weren't tied to it. Although the following short stories are in chronological order, I couldn't tell you exactly what day or time they happened. What mattered most to me were the people or events involved. Each story is a snapshot of something or someone I will never forget from Gracewood.

Hand-me-downs

Not long after my admission to Gracewood and my recovery from the seizure, I faced yet another one. As I prepared for the worst, a hand reached out from beyond my range of vision with a small cup of pills.

"What are these?" I asked.

"…and the white one is Ativan" was all I heard as a mystery person rattled off the names of several pills in the cup. I grabbed the small white pill, took the cup of water offered to me, and washed it down. Before I knew it, I was dead asleep somewhere in the bowels of a place called Gracewood.

I don't know how many hours passed before I awakened. I didn't know where I was, what day it was, or what time it was, but thankfully, I got some sleep and was through with seizures for a while. I sat up on my bed in the twilight of my new room. A translucent window glowed faintly in a corner of the room, lit by the glow of a streetlamp outside the building.

I took stock of my new surroundings. There were two blue plastic beds with thin, vinyl-covered foam mattresses resting atop them. Each had a fitted sheet, a sheet, and a faded blue blanket. One of the beds was bolted to the floor and the other was movable. There were two doors to the room: one was the entrance, and the other opened to a bathroom shared with a similar room. There were two plastic storage cubbies in the room, one for each occupant. Those were about two feet on a side and had a shelf across the middle. On top of the cubby nearest my bed sat a paper grocery bag.

I stood and searched for a light switch in the room. I found it and squinted after switching the fluorescent lights on as my eyes adjusted. I peered into the bag. It was half-full of clothing. I carefully turned it over on the bed and lifted the bag off to reveal a perfect stack of neatly folded clothes. Shockingly, they were *my* clothes. On top of the pile of clothes rested a blue plastic tube containing *my* travel toothbrush. It seemed impossible that anyone had a clue as to where I was with all the events that had gotten me there. I certainly had no idea. In my manic mindset, I could only conclude that they were a gift from God.

As I sorted through my pile of clothing, I couldn't help but try it all on. It was wonderful to have my own things. As I tried on various items, I was surprised that so few of them fit me, particularly my pants. Pants that used to fit me comfortably fell right off. I forgot how much weight I lost because of my surgery, and perhaps I lost more since then. I also noticed that some of the T-shirts in the stack were among my least favorite. *What was God thinking, giving me this odd collection of clothing?*

I divided the clothes into two stacks, the ones I liked and that fit (a very small stack) and the rest (a substantially larger stack). When I finished, I carefully tucked the two stacks of clothes onto the top shelf of my cubby with the intention that the top shelf would be my "clean clothes" shelf, and later the bottom would be for dirty ones.

The day after my arrival, a roommate joined me. His name was Rich, and he seemed normal enough. He and I got along well and spent a good deal of time together when he first arrived. He was quick to notice my stacks of clothes, since all he had was what he arrived in. I told him about the strange appearance of the bag of clothes and informed him of the fact that most of them didn't fit me.

He immediately stripped to his underwear to try on the ones that didn't fit. Surprisingly, Rich was the same size as the old me: everything fit him perfectly. I generously offered him any of the clothes he wanted, figuring that they were a gift to me anyway, and he claimed a goodly portion of them.

Eventually, word spread about all the unneeded clothes in my room that God so generously provided. They made their way to new owners: a shirt here, some pants there. One woman claimed two pairs of shorts. It was strange seeing her wearing my shorts. Some days she even wore my T-shirts with them.

One day Beth came to visit me. As we talked, she noticed a familiar shirt pass by.

"Hey, that guy has a T-shirt just like yours," she exclaimed.

"That's because it is mine, and those are my pants. He's probably wearing my underwear and socks, too."

Beth turned to me incredulously. "I went to all the trouble to bring you nice, neatly ironed and folded clothes and you gave them away?"

"What are you talking about?" I asked, confused.

"I brought those for you when you were admitted."

I smiled but didn't say anything. Things suddenly made sense, but I had to admit, I liked the idea better that God had given me clothes that didn't fit and that I didn't want so that I could share them with those less fortunate than me.

Covering for myself, I explained the clothing situation to Beth, making it seem as dire as possible. During our conversation, one of the other patients, Sandra, joined us. She and I had talked a bit and I told her Beth was coming by for a visit. She wanted to meet her. She quickly confirmed the clothing situation, and surprisingly, Beth, noticing they were close to the same size, offered to help her.

The next day when Beth visited, she brought a paper bag with freshly cleaned, ironed, and folded clothes for Sandra that she personally handpicked for her from her own clothes and from a local Goodwill. The clothes fit Sandra perfectly. She was delighted and wore them nearly every day for the remainder of the time I was at Gracewood.

As far as my own clothing situation, I quickly learned that the laundry services at Gracewood left much to be desired. You leave your crumpled, dirty clothes in a bag by your door at night with your name scrawled on it, and by morning, you have crumpled clean clothes returned in the same bag. The crumpled clean clothes looked worse than the dirty ones. Rather than deal with that, I instead decided to wear scrubs. You could get a clean pair of neatly folded scrubs any time. Unfortunately, the scrubs pants didn't fit me—they were either too tight and too short, or too baggy and too long. So, I wore the same pair of khaki pants nearly my entire stay at Gracewood. I did, however, have my underwear and socks washed regularly.

The Best Pillow

It was tough to get a good night's sleep at Gracewood because they had the worst pillows in the world. I wasn't alone in that fate. Everyone had the same dreadful pillow. The pillows were made of a solid piece of polyethylene foam with a sealed vinyl cover. They reminded me of an inflatable pool toy. Besides being uncomfortable, they were hot. When I lay my head on mine, it began sweating in no time.

After the first night, I had enough of that pillow and brainstormed ways to make a better pillow from materials on hand, which was almost nothing. The two plastic bed frames appeared fabricated from the same plastic as the blue garbage recycling bins in my neighborhood. The two cubbies were made of the same material. There was nothing else in the room.

Then, I noticed that the second bed, not yet occupied, had dirty sheets, a blanket, and a pillowcase on the pillow. I wondered if I could trade those for something to make a better pillow. I collected the dirty linens, took them to a PA, and asked if I could trade them for clean ones. He walked with me to the linen storage room and asked me what I wanted. I requested four sheets and two pillowcases. He must have thought that I intended to change both beds. He handed them to me without hesitation. I was delighted and quickly headed back to do some engineering.

I took each of the four neatly folded sheets, unfolded them, crumpled them loosely, and stuffed them into a pillowcase. When that was finished, I took my newly formed pillow and stuffed it open end first into the other pillowcase. That kept the sheets from falling out the open end of the first pillowcase. It was the most comfortable pillow imaginable and had the benefit of staying cool because it was so breathable.

I used that pillow my entire stay at Gracewood. It brought me countless extra hours of sleep, something that was always a necessity. On my last day, I disassembled it and deposited the sheets and pillowcases in a hamper. I didn't want someone to find it and get in trouble for having a non-standard pillow, even though I wanted to let everyone in on the secret so they too could share a little luxury in a place where there was none.

Girlie Pics

One thing that struck me about Gracewood was the lack of anything on the walls. It was like that everywhere I'd been so I shouldn't have been surprised. I was determined to make my own secret statement, however, to add a little color and spice to the place. On the table by the two phones in the main area was a stack of well-worn magazines. With little better to do, I often found myself flipping through them.

I was leafing through one of the women's magazines one day and noticed the makeup ads. The models for the ads were very pretty. I decided that was just the spice I needed. I took the magazine to my room, carefully tore the model's photo out, then tried to figure how and where to mount it. I could ask the nurses for tape, but they probably wouldn't let me have it—I might suffocate or strangle myself with it. I noticed there were pieces of masking tape on every door with patients' names written on them. The position of the tape on the door indicated their assigned bed. Some of the pieces were extra-long, so I tore off a bit of the extra and used it to mount my picture on the back of our room door where no one would see it.

I showed Rich the photo. Inspired, he rushed out to do the same. In no time, he had his own dream girl taped to the back of the door. I decided it would be fun to have a competition with him and fill the door with pictures. I went a little overboard on the endeavor, carefully tearing out many pictures to try to beat him. After acquiring a small stack of pictures, I carefully went around to all the rooms and pilfered small pieces of tape from everyone's names.

The only problem was that Rich was so dreamy eyed over his one girl that he had no further interest in the game. I was unstoppable, though. Soon, our door was half-covered with photos of models, and the magazines on the table were equally empty of them. Finally, I stood back and admired our accomplishments: Rich's one babe and my countless ones. Not only was it a good day's work, our room undeniably had some color.

The Bad Cuff

Grace was a real fixture at Gracewood. I don't know how long she'd been there, but everyone knew her and catered to her. I always jokingly called her "Your Grace," and the wheelchair I often wheeled her around in was "Your Rolls," but she stubbornly preferred Cadillacs, so that's what I ended up calling it. She was a feisty, redheaded Irish woman if I was to believe her stories, but if her hair had ever been red, it had long ago faded to white.

Once upon a time, Grace put her false teeth on a napkin and then mistakenly threw the napkin away. She'd been toothless ever since. I couldn't help but take most everything she said comically because of the way she scrunched her toothless face and slurred her words when she spoke.

Grace could walk, but edema swelled her calves almost as big as her thighs: walking was very painful. Mostly she parked herself in front of the center of attraction: the big screen TV in the main area. She usually sat in the second row and rested her eternally aching feet on an armchair in front of her.

Everyone had their blood pressure checked every day, and it was time for Grace to have hers checked. The nurse put the blood pressure cuff around her arm and then began chatting with another nurse as the machine inflated it. I wasn't paying close attention, but soon I heard, "Ow, ow, OW!" I looked over at Grace and she was obviously in extreme discomfort. The nurse, too distracted in conversation, failed to notice Grace's suffering, so Grace leaned forward in her chair and bit her. I mean, she gave a serious chomp to her arm. The nurse pulled her arm back and yelled, "Grace, what are you doing?" Grace matter-of-factly replied, "It's a guud fing I don't haf my teef in."

A few days later, I also had an opportunity to experience the bad cuff. Someone repaired an airline feeding the cuff with tape in such a way that it wouldn't release air between inflations as it was designed to. Consequently, it inflated without end. After the nurse placed the cuff on my arm and the air pump fired up, the pressure in the cuff built ceaselessly. It wasn't long before I yelled in pain as well. By coincidence, only Grace and I had the luck to experience the bad cuff. Thankfully, it is now resting comfortably in a landfill somewhere near Phoenix.

Too Many Footballs

It was 9:25 a.m. and everyone who wanted to go outside was lined up, including a few who always tried to sneak out but weren't on the "good behavior" list. It was always a small battle holding those folks at bay. It seemed the people who actually needed to go out the most were the ones who couldn't go. You had to earn the privilege to go outside.

Finally, with head counts tallied and names checked off, we shuffled in a line through the first level of security: a set of dark blue steel doors with wire mesh-reinforced glass windows. As the last person passed through, the PA locked the door behind us. Directly ahead was another set of locked doors, then another, and finally, one last locked door that opened to the outside. We hustled through all the doors as they opened and closed behind us until finally, we were free, to a point. PAs from multiple units sat in green plastic lawn chairs at strategic locations watching everyone carefully. In addition, a tall security fence surrounded the entire area.

The "rec yard," as I called it, was mostly grass dotted with small trees but also contained two enormous mesquite trees, each surrounded by a walled, circular garden perhaps twelve feet in diameter. The three-foot-high white stucco walls were so old that the mesquite tree roots outgrew them at points, lifting them off the ground and causing cracks that ran the full height of the walls. Each garden contained beautiful flowers of every shape and color. Normally it would be impossible to raise flowers in the Phoenix summer heat, but the mesquite trees provided so much shade that the gardens never saw direct sunlight.

We couldn't roam freely in the rec yard except on one day a week. On that day, we could walk the full perimeter and go wherever we wished. Otherwise, we were restricted to a small grass area and the concrete basketball court. There were weathered soccer balls, well-worn and underinflated basketballs, faded Nerf footballs, and some Hula-Hoops in a bin near the basketball court. In addition, you could draw on the concrete with colored chalk or play beanbag.

Whenever I was outside, I loved to engage people. One kid in particular, Travis, enjoyed tossing footballs with me. Travis very much liked to smoke pot. I believe he smoked so much that it remained in his system his entire stay at Gracewood. With his half-open bloodshot eyes, lazy smile, and slow reflexes, he seemed permanently stoned.

The footballs we tossed were Nerf balls of various sizes. I took all of them from the bin so I'd be guaranteed a good time. I usually found that if I nailed someone with a football, he'd get the message and join in. That in turn gave me more targets to choose from. I preferred picking on Travis and would wait until he was occupied throwing to someone else; then I hit him with as many footballs as I had—sometimes as many as six. As I threw them, I calculated the trajectories so that each football would hit at the same time. All of a sudden, every ball would pummel Travis at once. He always hunkered down in surprise with his hands protecting his head while I rolled on the ground laughing. With a big, stoned grin, he half-heartedly attempted to get even, but when the balls came my way, I merely collected them for my next barrage. Sure enough, in a few minutes, Travis would forget and I'd do it all over again.

One day Grace sat in her wheelchair watching us play. Curious as to what might happen, I tossed a football at her, and it landed squarely in her lap. A big, toothless grin spread across her face, she slowly pushed herself out of her wheelchair, took a few steps in my direction, and let loose. She wound that ball up like a professional slow-pitch softball pitcher and yelled "whoop, whoop, whoop" as she did, then let the ball fly. It was so comical I nearly died.

I tossed the ball with her for a while, and then Len came over and joined in. Len and Grace were mortal enemies. Len was a homeless veteran who lived on the streets for thirty-five years and was as hard as they come. Most words leaving his mouth were of the four-letter variety, and he long ago lost all conception of manners. Those two frequently battled it out verbally. It was a small miracle bringing them together. I stopped playing for a while and treasured watching them throw the ball, laugh, and enjoy each other's company.

A Single Ray of Sunshine

She was unquestionably pretty, with wavy, shoulder-length dark brown hair, a slender athletic build, and piercing blue eyes, but her most attractive feature was something people in the sane world wouldn't notice: she was able to interact with patients. The unspoken rule at Gracewood was that staff did not interact with patients. What it really boiled down to, I noticed, was that the female staff in particular did not interact with patients. This seemed to make perfect sense. Women are less able to defend themselves from patients, especially dangerous ones like us. In reality, however, it had nothing to do with that; it was all about control. With the exception of a very few, the female employees at Gracewood were strict and controlling. They were big on rules and quick with discipline. They were the top of the food chain. They didn't mingle because they were superior and they were in charge, regardless of what staff level they occupied.

Emma was the one exception. She calmly and compassionately crossed back and forth over that invisible line that divided patient from staff. I found it a wonderful quality. I did much the same thing, frequently interacting with both patients and staff, so when I saw that behavior in her, I recognized it instantly.

When I first saw Emma, she strolled into our unit with a box in her arms. It was hard to miss someone pretty in my unit, mainly because, unless someone pretty happened to walk in, there was no one pretty. Many female patients were missing a goodly number of their teeth, and more often than not, the teeth left were some shade of black. All of them wore scrubs, and most hadn't showered or brushed their hair in—well, a long time. Emma on the other hand had all of her teeth, aligned perfectly and highlighted by a beautiful smile. She wore a colorful print blouse and white slacks, clothes that might be commonplace on the outside but were something you just didn't see in Gracewood. Her hair was clean and shiny and fell loosely against her shoulders.

I had no idea why she was there or what she was going to do with that box, but I was intrigued, to say the least, and turned in my armchair by the television to watch her. She put the box down on the floor by the wall with the clock and proceeded to take colorful "splashes" of artwork from it. She took each splash of color and applied it to the wall, smoothing any air bubbles out by running her elegant fingers across it. They must have clung electrostatically or had some sort of adhesive.

The edges of the splashes were uneven, as if they'd been ripped instead of cut, and each contained a colored silhouette. The silhouettes were all of a sporting motif: a football player sprinting with a football in one hand and fending off unseen tacklers with his other outstretched arm; a basketball player leaping through the air to make a dunk; a golfer smacking a ball down a fairway with his driver. There was also a number on each splash. As she continued, I realized it was a calendar. *Now I can count down the days until I get out of here.* Being able to know the day and date seemed like a miracle. Even though I could probably figure out those things from TV or even by asking someone, my reconfigured mind could better relate to the new calendar. It was the first time I realized how important that was to me; it connected me to my wife and children. It was as if she had secretly brought a piece of the real world inside Gracewood.

Each day from that point on, a splash disappeared from the wall, banished from life and forgotten. I never actually saw it happen; the next day it was simply gone as if by magic. The calendar was a constant reminder of the days that really mattered: the days still ahead. Today stood as a boulder perched precariously on a cliff's edge, ready to roll off at any time into the abyss. I couldn't miss today, everything preceding it was gone. Each morning from then on, I came out to her calendar and rested my hand on today. That act started each day with special meaning and recharged my soul.

The next time I saw Emma was at the 5:30 p.m. recreation time. That evening I quickly rushed to get a good basketball from the ball bin as I usually did. Unless I was the first to get one, I was lucky if it bounced at all. There is nothing worse than trying to bounce a basketball and have it stick to the ground like a wet rag. I figured out early on that there were only two halfway decent balls in the whole bunch, so if I was in the mood for basketball, I didn't waste any time getting to the ball bin. I beamed with accomplishment if I seized one of the better ones.

Even the best balls were underinflated, so I devised a scheme to fool my mind starting by dribbling the ball in the grass. It was so dead in the moist grass that once I progressed to the concrete, it transformed into the finest ball imaginable. When I finally crossed that threshold between damp green grass and hard concrete, I always marveled at how the ball came alive.

Once, as I dribbled on the court, I looked to see if anyone might want to play a game with me. Instead, my eyes came to rest on Emma at the other side of the court. She was playing beanbag with one of the patients—a short, heavyset man wearing small oval-frame glasses with thick lenses that made his dark brown eyes look beady. He had a thick head of black hair. I noticed him before, and he always seemed in a foul mood. I was surprised that she got through to him. I threw Nerf footballs his way, rolled basketballs at his feet and even asked him point-blank if he'd like to play. He always scowled at me. I was anxious to meet her, so I left my ball on the court for someone else and walked over to her.

"Hi, I'm Ken. Could I join you?" I asked.

"Hi, Ken. I'm Emma and this is Robert. Sure, you can play with us."

"Hi, Robert," I said. He ignored me as he focused for what seemed an eternity on a chalk-outlined target, then slowly tossed his beanbag, and undershot it by several feet.

"Frickin' dangit!" he yelled, scuffing his right foot across the concrete. He was obviously upset, but his creative language nearly caused me to laugh. His bad attitude did give me an idea, though. I waited for Emma and him to finish their game; then she explained the rules to me and we began to play together. During the first game, I kept my mouth shut and played by the "normal" rules. Each time Robert's turn came up it was always a disaster. "Gosh dang frickin' ash game!" he exclaimed. I sometimes couldn't keep from laughing when he did that, but whenever I did he looked like he wanted to kill me.

When that game ended, I said, "I have an idea for a new game. Each round, one person gets to decide how we are going to toss the beanbags, and then everyone has to do it that way. We keep score just like before."

"OK," Emma agreed. Robert grumbled.

I started the game by throwing all three of my beanbags at once. I actually got two of them in the target. As we played, we tossed beanbags backward over our heads, between our legs: you name it. The plan was to make it so impossible that Robert couldn't worry about being a perfectionist. Soon everyone was having fun. It was especially enjoyable watching Emma contort her body various ways and laugh as she missed with every one of her beanbags. Most importantly, I got to know her as kind, calm, and considerate. It was relaxing to be around her. I learned that she was a recreational therapist. Her job was to plan and direct games, arts and crafts, or other activities with the patients.

There were three recreation times at Gracewood: 9:30 a.m., 1:30 p.m., and 5:30 p.m. Hardly anyone went outside at 1:30 p.m. because of the miserable heat and the sun blasting straight down. The morning was most popular because it was still relatively cool. The next morning at recreation time, I saw Emma unwinding a hose from a reel. She pulled the hose over to one of the gardens under the big mesquite trees and commenced watering the flowers. I walked over to the tree.

"Hi, Emma," I said

"Hi," she responded, seeming not to remember my name.

"Why do you have to water these flowers with a hose?"

"I planted all the flowers around the two mesquite trees myself. Unfortunately, there's no automatic watering system."

"Wow, it's amazing that you've been able to keep them looking so great watering them by hand. I would expect the heat would kill them by now. What do you do on the days you aren't here?"

"I have another recreational therapist water them for me; otherwise they'd die."

"It sure is a big responsibility."

"I love flowers, so I don't mind. I have a large garden of my own at home as well. I find it therapeutic caring for them."

"I bet your garden is amazing. I wish I could see it. You must really have a green thumb." Emma smiled but didn't respond. "Can I help you with them?"

"Sure. I could use some help," she said, handing me the hose. That was the beginning of my most precious time at Gracewood. Each day for half an hour, I helped her tend the gardens. We watered, pruned, removed debris that the wind had blew in, and even planted new flowers, all the while talking or just quietly working together. Over time, I learned a little about her family, more about her garden at home, and various other facts about her life, but mostly we made small talk as we worked together. Sometimes Emma sang softly. Her voice was beautiful, and I knew all the songs that she sang. Her singing never failed to make me smile.

I wanted more than anything to be free someday, but when that day came, gardening with Emma was the only thing I would miss. I wished there was a way that I could have my life back and still tend gardens with Emma.

Smuggling Food

My heart rate and blood pressure were elevated for weeks when I arrived at Gracewood. Somehow related to that was a ravenous hunger. In addition, I squeezed as much physical activity as I could into the few hours outside every day. Overall, I burned a lot more calories than I consumed.

I estimated the meals at Gracewood were around five hundred calories each. I put in a request for double portions, but after several days, nothing changed. In desperation, I begged for leftovers from the other patients. Sharing food was strictly prohibited in part because some patients had medical problems and related food restrictions. After the PAs admonished me several times, I backed off and suffered with the hunger.

In general, the female nurses stuck to the rules, but the male PAs and nurses bent a little. Sympathizing with my dilemma, they started to slip me food. I always treated them with respect, behaved, knew them all by name, and frequently spoke with them. We became friends of a sort. It was much like being in prison and befriending the prison guards.

After a few days of suffering, George, a black man and the heaviest of the PAs, slipped me an extra piece of cake on my tray. After that Alphonso, or Al, included an extra roll with my meal. I knew I had it made when an entire extra plate of food appeared on my tray one day. It took over a week for my double-portions request to go through, but in the meantime, my friends took care of me.

Stolen Glasses

When Rich first arrived, he was on prescription medication that seemed to work for him. Immediately after his arrival, the head psychiatrist, Dr. Davis, initiated a treatment plan that started by cutting off his prescription medication cold turkey. Taking Rich off his meds so abruptly took its toll. In only a few days, he went from "regular Joe" to "raving lunatic" as he spiraled into withdrawal. During my time at Gracewood, I witnessed two cold-turkey withdrawals: Rich and Sandra. It was brutal watching my friends suffer so much and unbelievable to me that they were forced to do so among the general populace.

Nearly everyone ignored Rich's agony except for me; he was my roommate after all, and I felt responsible for him. As his condition worsened, he lost his temper quickly and frequently. Desiring to ease his suffering, I informed a nurse of his rapidly deteriorating condition. The nurse spoke with Rich in private. I don't know what they discussed, but it didn't lessen his suffering. Instead, the nurse evicted me from the room and escorted me to another.

My new room was much larger, but had two roommates instead of one: Len and Robert, and room for a third. The room was split into two halves with two beds in each half separated by a partial wall in the middle that ran half the length of the room. On my half was a bathroom that we all shared. Robert and I slept right next to each other, and Len and an empty bed were on the other side of the partial wall.

One evening, as I lay on my bed jotting down ideas on a piece of paper with a stubby pencil, a huge commotion erupted near the main entrance of our unit. Living in Gracewood was like living a tabloid reality show: there was always something of entertainment value going on. I left the room to see what was happening.

What I saw was quite different than I expected. Most of the patients were frail-looking drug addicts, and the few who weren't were just normal-looking folks. Near the entrance were four PAs: the swing shift PAs: Jose, Antonio, and two others apparently from another unit. Instead of being in control of yet another spindly, still-high drug addict, they kept their distance from the new patient, who just arrived. It reminded me of a show I saw on TV in which they released a lion back into the wild. Once the cage door on the back of the truck opened, everyone scampered for cover.

At the center of the action was Nick, a former champion cage fighter, or at least that was his story, and I believed it. He was tall and massive. Every square inch of his body rippled with intimidating muscle. His eyes were dark and wild, his arms were covered in tattoos, and his gray hair was pulled back tightly into a ponytail. "Where's my fucking cell phone?" He demanded." If I have to ask for it one more fucking time, I'm going to call 911. You hear me? I'm going to call 911. Get me my cell phone NOW!" Anyone could see that drugs were involved. The great news: that raging lunatic was my third roommate.

Nick never did get his cell phone, but he did come down to earth over the next few days. It was pretty touch and go during that time, and I elected myself as his champion. I showed him around, introduced him to the male nurses and PAs, and told him which of the female staff he needed to avoid pissing off. I showed him all the things that no one showed me when I arrived.

I got the impression that Nick appreciated that I took him under my wing. We hung with each other almost all the time, and I have many fond memories of him. We played basketball, threw footballs, argued about religion, and even figured out how to exercise using towels and chairs. Overall, Nick and I had about as normal a relationship as an engineer and a broke ex-cage fighter, who'd just spent his last twelve dollars in the world on a large pizza and two cans of pop, could have. I loved him. He made me laugh and he made me think.

You wouldn't know it, but Nick was a year older than me. He was quite handsome, and women swooned over him wherever he went—even toothless ones at Gracewood, much to his chagrin. He did have one problem that we older guys have: he needed reading glasses. Nick usually kept his reading glasses on top of his cubby, but one day he left them on a table in the main area. Shortly afterwards, Robin, a gal who was released a few days earlier, came in to visit Sandra. They both sat down at the table with the glasses to catch up, and, knowing both of them, I pulled up a chair to join them. Eventually Robin inquired about the glasses.

"Whose glasses are those?"

"I think they're community glasses," I said. "Someone left them in their room when they were released, so now anyone can use them."

Robin picked them up and inspected them. "These are nice." She removed her own glasses, set them on the table, and put on Nick's. Then she looked around. "Wow, I can see a lot better with these than with mine." She kept them and no one thought anything of it. There were still glasses on the table for everyone to share. Soon, Robin said good-bye, taking her new glasses with her.

About an hour later, Nick came into the room. He looked around, picked up the glasses on the table, and set them back down. "Who the fuck took my glasses?" he asked. I felt like crap. I had no idea those were his. I squeamishly told him what happened. To my surprise, all he said was "Hmm." Then he picked up Robin's small, black, horned-rimmed glasses, which looked like throwbacks from the fifties, and put them on. He looked ridiculous. He gazed around and exclaimed, "Hey, I can see better with these than with my own damn glasses."

Nick used those glasses the entire time he was at Gracewood; then he left them for someone else to use when he was released. Nobody made fun of him, in part because we were all funny in our own ways, and because we were afraid he'd beat the tar out of us if we did.

Room 1149

The roommate who slept next to me, Robert, was the crankiest person I ever met. Despite the fact that he, Emma, and I played a few fun-filled rounds of beanbag together, he was no friendlier toward me. Before landing there, Robert lived his ideal life: surviving off taxpayer money while secluded in his apartment watching TV and chain-smoking cigars. Robert was probably in his late twenties, and looked very unhealthy. He had dark circles under his eyes and looked like he hadn't slept in weeks. I consistently made efforts to befriend him but always met outbursts of mock cursing in response.

That first night I went to bed about 10:30 p.m. I soon found out why Robert looked like he hadn't slept. At first, he lay on his belly, breathing normally. Then he rolled over onto his side and began to snore. The snoring was bad, but tolerable. Finally, he rolled onto his back and the real party began. Robert generated the most inhuman racket I ever heard. Intermixed with periods of gurgling, gagging, and sputtering were long, irregular spans of silence during which I wondered if he died. Worst of all, he was five feet away, and there was no escaping it. After an hour or so, I got up and stood next to him in the dark, trying to figure out what to do.

"Robert...Robert, wake up," I said with no response. Then I poked him. "Robert, turn over on your belly. You'll sleep a lot better." After again getting no response, I shook him. He awoke like a grizzly bear roused from hibernation.

"Gosh dang it. What the frick are you doing? Get the hey away from me." Then he turned onto his belly, and I had some relief for a while before the cycle repeated itself. By the third night in the room, I had so little sleep I was approaching my seizure threshold. Nick was likewise having trouble sleeping, so we both spoke to a nurse. Unfortunately, it wasn't possible for her to do anything. I convinced her of how important a night of good sleep was for my health. She let me take my sheet, blanket, and pillow to one of the quiet rooms, room 1149.

I was excited to have my own private room for a night. I grabbed my things and hustled over there as quickly as I could. The quiet room was where they put violent patients until they settled down. At that point, I didn't know much else about it. There were two steel doors to the quiet room further isolating the patient from everyone. That way, they could pound or kick on the inner door, and with the outer door closed, no one could hear very much. In between the two doors was a small bathroom area to one side with a very basic sink and toilet. The sink had no handles, just push buttons for hot and cold water like all the other sinks there. The water only stayed on a short time when you pressed the buttons. On that particular sink, the hot water button didn't work at all. In between the buttons was a small stainless steel dome the size of half a golf ball with a hole aimed at 45 degrees, from which water spouted, much like a drinking fountain.

A stainless steel mirror stood above the sink covered with fine scratches from years of cleaning. I couldn't see myself very well in the foggy mirror. It gave the illusion that I was younger; the wrinkles near my eyes and on my forehead vanished into the haze. The toilet was solid stainless steel. It had no lid or seat, just a seat shape as part of its design. The reason for the odd design of everything was to prevent people from hurting themselves or others. I felt privileged to have my own personal bathroom, since at least one of my new roommates, probably Robert, had bad aim.

I flipped on the switch next to the bathroom to illuminate the quiet room. With pillow, sheet, and blanket in hand, I stepped into the room and froze. Chills ran up my spine, goose bumps sprang to attention on my arms and my hands trembled. I sat on the bed thinking I might collapse otherwise, and took it all in: the harsh, white, windowless concrete walls and ceiling, the steel frame bed bolted to the floor, the quiet emptiness. *I know this room.* It was where they abandoned me on my first day when I arrived by ambulance paralyzed.

Tears filled my eyes and soon, I was so sobbing uncontrollably. For the first time in a long time, I experienced a negative emotion—sorrow. I couldn't help myself. The room brought back all the memories of the PDC, the ambulance ride, and my abandonment. I never felt as helpless in my entire life as I did on that day. Seeing the room again was also a relief; it put a face on a mystery that plagued me since the day I arrived. Until that moment, I had no idea where that place was. I wasn't sure if it was real or a dream. Now I finally knew, and it put an end to the nightmare.

Though it was once been a place of horror for me, room 1149 ultimately was my salvation. With the light off and both doors closed, the darkness was nearly total and my isolation from the world of Gracewood complete. The sleep I found in room 1149 was like a gift straight from God.

Angels Among Us

One of the patients at Gracewood was an older woman suffering from anorexia. She was so weak and frail that she needed help getting around, and she shook constantly as if her nerves all misfired. Frequently family members visited and tried to spoon-feed her. At meal and snack times, I never saw her. One day, as I sat by the nurses' station on my favorite sofa, I watched her family try to spoon-feed her at one of the tables. It was always a losing battle, and they'd always leave frustrated.

That particular day I focused my thoughts on her and in my mind told her that she could get better but that she had to choose to do so herself. Although she had her back to me at the time with her daughter's arm resting on her shoulders, she turned all the way around and looked me straight in the eye as if I'd spoken aloud.

That afternoon at snack time, she joined everyone else and I swear that she salivated and licked her lips. I whispered words of encouragement to her in my mind, and sure enough, she accepted a snack and ate it all. Over the next few weeks, she never missed an opportunity to eat. I watched her gain weight and become a semblance of the beautiful woman she obviously had once been.

I can't explain that incident. Perhaps we do have some kind of ability to communicate with others in a heightened state. My dogs certainly seemed different around me, after all. I'll always remember that incident. It's the one time in my life I truly felt like an angel.

Sadly, despite all that she accomplished, her family continued to attempt to force-feed her whenever they visited, and at those times, she retreated into her shell. Just before I left, she was forced to undergo electroshock therapy.

Getting Out AMA

As time passed, Rich drifted further and further from reality on Dr. Davis's treatment plan. At one point he complained of the lights being too bright, so one of the other patients gave him some cardboard, fold-up 3D glasses to wear. He happily donned those. Still having glare problems, he managed to talk another patient out of a baseball cap.

The 3D glasses and baseball cap solved the glare problem, but then he had another issue. He disappeared into his room for a while, and then reappeared with a makeshift turban made from a T-shirt wrapped around his baseball cap. He claimed it made him feel better. He was then frequently seen worshipping the ceiling speakers near the TV with his 3D glasses, cap, and turban, particularly if a loud movie was playing. He faced upward with his arms outstretched and swayed back and forth.

Eventually, things got nasty as Rich's withdrawal took him to the very bottom. During that period, Rich was a firecracker with a short fuse. The least provocation sent him into fits of rage. One day, during a particularly bad outburst, he threw an oak chair across the room, narrowly missing the windows. Everyone scampered as Al and George rushed to gain control of the situation.

At that point in Rich's withdrawal, Dr. Davis put the next stage of his plan into action and flooded Rich's body with new drugs. Rich's mental function rapidly morphed in a different direction. I noticed in particular that he talked constantly. It was difficult to distinguish whether he was having a conversation with himself, with someone else, or just verbalizing his thoughts. Gradually his behavior settled down, but he continued to have outbursts. During one such outburst, he decided he had enough and wanted out. He walked around the facility asking everyone what he needed to do to get out. Finally, a patient told him he could fill out an AMA form. Rich went to the nurse and she reluctantly gave him the AMA paperwork to complete.

I wasn't paying attention at first, but what transpired from there migrated toward the sofa on which Grace and I sat, and was unavoidable. Nick seized an opportunity to have some fun by putting on a show for us. In a serious voice, he assisted Rich in his attempts to fill in the required information on the form, periodically winking at us during the process.

Rich was so mentally incapacitated that it was impossible for him to actually read or write anything, so Nick would feign reading the form for him, fabricate some outrageous instructions, and indicate to Rich where to sign. Rich would then spend five minutes painstakingly scribbling everywhere but the signature line. At first, I thought Rich was playing along, but he was dead serious and one hundred percent focused on completing that form. Both Grace and I rolled with laughter, which didn't affect Rich in the least, making it all the more hilarious. Nick tried so hard to maintain a straight face as he continued making things up that tears streamed from the corners of his eyes, and though he needn't have bothered, he turned his head before wiping them away so Rich wouldn't notice. Soon, a small crowd gathered. Rich remained as dedicated and oblivious as ever, and before long everyone laughed until our bodies ached.

When Rich finished entering all the information, he scrawled a big, nasty-looking X on the final signature line, as per Nick's instructions, to complete the document. I made him take it to the nurse to make a copy for me for safekeeping in case Gracewood lost the original, but in reality. I wanted that copy for myself to remind me of that hilarious time.

The Scandal

After I was in my new room for a while, it bothered me that all the girlie pictures were still on the back of the door to Rich's room. I didn't want to put them on my new door but felt that they were mine, so one day I walked in and took all but Rich's down. I folded and stuffed my favorite one—a pretty, brown-haired woman with striking blue eyes—in my left pants pocket and put all the rest in a stack. I took them to my room and hid them in some of my clothes.

Those pictures weighed heavily on my mind. I don't know why; they were just cosmetic ads after all. Over time, I felt guiltier and guiltier for stealing them. One day I removed the emptiest magazine from the table, took it to my room, and filled it with the girlie pictures. I returned it to the table, placing it at the bottom of the stack of magazines, satisfied that I did the right thing.

A few hours after that, Nick opened the door to our room just as I was about to walk in.

"Uh, you might not want to go in there right now," he whispered.

"What's going on?" I whispered back.

"I just walked in and Len is choking the chicken," he whispered, trying his best not to burst out in laughter.

"What? You've got to be kidding."

"I swear to God. He took a magazine from the table, tore a whole bunch of chick pictures out of it. He's got them scattered all over his bed and is going at it like a madman."

I almost died. Rich was the only other person who knew about those photos, and he was in another world. No one but me knew that they made it back into the very magazine Len had stumbled upon. By accident, I created an excruciatingly good scandal. Word got around as to what he was doing, and in record time, a couple of nurses burst into the room to do a contraband check. Len lost all his treasures, and cursed and swore for days. On top of that, all the magazines disappeared from the table, replaced by black-and-white coloring books and a tin of Crayola crayons.

The Cat Lady and the Evil Asian

A moody, gaunt, and wild-eyed woman, Sara acted as if she was on meth: speaking rapidly, repeating herself, and yelling as if everyone were deaf. We called her "the Cat Lady" because she obsessed over the health of fifty stray cats in her neighborhood that she fed and cared for. She spent hours on the phone trying to find someone to feed them while she was in Gracewood. It was impossible to ignore her loud and incessant babbling as she phoned acquaintances, sometimes with both of the wall phones at the same time. We tried to no avail to convince her that the cats were feral and could take care of themselves.

Sara's nonstop babbling infuriated Grace. She made that clear to her on many occasions, verbally attacking her from across the room. Although managing conversations on both phones, Sara somehow found time to respond in kind. The two women's dislike for each other was obvious.

As fate would have it, a new roommate joined Sara: a short, creepy, Asian woman with wide unblinking eyes, a permanent scowl, and an impossibly tight bun of black hair atop her head. She never said a word and shuffled everywhere she went, with her arms, which appeared too long for her body, hanging limply at her sides. Since they were roommates, Evil Asian (the only name I knew her by) promptly assumed the role of Sara's minion.

One day, Evil Asian crossed the room with a large cup filled to the brim with water, walking slowly and carefully so as not to spill a drop. Mesmerized by her peculiar behavior, I couldn't imagine what she was doing. She continued along her path until she was right behind Grace, and then appallingly, she poured the entire contents over Grace's head.

Grace, who'd been sitting with her puffed-up feet on the armchair in front of her watching television, sputtered, coughed and let out a string of profanities from her toothless mouth that made everyone's ears burn. I sprang to her aid, protecting her from further harm with my own body. "Get away!" I screamed venomously, inches from Evil Asian's face. Stunned by my swift response and aggressive demeanor, she stumbled backward. Her lifeless eyes blinked for what seemed the first time, and an odd look crossed her face as if a spell had just been broken.

She was different after that. She began talking to people, and let her hair down. She even wore makeup when her family visited. A few days after the water incident, she slowly approached Grace. My senses buzzed in alarm, and I readied myself for the worst until I observed the tears streaming down her cheeks. She stopped next to Grace, hung her head, and humbly apologized. As the Asian woman wept, Grace embraced and comforted her as if she was her own child. From that day forward, Grace and the Asian woman were friends.

Jimmy

Jimmy was the only patient who I felt truly healed during the course of my stay. He was schizophrenic and generally kept to himself except when we all attended our "goals" meeting at the end of each day. At that meeting, we all shared our achievements with the rest of the group and set a goal for the next day. Most of the patients couldn't care less about goals, but a few, like me, tried to come up with something inspirational to strive for.

Each meeting, when the group leader called on Jimmy, it was always the same. Jimmy never listened and never had goals. "Jimmy…Jimmy…JIMMY!" the group leader shouted, trying to get his attention. Eventually Jimmy responded with gibberish. No one understood a word he said, and once he started, it was almost impossible to silence him. We nearly had to wrestle him to the ground to get him to stop, but at least he contributed. That was very important to the group leader and after getting him to stop; she always thanked him for sharing.

At recreation time one morning, I was tossing Nerf footballs to some of the guys when along came Jimmy. With his bright eyes, big grin, slicked-down black hair, colorful plaid shirt, bowed legs, and big feet, he looked like he walked straight out of a cartoon. I tossed him a ball to see what would happen and he snapped it up like a pro. Jimmy was quite talented passing and throwing, and soon both of us were running for "long bombs." All the while, Jimmy never spoke, he just played ball.

After that day, I made sure to include Jimmy whenever I could. In time, Jimmy started joining me for lunch. As soon as they handed him his tray, he looked around for me, and if I was alone, he joined me. He didn't say anything in the beginning; he just grinned like always and ate his meal. Eventually I attempted to engage his mind. I asked questions about his life and, to my surprise, he answered. His response was at first understandable, but he inevitably transitioned to gibberish. It seemed that he couldn't help himself and that he was very frustrated by that. Eventually, the gibberish portions of the conversations grew shorter and shorter until, without either of us even realizing it, they disappeared completely. By the end of our time together, Jimmy and I had completely normal conversations on a regular basis.

Chapter 25

UTOPIA: PUTTING PENCIL TO PAPER

May 27, 2011: I obsessed over Utopia often. Now, it was time to put pencil to paper and record my ideas to share with the world. There was plenty of time to kill at Gracewood. I literally had no responsibilities at all: I didn't have to go to any groups I didn't want to; I didn't have to shower or change my clothes; I didn't even have to make my bed. I spent some of that time writing.

It was awkward lying on my bed and writing, so I often wrote later in the evening at a table in the main area. During the day, it was too noisy, with too many distractions. I wished I had a computer, but instead, all I had was a two-inch stubby pencil and white printer paper. I asked the nurse once why we couldn't have pens, and she told me that people broke them apart and used them to crush and snort pills that they'd secreted or acquired in various ways.

Those pencils didn't come with erasers, and I was only able to get a slip-on one because a nurse was in a good mood when I asked and was willing to take time from filling out her endless paperwork to find one for me. There was a whole box of stubby pencils, but aside from a few scattered in drawers, the erasers had all but disappeared. Most people there weren't interested in correcting their mistakes anyway. I was apparently one of the few who ever showed interest in an eraser.

It was difficult writing with stubby pencils, and the points became dull in minutes. I was constantly pestering the nurses to sharpen them. Finally, ignoring rules, they gave me a few spares. When I wrote in normal life, I used lowercase print and capital letters as needed. I gave up cursive years ago because it was so illegible that even I couldn't read it. When I wrote in Gracewood, I wrote in all capital letters. That was something that I never did in my life. I decided to change because my printing had gotten as bad as my cursive. It was difficult for others to read, and the stubby pencils only made it worse. Once I started, my new brain switched gears instantly and never missed a beat. In no time, I could print in uppercase quite rapidly. As a consequence, I consumed paper as well as pencil points in a hurry jotting down all my ideas, including those relating to Utopia, so the nurses broke another rule and let me have as much paper as I wanted. Among the many pages I wrote, there were four that dealt strictly with Utopia. Three were text and the fourth had hand-drawn images. All of those handwritten pages were on plain white printer paper with no lines or margins. They were certainly unsophisticated for an engineer used to creating fancy PowerPoint presentations, but that was all I had. What follows is the text of the pages I wrote in Gracewood that dealt with Utopia.

Utopia

The idea behind Utopia is to capitalize on a changed human psychology due to the loss of negative emotions and to reinvent society by redesigning it from the ground up. People without negative emotions will naturally get along. They will require less space for material fluff and be more interested in interacting with their community. Instead of an urban sprawl, the society of the future might be more like a beehive. People will be able and will want to live in closer proximity to the ones they care for and they will care for more people.

There are three phases to the Utopia project. The first phase generates funding for the project and conducts social experiments to confirm and refine how humans without negative emotions interact. The second phase builds the teams who will create the final Utopia and continues to generate funding. And the third phase builds Utopia.

Phase 1

In phase 1, a small community will be established (Utopia 1), probably by selling existing larger homes and moving families involved in the project to a smaller tract home community. This will generate some cash to get the project going. Experiments will then be conducted in these homes to create more efficient living spaces and furnishings, and determine if more people can live in the same space. Some modifications may be made to both interiors and exteriors of the homes.

Phase 2

In phase 2, the passion groups who will build Utopia will be populated. These groups will consist of people naturally passionate about their particular group. The groups will be: finance, agriculture, parks and recreation, human needs, transportation, technology, utilities, protection, infrastructure, governing, and others as necessary. With some results of phase 1 known, it may be possible to sell additional real estate to fund the project, and that will be done at this time.

Phase 3

In phase 3, everything will come together and the final Utopia (Utopia 2) will be built. Utopia will be a self-contained city, using many green principles to achieve that goal. Such technologies as solar power, micro wind turbines, hydroelectric generation and storage, and burning of biogas from human and animal waste will be used. Utopia will be built down instead of up to reduce energy demands for heating and cooling. Utopia will seamlessly integrate into the local environment. It will have underground walking and bikeways as well as personal rapid transit: small electric vehicles that can hold as many as six people. Utopia will be constructed like a many-layered wheel with living spaces on the outer rings and social, entertainment, shopping, government, and work functions toward the center. Utopia will produce all its own power and food. There will always be interaction with the outside world, so Utopia will remain an open community, trading necessities and ideas with the rest of the world.

Technology Transfer

The primary goal is to develop Utopia, not to spread knowledge to the world. The ultimate ambition, however, is to create a template for the rest of the world to follow. Communication during early phases will be restricted to Utopia 1, Utopia 2, and satellites, small off-site organizations spread across the country or even the world that have stakes in Utopia. As Utopia 2 nears completion, communication will shift, making technology and concepts from Utopia an open book to the world.

A fourth page contained two drawings, which contrasted room size in Utopia with conventional design, illustrating the inefficient use of space in a typical bedroom/bathroom. There was a flow chart showing how Utopian technology would be developed and spread to the United States, then to the world, and finally there was a drawing of a wheel with different passion groups as the spokes and me as the leader at the hub.

Utopia would be primarily social in nature, since putting together people without negative emotions was the most important aspect to work out. Future communities might focus on music, art, technology, etc. as people's passions dictated. Those communities would be like self-contained islands, each having a unique flavor, but there would always be a desire to share products and experiences among communities.

Since I knew that everyone would lose their negative emotions, and since I was the focal point from which all change would radiate, I was in a unique position to guide the creation of the first community. I felt strongly that my vision of tomorrow should be anchored here in America, and I didn't want to sit around and watch while others struggled with all the changes. Instead, I wanted to jump-start the process so we could circumvent what would otherwise be a clumsy learning curve fraught with missteps.

It was for those reasons that I wrote so feverishly and passionately, and I firmly believed everything I wrote. I had individuals already picked for specific positions. Those positions provided them with opportunities to do what they loved most. Dad loved photography, so I hoped he and Mom would join the Utopia 2 site location team to help find and photograph our eventual home. I wanted my nephew Justin, who was studying to become a doctor, to be on the medical team. My brothers Alan and Dana had years of business experience and would be perfect at figuring out creative ways to fund the venture. Beth and my children would be key players in the Utopia 1 experiments in Ahwatukee. Many other family, friends, and community members would qualify for roles they would be passionate about.

Chapter 26

THE LAST VISITOR

On May 27, my dad and my nephew Justin stopped by for a visit. At that time, I just finished writing my papers on Utopia and was anxious to share them. Dad and Justin sat on a sofa near the window, and I pulled up a chair in front of them. I handed Dad the papers and waited as he got comfortable, adjusted his trifocals, and read my pencil-written, all-caps documents. I hoped he would see beyond the pencil writing on unlined paper and focus on the content. The all-caps script alone lent a disturbed look to the documents.

Dad made it through the first page and then lifted it to see how many more there were. He peered at me over his glasses and said, "You do realize this is crazy, don't you?" It wasn't the response I wished for. I hoped that he might find it interesting on some level. It was just an idea, a rough draft. I put much work and thought into those papers. After scrutinizing the remaining pages, Dad handed them back. Justin asked if he could read them. I offered them to him. He read them all and said, "You're a good man, Uncle Ken. Do you mind if I keep these?"

"Not at all," I said. Perhaps it was for the best that he took them. No good ever came from sharing my ideas about change and new societies. In fact, those topics seemed to be at the root of many of the bad things happening to me.

The rest of the visit was uneventful. Justin remained quiet, and Dad seemed to be fishing for information. It was, after all, the first time he saw me that way face-to-face. When they left, I felt hollow.

On May 28, Mom and Dad visited. Mom brought orange soda and peanut butter crackers. I couldn't remember the last time I had orange soda. It was a welcome change of pace. Mom is a real health food nut and I'm sure she intended to bring something healthier, but they didn't know the area and were reluctant to search for a grocery store. The orange soda and crackers were the healthiest foods she could find in the vending machines in the lobby. We talked about what was going on back at their home in Utah, how their cats were doing, and how their new fishpond was coming along.

On May 29, Mom and Dad visited again. Dad entered the main area with a somber look, and Mom followed him in silence. Dad apparently completed his fact gathering and was ready to get down to business. He and Mom had just spoken with Dr. Davis. They held him in high esteem and agreed on a plan with him for my release.

I felt the complete opposite of my parents regarding Dr. Davis: he was pompous, arrogant, and more interested in satisfying his own giant ego than healing his patients. I witnessed Dr. Davis at work every day with patients and families. He frequently met with patients, and sometimes families, in the main area where anyone could hear, so I often sat on a sofa within earshot and listened to him manipulate both the patients and their families. I knew many patients personally and spent a great deal of time with them one-on-one, so I felt it was my business to know what he was up to, even though I was powerless to do anything about it. What appalled me the most was when he used families to manipulate their sick loved ones to his benefit.

Dr. Davis took advantage of the fact that families were desperate for anything to help their loved ones. Without fail, he convinced them that drugs were the only solution. I couldn't help but wonder if he received a kickback from drug manufacturers. His policy seemed to be this: overdose the patient on one drug, and then overdose them on additional drugs as required to counter the adverse side effects of the first overdose. In the end, I was stuck with the aftermath as I watched one of my friends after another spiral down into seemingly bottomless pits of suffering.

The plan my parents agreed on was that I was to go live with them in Utah under the care of a psychiatrist there while I stabilized into a life of medication. I could hike, swim, anything I wanted. I could relax and get better. That all sounded much nicer than being at Gracewood. There were just a few things wrong with the plan. First, the reason for the offer was that they were convinced that I was dangerous to Beth and the children, and that being in a different state was the only way to protect them. Second, when and if I could return to my "normal" life was up to a psychiatrist who never met my family or me. Lastly, the bomb: Dad looked me straight in the eye and said, "Your mother and I have a perfect life together. Caring for you will be a big burden for us."

He spoke more after that, but I didn't process it. Of all the brothers, I am the most independent. I rarely ask anyone for anything, and I always pay back right away, often with interest for the small amount of help I ask for. I take great pride in being a burden to no one. In fact, I consider it one of my greatest faults that it is so difficult for me to accept help from others.

To me, what started as an offer of help ended as another manipulative way of trying to get me to snap out of it, to make me come to my senses. I could handle that, but I was suddenly no longer interested in family and friends' so-called help. Every interaction with them of late had only ended up putting me in more jeopardy of one kind or another, regardless of their good intentions. That final attempt at help just made me want to be alone.

Throughout my stay at Gracewood, I periodically got "slapped in the face." That was a phrase I used to describe an overly strong reaction by people to something I said or did. Eventually, I came to realize that it mostly happened when I attempted to force my opinion or control a situation.

Because of my mental state, I lost a few social skills. I wasn't getting them back any time soon, so by trial and error I learned new ways to interact with people. One such way was to offer choices. It required much more thought and creativity than just blurting something out, but the results were more satisfactory. I genuinely wished to talk with my parents, just not about fixing me. So instead of being confrontational and getting nowhere, I offered them a choice.

"We can continue down this path if you want. If we do, our conversation will be finished. Or, you can change the subject and I'll be happy to spend time with you. I'll give you ten seconds to decide what you want to do." With that, I looked at my wristwatch and mentally began counting the seconds down in unison with the changing second digits.

Rather than take the time to decide, they ignored what I said and continued from where they left off. Ten seconds listening to my parents unable to veer from their own agenda was agony. At the end of the time, they didn't even stop to take a breath. When the last second transpired, I looked at both of them and said, "We're done." I stood and escorted them to the door. I hugged Mom and shook Dad's hand.

"Think about it," Dad said.

As they departed, I turned and knocked on the nurses' station door. The nurse opened it and I said, "I want to request that I have no more visitors."

"Are you sure?" she asked.

"Yes, no one."

Beth came to visit the next day, and they turned her away. I watched the clock pass 2:00 p.m. knowing it would happen, but I never expected the empty feeling that came over me. I missed her. Even though she mostly talked about more testing, another doctor or some other way we could try to help me, sometimes she was just herself. It reminded me of someone with Alzheimer's becoming lucid for a moment. I don't mean that in an unkind way, but my family and friends all seemed sick to me in a similar way that I seemed sick to them. I couldn't let go of being sick, and they couldn't let go of trying to fix me. We were codependents to addiction.

The problem was that many of them seemed to think that like a drug addict choosing to be sober, I could choose to be normal. What they didn't understand was that, like it or not, my body was forcing me to be that way. I could no more fix myself than I could jump over the moon.

One thing I did realize: in a place where everyone was a danger to themselves and others, I finally found safety. All the seizures, the whirlwind of ambulance rides, police rides, hospitals, and psychiatric institutions were finished because I couldn't get out, and now no one could get to me. I breathed a sigh of relief.

Later I knocked on the nurses' station door again. The nurse stood from her chair and walked to the door. She unlocked it and asked, "Yes?"

"I want to give my wife permission to visit me again," I said. From then on, just as she had prior to me shutting her out, Beth visited me every day, and I lived for her visits.

Chapter 27

THE BURDEN

I understood what Dad meant when he told me that I would be a burden. He meant that they were almost eighty years old, they had their routines, and they had things set up just the way they liked for their golden years. The last thing they wanted was to have to take care of one of their children again. It did make me contemplate what being a burden meant. Though I never imagined it, over the next two weeks I would become an expert on what a burden was. I was going to have a master teacher on the subject: Matthew.

***

"God damn it, this food tastes like fucking garbage!" I heard a tinny, raspy voice yell. I looked around, but couldn't locate the source of the angry voice. "They never fed me dog food like this at Estrella. They treated me like a *king* over there!" Then I noticed that it came from a hospital bed parked in the corner, shoved as far away from everyone as possible. Right about then a tray went flying out of the bed, sending finely chopped food everywhere, the kind of food they gave Grace, who had no teeth. I could hardly make out the frail man covered in blankets there. His name was Matthew.

Estrella transferred Matthew because they could no longer deal with him. No one could deal with him or wanted him. He was the epitome of a burden. He was booted out of every place he went, and that only made him more ornery. Everyone at Gracewood avoided Matthew. Not only did he stink to high heaven from poor hygiene, he verbally bit anyone's head off who got within sight.

Matthew intrigued me. In my book, it didn't matter what his sins were yesterday; what mattered was his potential today. Matthew had spirit, that's for sure; it was just misdirected. Matthew was a magnet to my steel. Over time, I drifted closer and closer to him. I did get my head bitten off a few times. However, once I was able to talk to him from a distance, he settled down. As he did, the staff addressed his hygiene needs and worked with him to build his strength.

Matthew was the most emaciated person I've ever seen. He was my height, about five foot eight, but weighed barely one hundred pounds. Soon Matthew's bed was no longer lying flat. The staff inclined it and turned it so that he could watch TV like anyone else in the main room. Before long, his strength improved enough that he could take a few wobbly steps to a table for meals. I started sitting with him at lunch occasionally. We didn't really speak much, I just said hello and made small talk while we ate.

One day I witnessed a small miracle. Matthew got out of bed (which was a long, drawn-out process), stood hunched over, and hobbled a few feet to the nearby phone. Then, in slow motion, he picked up the receiver and pressed the buttons. He unsteadily moved the phone to his ear and, after a lengthy pause, asked in his scratchy voice, "Is this Papa John's Pizza?" I felt like cheering. He continued slowly and distinctly. "I want a medium thin-crust pepperoni, please." He then gave the address from the paper on the wall near the phone. After that, he shouted for the nurse and had her retrieve some of his money, which they kept in an office safe. He then hobbled a few steps to the table, sat down in slow motion, and waited patiently for his pizza to arrive. He ate alone, but right then and there, I made it my goal to share a pizza with him some day.

As fate would have it, Gracewood freed my obnoxious, snoring roommate, Robert, to return to chain-smoking cigars at taxpayer expense. I would finally get some decent rest. Within hours, however, they removed the bed and wheeled Matthew and his hospital bed into the spot. I was immediately thankful that I invested the time building a relationship with him. Matthew was in that room nearly twenty-four hours a day after that.

In the beginning, Matthew only spoke when he needed something: water, an apple juice box, or graham crackers (he was especially fond of those). It wasn't long before we talked about everyday things such as our families. One evening he made a comment to Jose and Antonio, the evening PAs, about needing a few spotters for something they wanted him to do. My ears perked up immediately. Spotters were people who caught gymnasts if they fell while learning or performing a difficult trick.

"You must have been a gymnast," I said. "I haven't heard that term in a long time."

"Yes, rings for three years in high school," he replied.

"Me too, I competed on the pommel horse."

I couldn't imagine that Matthew, so frail he could barely stand, once performed on an apparatus requiring the most strength of anything I could imagine. I learned that as his gymnastics career was ending, mine was just beginning. I was a very strong young man back then and could press from an "L" to a handstand on the rings myself, but that was about all I could do. I didn't have near the strength to perform an iron cross or inverted planche, and Matthew could do those things and more.

I immediately felt a kindred spirit with Matthew, and from then on saw him in a different light. As we lay in our beds late one evening, Matthew shared stories about his youth as an underage, red-haired troublemaker. He created a fake driver's license and took his buddies driving down Central Avenue in Phoenix on Saturday nights back when everyone cruised. It was the late 1960s and all the teenagers came in force in their fifties and sixties hot rods. Afterward, he bought them all beer using his fake license, and then they headed to their favorite pizza joint. He raved about that restaurant, which still exists today.

As Matthew and I shared stories, we laughed and Matthew grew stronger. I convinced him that he should get out of there and into a place that provided physical therapy. I bet him that he could gain all his strength back and be independent again. Right away, he requested double portions at mealtime and started to beef up. It was a long, slow process, but I watched him change before my eyes.

The most difficult thing about having Matthew right next to me was getting quality sleep. With no call button on his bed, Matthew called a nurse with his frail, scratchy voice whenever he needed something: "Nurse...nurse...nurse..." No one heard him through the door, so I left it open just enough that they might hear. Even then, no one heard unless someone happened to be walk by, which rarely happened on the grave shift. I took it upon myself to get up and find a nurse whenever he needed help going to the bathroom. It was usually a fifteen-minute ordeal getting the nurse and the nurse getting him to the bathroom and back. By then I was wide-awake.

That usually happened at 2:00 a.m., then again at 4:00 a.m. I knew it was a risk for me: I hadn't experienced seizures since my arrival at Gracewood, and hadn't needed Ativan for a long time. Concerned, I took some again, but it didn't help: I kept expecting him to wake me again. It was like someone poking me every time I neared sleep.

I never complained, and Matthew started telling people that I was his angel. I sacrificed sleep every night, and after three nights in a row with only a few hours of sleep, the monster came calling. It occurred around 9:00 p.m. while most patients were watching TV. I felt him stir and sought the nurse right away. "I'm starting to have a seizure. I need Ativan *immediately,*" I implored. In no time, the monster was after me. Some old memories returned, and I recalled "changing up." I ducked, dodged, and never ceased moving. I paced, grimaced, and growled. I drank water from a cup and splashed the rest on my face. Most patients and staff paid little heed with numerous individuals exhibiting similar behavior on a regular basis. A few recognized that I was not myself and asked what was going on. "I've got a tiger on my tail," I told them. They laughed.

Though I made light of my struggle, it was serious business. If it was within my power, I was never going to submit to the monster's will again. Ten minutes later, the nurse brought me Ativan and some water. I downed that pill as quickly as I could, and returned to fending off the monster. After a few minutes, the drug took hold. I closed my eyes and in my mind faced the monster head on. Though he towered above me, it felt as if we were equals on the battlefield for the first time. He clenched his gnarly fists, tipped his head back, and let loose a mighty roar that reverberated to the farthest reaches of my mind. Then he lowered his head and glared at me with his glassy, soulless eyes. He hissed and reached for me one last time, but as he did, I opened my eyes, and as quickly as he first appeared in my life, he vanished. With an exhausted sigh of relief, I made my way to my room and slept. After that narrow escape, I made sure to take naps whenever I could as insurance against the monster's return. I never experienced another seizure and never faced the monster again.

Matthew reached a point where he could really appreciate what I was going through for him. I think it was eye opening having a stranger care for and sacrifice so much for him out of the goodness of his heart. He asked his brother if he could bring a cell phone to call the nurse and give me some relief. It was a great plan but never happened. The only thing that did happen was that Jose gave him a bell, the kind that sits on a hotel's front desk. You hit the button on top and it goes "ding." Unfortunately, it was barely louder than his frail voice. The only thing that changed was instead of "nurse...nurse...nurse...," I woke up to "ding...ding...ding..."

I made a decision after that to give everything I had to Matthew during whatever time I had left. I got him graham crackers and drinks; got up at all hours of the night to fetch a nurse; ate with him; and was his friend. I was a perfect angel. There was no reward in it for me; I would probably never see him again after my release. There would be no happy ending to look forward to; it was just the right thing to do. I showed Matthew how good a person could be and continued to push him toward physical therapy so that he could get better and perhaps be that good person, that angel, to someone else.

I didn't know if Matthew ever conceived of such a thing, but here was a chance to open his eyes to it, and I would plant that seed in his mind. It was an opportunity to give him purpose in life and a means of escape from being a burden, rotting in a forgotten bed in the furthest reaches of a darkened room in a psych ward.

Chapter 28

COMING OFF ADRENALINE

June 3, 2011, is a day I will always remember: the beginning of my mania ending. Every day at 5:00 a.m., techs made their morning rounds, measuring temperatures, pulse rates, and blood pressure. If I was asleep, that was usually the end of it. Afterward, I typically tossed and turned in bed, or took my pillow out to the main area in hopes of finding an empty sofa. That often worked because there was rarely anyone snoring. There were overhead lights, but most of them were turned-off. One downside was that the vinyl sofas made poor beds: they were too short, too firm, and rounded. If I managed to fall asleep, I stood a good chance of rolling off at some point. The worst problem was that it was only two hours until breakfast. In addition to being awake, I spent that time hungry.

June 3 started no differently than any other day. The door cracked open, I instinctively hung my arm out for the cuff and opened my mouth for the thermometer. I always watched the machines when they took my blood pressure and heart rate, ever since Desert Hope, making a mental note of any significant change. My normal blood pressure prior to surgery was 120/70. After surgery, it steadily climbed as my body ramped up. My normal now was 155/85 at rest at 5:00 a.m. No one thought anything of it even though I repeatedly pointed it out to medical professionals. Today things were different. I did a double take when I saw 140/80 on the machine. Over the next few days, the downward trend was undeniable; the adrenaline (at least that was my assumption) was leaving my system and my blood pressure was returning to normal. The ride was ending, and my body and mind would soon be my own again.

I didn't notice anything immediately—it took time for my body to accept a new reality, but it wasn't long before changes became apparent. The biggest difference was the chatter in my mind. When other parts of my brain came back online after mania, it was like a quiet, empty classroom filling with noisy students or like a freeway going from no traffic to morning rush hour. My narrow, focused mind with its crisp memories altered as it widened once again, bogging down due to all the competition for bandwidth. Memorization and recall became more challenging and my jazzed-up senses returned to normal. I couldn't see or process things quickly or sense people's shields anymore. Everyone seemed to become as flat as a cardboard standup and I could only see what was on their paper surface. I missed being manic. I felt like half a person. Even though my mania was subsiding, I still had a big hurdle to jump through before I reached the end of my journey: my courtroom battle.

Chapter 29

TAKING THE STAND

A few days after arriving at Gracewood, my psychiatrist pulled me aside and attempted to convince me to take medication. Considering my bad track record with medications, I refused. This chapter steps back in time to revisit that conversation, then details the aftermath of my decision: having to take the stand in court to defend myself.

The Grievance

On May 29, Dr. Davis tracked me down and asked if I would come with him. He took me to his office, a place I hadn't been to since he interviewed me after my arrival.

"How are you doing today?" he asked.

"Fine."

"Is everything going all right? Are you having any problems? Have you been feeling well?"

"I'm doing OK."

Dr. Davis took a seat behind his cluttered desk and directed me to a chair across from him. I obliged him and made myself comfortable.

"The reason I've asked you to my office is that I would like you to start taking lithium, or more specifically, a prescription medication called lithium carbonate. It's a mood stabilizer. I use it myself."

"Why do I need to take it?"

"Well, I want to give you something to prevent something."

Those were his exact words and they weren't a convincing argument for taking lithium, or any other drug for that matter. "Dr. Davis, I've avoided drugs, prescription or otherwise, my entire life. I've never smoked anything, tried any illegal drug, and I rarely even drink, not because of religious reasons, I firmly believe that I only get one body with which to live out my life in, and I choose not to abuse it. On top of that, I've had many complications from medications lately. In fact, the only medication I trust is Ativan, and I only take that sparingly. If lithium is something that comes in an over-the-counter multivitamin, I'll be glad to take it. If not, you haven't given a good enough reason to take it.

"I understand, but you really should give it a try. It works very well for me."

"I'm sorry, Dr. Davis, I don't want to take it."

"OK," he said with frustration in his voice.

That was the end of our private discussion. The next day I received written notice to appear in court. In Gracewood, everyone had the right to refuse their medications, but if they did, they risked a court order forcing them to do so. A typical scenario went like this: first, we received notice that a court date would be assigned for a hearing (the notice I just received); second, we waited up to ten days before learning the actual court date; and third, we waited up to ten more days for the actual court appearance. After the appearance, if the court ordered us to take medication, Gracewood administered the medication and monitored us for a time to make sure it was effective.

By refusing to take lithium, I potentially added twenty-five days or more to my stay. That didn't deter me. It was a small price to pay to protect my body. Fortunately, I received notice of a court date on May 31. The hearing was set for June 7. I don't know for sure if I would have been released sooner had I agreed to take the medication, but I was dead set against taking anything without good reason. The next day, after receiving the initial notification, Dr. Davis passed me near the nurses' station.

"Have you changed your mind yet?" he asked with a smirk.

If I were a different type of person, I would have decked him. Instead, I replied "No."

When I received notification of my court date, I also received a brochure from the Maricopa County Public Defender's office with the name of my public defender. In addition, I received a copy of the petition that landed me in Gracewood as well as two psychological profiles written by Dr. Davis and another psychiatrist, Dr. Borova. Both documents borrowed heavily from the petition from the crisis team that originally forced me into the PDC and Gracewood. It seemed that the psychiatrists could only see me through the eyes of the crisis counselor.

What I read shocked me. The petition from the crisis counselor included these statements: "He physically assaulted his wife"; "He lay in the street in a fetal position"; "He ran around the neighborhood late at night ringing doorbells and hiding behind bushes"; "He purchased a dream car, then went out and attempted to purchase another." I noticed in particular two boxes checked: "Patient is a danger to himself" and "Patient is a danger to others." Another statement stood out: "Persistently or acutely disabled." Those were the reasons I was in Gracewood, a place for people who were a danger to themselves and others.

The statements were lies. Unbeknownst to my family and me, the crisis counselor took bits of truth and distorted them to make me look both insane and dangerous in order to ensure that I was placed in a maximum-security facility, which I couldn't leave. I couldn't believe what I read. I've never had anyone make such claims against me before. To make matters worse, according to the paperwork, my wife and my older brother were going to testify against me in court. I called my public defender immediately and made an appointment. He agreed to see me at Gracewood on the morning of June 6.

The Preparation

The evening before my attorney arrived, I collected my court documents, some blank paper, and two stubby pencils from the plastic cubby by my bed. Then I asked Jose if I could borrow a roll-around cart and a chair so I could sit and review my legal documents in private. He got me the cart and chair, and I asked if I could place them in the hall outside my room where it was quiet. "No problem," he said. I thanked him, sat down, and got to work. Moments later a black woman with close-cropped hair and an eternal scowl appeared before me: the charge nurse.

"It's against regulations to have that table and chair back here. You have to put them back," she said.

"But I'm reviewing my court documents," I pleaded, pointing to the small stack of papers that lay in front of me.

"You can work at a table in the main area."

"It's too noisy out there. My case is in two days. My attorney is coming to talk to me tomorrow. I need to be in a quiet area where I can focus."

"I'm sorry, it's against rules."

"Could I use one of the quiet rooms?"

She turned and looked at the empty room less than six feet away. "Well, OK, but you can't have the chair."

I thanked her as she turned and took the chair away. I rolled the cart into the quiet room and up against the steel-framed bed. I sat cross-legged on the mattress and pulled the cart in front of me. As I waded through the documents, I circled or underlined things that seemed important and wrote questions for the attorney on the blank sheets.

As I worked, I remembered seeing other patients go to court, but I never saw anyone review their paperwork beforehand. I was probably one of a few with high enough function to do so. After an hour and a half, I was finished, ready for my attorney.

The next morning my attorney arrived. He was short, probably five foot six, thin, and mild mannered, his dark brown hair perfectly cut and styled. His suit, however, looked like it came off a rack at Goodwill. It wasn't a bad suit; it just looked beaten down. It was a good choice for him though; he seemed equally beaten down, like he lost a lot more cases than he won.

"Hi, I'm Roger Lermer."

I shook his hand. "Ken Dickson. Nice to meet you in person. I've got a room set up where we can have some privacy."

Roger followed me into the same quiet room I was in the night before. There was no handle on the inside of the scratched, dark blue steel door of the quiet room, so I took a shoe off and placed it between the door and the frame so it wouldn't swing shut, as I had other times I used the room. I directed him to take a seat on one end of the steel bed while I sat on the other end, rolling the cart between us so he could see the documents. It was deathly quiet in the room, and I could sense the public defender's unease as he took stock of his surroundings.

To me, that room was a safe haven from all the madness, a place where I could count on getting good sleep. As I observed his eyes darting nervously around the room, I tried to imagine what was going through his mind.

Perhaps he sensed poor Andy, the tall, lanky, dark-haired young man who lay restrained on that very bed only a few days earlier, his wrists, ankles, and head bound to the gray steel bed frame by heavy leather straps with cold, chrome steel buckles as he screamed and writhed madly, trying in vain to escape. Or maybe he sensed Len cursing and pacing like a trapped panther, kicking and punching the door and walls with an animal vengeance, and ranting about how the Risperdal the doctors forcibly injected into his thigh caused him to have a heart attack before and was going to kill him this time for sure.

On the other hand, possibly, he noticed the outline where the domed security mirror was missing from the ceiling, ripped down by a patient with his bare hands, leaving rough holes in the wall and ceiling where the mounting bolts tore out chunks of concrete. Maybe he sensed me lying face down and paralyzed on this very bed. I ran my hand over the sheet where I used to be, and I shuddered.

Roger eventually relaxed and we started reviewing my case. As I led him through the documents, he became more and more animated. I was a very capable client who seemed a welcome change for him. I started by pointing out the glaring lies in the petition.

"The biggest problem I have is that it says I physically assaulted my wife."

"*Did* you assault her?" Roger asked.

"No, I've never assaulted anyone. You can even ask my wife in private if you want. I'm not an aggressive person, and besides, I care a great deal about other people."

"What about this? 'He lay in the street in a fetal position?'"

"Sometimes, when I'm really sleep deprived, I collapse, paralyzed, wherever I am. I can't talk or do anything. That happened as I walked with my brother. My neighborhood doesn't have much traffic, and in some places the oleander bushes overhang the sidewalk, so we were walking in the street when I collapsed."

"Why were you in a fetal position?"

"I guess I collapsed that way. It wasn't intentional. My brother dragged me off the street afterwards."

Roger read some of the other things I circled. "Why were you running around the neighborhood late at night ringing doorbells and hiding behind bushes?"

"I never did that. My wife was staying at a good friend's house right behind ours. We've known them for many years and even have a ladder over the fence so their daughter can come over anytime. She's been coming over the fence to visit us since she was only a few years old. Now she's old enough to drive. I went over at maybe 9:30 p.m. and rang the doorbell twice. I only rang a second time because no one answered the first time and I wondered if it rang. Then I noticed that the lights were off and assumed everyone was in bed. I never hid in any bushes, and I certainly didn't ring anyone else's doorbell."

"What about buying a dream car?"

"I did buy a car, but it wasn't my dream car, just a very practical car: a Hyundai Elantra. I already test-drove two Elantras in prior months and my wife even test-drove one with me after that. I have good credit, no debt, and I wanted to reward myself for surviving my surgery. It wasn't even top of the line; it was just a middle-of-the-road model."

Roger asked about my surgery. I told him about it and everything that transpired afterward.

"It says here that you also attempted to purchase another dream car."

"That never happened. My wife told me that they were taking the car back to be stored for thirty days. Later, I went back to see if I could at least take it for one more drive. After arriving at the dealership, I changed my mind and left. Somehow that evolved into me trying to buy another car."

"Are you telling me that these are all lies?"

"Yes."

"Why would the crisis counselor do that?"

"To build a bulletproof case against me so they could put me in here, where I can't escape."

"Did you talk to the crisis counselor?"

"I just introduced myself, that's all."

"Hmm," he said, paging through the petition.

I finished by pointing out that nearly everything in the doctor's affidavits came directly from the crisis counselor's petition. In addition, they were created on the day I first arrived at Gracewood and had not been updated at all in the weeks since. There was no mention anywhere of how helpful and cooperative I was or how I had been a problem to no one. Perhaps my condition had even significantly improved during that time. By the time we finished preparing, I was confident it would be impossible for Dr. Davis to force lithium or any other drug on me. We were going to be an unbeatable team—we *were* an unbeatable team.

The next morning I dressed in some nice clothes that Beth left for me. As I walked out to the main area to wait for the shuttle to the court, there were a few catcalls from the female psych patients. *Even crazy women can appreciate a well-dressed man.* I strutted like a runway model for them. It felt like the judge would throw out my case and let me go home; remove my imaginary shackles, and shout, "Mr. Dickson, you are free to go."

The Hearing

My hands were laced together between my knees as I sat, leaning forward in a wooden chair. I stared at the immobile police officer guarding the two oak doors of the courtroom with his arms crossed imposingly across his chest. Tall, tough looking, and sporting a buzz-cut, he was dressed all in black with a yellow X26 Taser on his left hip and a Glock firearm on his right. A thin, nearly transparent coil protruded from an earpiece in his left ear; a push-to-talk microphone hung from his lapel; and a silver and gold police badge decorated the left side of his chest. Roger, sitting at my right side with his briefcase on his lap and his arms resting over it, tapped his foot anxiously on the floor as we waited. The officer pressed the button on his microphone to reply to something he heard in his earpiece, and then proceeded to open the courtroom doors one at a time. Witnesses, visitors, attorneys, and clients from the previous case meandered out, followed by another officer, who nodded his head in acknowledgment to the one at the door. There were no happy faces in that crowd.

"You may enter the courtroom now," the officer stated once everyone left. I let Roger lead the way. As we entered the room, its small size struck me. It was unlike any courtroom I'd ever seen. There was no place for a jury, and room for perhaps only a dozen visitors and witnesses in the few rows of seating at the back of the court. Everything in the room was either oak or leather. The officer made his way to an area to the left of the judge's bench, spun, and crossed his arms. Roger and I made our way to an oak table on the right side of the courtroom and sat in two gray leather roll-around chairs.

On the left of the courtroom was the clerk of court's post. In the center was a tall judge's bench with the judge's name emblazoned on a brass placard: Judge Veronica Graham. The great seal of the State of Arizona filled the wall behind the bench, and the American and Arizona flags hung freely from poles on either side of it. There were several cameras and microphones scattered around the courtroom. The witness stand loomed directly in front of us.

Moments after we sat, I heard a rustling in the back of the deathly quiet courtroom. I turned to see my wife, two brothers, the plaintiff, and her attorney walk in. My family looked very solemn, as if they were attending my funeral. For the first time in my life, I didn't acknowledge them. I couldn't imagine them testifying against me. I wasn't angry or upset; after seeing the lies in the petition, I was simply dreading hearing more of the same. The plaintiff and her attorney took a seat at the other table while everyone else filled the seats on the left-rear side of the courtroom. I turned a little farther and noticed sadly that there were no witnesses or visitors on my side of the court. It was a humbling observation.

Everyone sat quietly awaiting the clerk and judge. Within a short time, they arrived.

***

The following is a condensed version of the actual court transcripts, painstakingly compiled from the audio record:

***

"All rise for the Honorable Judge Veronica Graham," the clerk said. We all rose and the judge, a short, heavyset black woman, entered the courtroom and took her seat behind the bench.

The judge introduced the case. "Thank you, you may be seated. We're here this morning to consider case number

MH3033001424 filed on June 1, 2011. The allegation is 'persistently or acutely disabled.' The patient's name is Kenneth Dickson. Please announce the petitioner."

"Good morning, Your Honor. Katherine Cuomo, deputy county attorney on behalf of the petitioner."

"Your Honor, Roger Lermer on behalf of Mr. Dickson."

"Sir, can you state your name for the record?" asked the judge.

"Kenneth C. Dickson," I said.

"Thank you. Ms. Cuomo," said the judge.

Ms. Cuomo mentioned the affidavits from two psychiatrists at Gracewood admitted as evidence and that my brother Dana and Shirley Steinfeld would testify against me. My wife and my brother Cole were present but elected not to testify. It was clarified that I was released AMA from Pinecrest by my wife and released under my own recognizance by a doctor from Phoenix Mercy. The Judge asked the two witnesses to stand, and be sworn in by the clerk.

"Do you and each of you solemnly swear or affirm that the testimony you are about to give will be the truth, the whole truth, and nothing but the truth?"

"I do," they replied in unison.

Dana took the stand. Ms. Cuomo questioned him first. She asked why he had come to Arizona, and he responded that he was here to help me. He came for five days from May 23 through May 27 and flew back today to testify.

"Mr. Dickson, did you have frequent interaction with your brother during the five days you were here?" asked Ms. Cuomo.

"Every day," Dana replied.

"Was he very different than how he normally is?"

"Yes, he was very intense, he spoke rapidly. It wasn't what I was accustomed to seeing from him."

"Did he say things that didn't make sense?"

"He talked about things that were way out of the ordinary for him in terms of his family, work, and his future."

"Could you give the court an example that was out of the ordinary?"

He mentioned my ideas regarding a society without negative emotions, and how the condition could potentially be spread, then added, "The ideas were very well conceived but not probable."

"Was his physical behavior different?" asked Ms. Cuomo.

"He was excited about how these new abilities were going to affect everybody."

"Did he indicate to you that he wasn't going to work anymore?"

"In his new social system, people wouldn't have to work. That definitely was out of character for him. He's a good employee, loves his job. But work didn't seem to be on his radar anymore."

Ms. Cuomo asked him if he saw me sleep while he was here. He responded that he only saw me sleep at Phoenix Mercy: a two-hour nap and a four-hour nap.

"Previously, did he sleep regular hours?"

"Yes. He's very fit; he exercises regularly, sleeps, and eats well. Much better than I do."

"Did you at some point go for a walk with him?"

"We went for a walk in his neighborhood the second morning I was here. Suddenly his speech became slurred and he stumbled and then collapsed in the street. I pulled him onto the grass in someone's yard, went and got the car, and took him home."

"Did you see any aggression toward anybody recently?" asked Ms. Cuomo.

"Objection: relevance," Mr. Lermer cried out.

Ms. Cuomo continued. "I would argue that it shows his 'persistent and acute disability' and shows a change in character."

"I'll allow it," said the judge.

"Did you see any aggression or anger toward anybody that your brother would normally not exhibit?"

"I just noticed some agitation. I never had to intervene or protect Beth."

"Did you ever suggest that he get services other than medical treatment?"

"He was very unaccepting of that if I brought it up, so I just let his wife and doctor deal with that."

"In your opinion, did you feel he was unwilling or unable to get help on his own?"

"Well, he was willing to take an occasional Ativan, but that was all. He didn't feel like he needed mental health treatment."

"No further questions, Your Honor."

"Mr. Lermer," the judge called.

Roger asked Dana again how long he was here and where he stayed, then attempted to undermine some of his testimony. "When you testified about Ken discussing new abilities and talking about a new kind of society, how long of a conversation was that?"

"Hours. It wasn't a casual fifteen-minute conversation."

"You testified that Ken only slept at Phoenix Mercy. How do you know that?"

"I was there the whole time. We brought him in at ten thirty a.m., and I was with him until four o'clock the next morning. During that time, he slept for two hours, from around one to three p.m. They gave him a shot of Ativan, and he slept for four hours sometime after that."

Mr. Lermer interrogated Dana with regard to my sleep patterns. It was clear that Dana had no knowledge of my sleep aside from Phoenix Mercy. Then he revisited my collapse.

"Do you know why Ken collapsed when you were walking with him?"

"Well, my guess is from fatigue. I put him in the car afterward and we drove around; he seemed to recover a little."

"Do you know the specific reason?"

"No."

"So you're just guessing that it may have been because of fatigue?"

"Well, he just seemed to run out of gas. He was talking to me one second, then something went wrong. It could have been anything."

Roger asked Dana if he'd asked me to get medical treatment. Dana reiterated that I was resistant to that suggestion.

Roger continued. "Ken had already been to a couple of other medical facilities previously, right?"

"Yes."

"So he had already gotten some mental health care?"

"I wasn't involved in that."

"Nothing further, Your Honor."

"Ms. Cuomo," called the judge.

"Why are you testifying today?" asked Ms. Cuomo.

"To help Ken get restored to where he was before his surgery so that he can return to his wife and children."

"It's not to punish him?"

"Ken and I have never had any kind of punitive relationship in our lives."

"Thank you."

"You may step down," said the judge.

Dana stepped down from the stand. As he passed me on the way back to his seat, he glanced at me briefly. I don't know if he noticed, but I had tears welling in my eyes. Regardless of whether his testimony hurt or helped me, his honesty and accuracy overwhelmed me. Dana traveled seven hundred miles to testify against me and force me to take medication. I fully expected that he might lie or twist the truth in order to accomplish that goal. Instead he paid me, a person who values the truth above all else, a supreme compliment. As our eyes met, I gave him a subtle thumbs-up and mouthed the words "thank you."

Shirley Steinfeld then took the stand, and Ms. Cuomo questioned her. "Were you recently called to Mr. Dickson's home?"

"Yes."

"Besides the family, was there anybody else there?"

"A neighbor and the other three individuals in court."

"It wasn't a police call?"

"No, it was not."

"When you met with Mr. Dickson, how did he present?"

"He was in constant motion. He rarely sat down. When he would sit down, it was for a minute or two at the most."

"Was he calmly doing something, or was it an anxious, restless motion?"

"It was restless. He was constantly moving, playing with the dog, walking from outside to the garage and back."

"Did he know why you were there and the purpose of your evaluation?"

"We explained that we were a crisis team, that his family was concerned about him. He didn't seem to understand that."

"How was his speech?"

"I found his speech pressured, rapid."

"How long have you been doing this?"

"Over four years."

"How would you describe his overall presentation? Was he manic? Was he depressed?"

"He was extremely manic. I do not believe he was oriented to the situation. It didn't seem to bother him that there were two strangers in his home, even when we explained why we were there."

"Did he want to answer your questions?"

"No, he didn't."

Shirley could certainly read a lot into our brief introduction, me playing with my dog and talking to my brother and friend. It wasn't that I didn't want to talk to her; I had nothing against her, I just didn't want to be involved in whatever was being discussed. I had enough of people trying to fix me.

"After watching him and attempting to interact with him, you filed an involuntary petition. Why was it involuntary?"

"In speaking with him when he would sit down, I believe my comment was, 'Your family is concerned about you; would you be willing to see a doctor?' He was not interested."

I shook my head and whispered to my attorney that what she was describing never happened. I was to repeat those actions several more times during her testimony.

"Is there anything else that he presented at that time?"

"He seemed extremely tightly wound; I felt he would be extremely unpredictable."

"Agitated?"

"Yeah, I guess you could say that."

"Thank you. I have no further questions."

"Mr. Lermer," called the judge.

"Thank you. Have you ever met Mr. Dickson before?"

"No."

"You were at his home for two hours?"

"That's correct."

"It's your testimony that you explained to Mr. Dickson why you were there?"

"Yeah."

"And you're saying he did not understand why you were there?"

"He didn't seem to understand when I said, 'Your family is concerned about you.'"

"Where were you in that two-hour period, inside or outside the house?"

"I was inside sitting on a couch. I had a clear view of the backyard and the path that was continually taken by Mr. Dickson."

"Where was Mr. Dickson most of the time during that period?"

"He probably was outside more than inside."

"When he was outside, was he mainly playing with the dog?"

"He was playing with the dog and talking to his brother and a friend."

"Could you hear the conversation?"

"No."

"What you mainly observed when Mr. Dickson was outside was him moving around rapidly?"

"I observed a hyper level of activity, constant motion, what appeared to me to be an inability to sit down and relax."

"You mentioned that Mr. Dickson was irritated when you told him that you were there because his family was concerned about him?"

"He wasn't irritated with us; he really didn't even acknowledge us."

"You made a comment before that Mr. Dickson really wasn't bothered that you were there, right?"

"He didn't acknowledge us."

"But you did testify that he was irritated when you asked him questions though."

"Once, we asked him if he would sit down and chat with us for a while. He became irritated."

"I have nothing further."

"You may step down," said the judge.

"The petitioner rests," said Ms. Cuomo.

After taking the oath, I took the stand and Roger questioned me. He asked what my marital status was and if I had children. He asked if I loved my wife and family. I replied that I did and that I had a good relationship with both my wife and my children.

"Have you ever had any mental health history before?" Mr. Lermer asked.

"Never in my life."

"You've never gone to the doctor and complained about depression?"

"No."

"You've never been in a hospital like this before?"

"No, except for the other ones in the last few weeks."

"You had a surgery to your bowels recently, right?"

"Yes, I had a micro-perforation of my colon due to diverticulitis. I had to have ten inches of my colon removed."

"Were you in the hospital for quite a while?"

"Twelve days, from April fourteenth to the twenty-fifth."

"Have you ever had that serious a surgery before in your life?"

"No, just a minor hernia surgery a few years back, and resetting a broken leg when I was five."

"So you're a healthy person?"

"Yes."

"Do you believe that when Dana was at your house that you were having mental health issues?"

"No."

"So when your brother was describing the issues, what are your comments regarding that?"

"I agree completely with his testimony." That was perhaps the worst thing a defense attorney could hear from his client, but I wanted to make it clear that I didn't want to discount or distort my brother's truthful testimony. "I definitely had some ideas in my head that were very interesting, and I was very excited about them, but I've since realized that some of those things are not possible."

"He mentioned that you expressed some new abilities and talked about a new society. Did you talk to him about those topics?"

"Yes."

"Are those topics that you normally talk to him about?"

"No, just after the surgery."

"Were you behaving any differently because of loss of sleep?"

"Only when I collapsed. If I go too long without sleep, I have a seizure. I'll be temporarily paralyzed and lose speech."

"Is that what happened when you went for the walk with your brother?"

"Yes."

"Were you having seizures prior to that?"

"I had several: one at Desert Hope and another in an ambulance on the way to Pinecrest. I also had two in the PDC."

"You never had these until after your surgery?"

"No."

"Did you have trouble sleeping after the surgery?"

232

"Yes. Something happened as a result of the surgery, and it made it impossible to sleep. Eventually, I began to use Ativan to help myself sleep."

"Were you having sleep issues when your brother was visiting?"

"Just the night my wife was at the neighbors'. I was restless because I wanted to see her."

"You said you were having trouble with your adrenal gland. Did it make you hyper for that night?"

"No, that wasn't adrenaline. I was agitated because of all the people in my home and the fact that my wife was suffering under all the stress and needed help. When she is under stress, she doesn't eat well and loses weight. It turns out that one of the women was a recovering anorexic and recognized that Beth was undernourished. So she offered to help her. They also took her away to let me sleep in the house that night instead of at a hotel."

"I see. Do you believe you were a little hyper that night when you were talking to your brother?"

"Yes, because of everything going on. There were maybe nine people in my home, all telling me I had a problem. I was trying to convince them that my wife had a problem because she was so stressed from my surgery and she'd lost a lot of weight. I felt attacked by all these people. Some of them I didn't even know."

"Let's talk about when the crisis worker came. Do you recall the crisis worker telling you why she was there?"

"No, I don't recall that they asked me questions. I would have been happy to sit down and talk to them, but I didn't know that I was required to. I didn't know why they were there. They were talking to my wife and I just stayed out of it."

"Were you irritated that the crisis worker was there?"

"No, not at all. I just wasn't aware of why they were there, and I just tried to stay out of it. If anyone had asked me to come over and talk, I would have been happy to."

"Do you have a job, Ken?"

"Well, I hope I still do."

"What is your profession?"

"I work at Nanosys; I'm a principal test engineer."

"How long have you worked there?"

"Since last July."

"How long have you been in that profession?"

"About thirty-two years."

"When you're sick, do you go to the doctor?"

"Yes, but I rarely get sick."

"Did you agree to go to the doctor for your bowel issues?"

"I admitted myself."

"Did you go to a couple of facilities for your behavior prior to coming to this hospital?"

"I did everything I was asked."

"You thought you were having some issues and you cooperated and went to those facilities?"

"I didn't believe that I had issues, but I agreed to go because my family felt it was necessary."

"When you get out of the hospital, are you going back to work?"

"Yes, that's my plan."

"Do you feel ready to go back to work and able to take care of yourself?"

"Yes."

"Do you want to see your wife and family and work through this whole process with them?"

"Yes I do. I've wanted to for a long time. I am concerned they'll continue to put me in institutions until they think I'm cured. I have a lot of anxiety about that."

"Do you have anything else to comment on regarding why you're in here?"

"I'm concerned that the doctor wants to force me to take lithium. I told him that if lithium was something that came in an over-the-counter multivitamin, I'd be glad to take it. Since I refused to take it, they forced me to come to court. I've never taken any drugs in my life except antibiotics. I feel like lithium is being forced on me."

"Thank you, Ken. That's all I have, Your Honor."

"Ms. Cuomo," the judge stated.

"You had up to nine people in your house urging you to get some help?"

"There were neighbors, friends, and some people I didn't know."

"Why did they agree to take your wife out?"

"One of the women there was a recovering anorexic. She recognized that Beth was undernourished, and took her under her wing. They all took Beth over to Caroline's house, my neighbor behind us, so I could stay at the house instead of at a hotel."

"Could it have been that it was because you had attacked your wife?"

"Objection!" Roger exclaimed.

"What reason?" the judge asked.

"Relevance: there is no evidence of that that was introduced prior."

"Ms. Cuomo?" queried the judge.

"I believe it's relevant to his 'persistent and acute disability' and once again that it's not out-of-character behavior for him."

I attempted to make a comment. "I just want to say that I never..."

"Stop...stop...stop! Sir, when you hear the word 'objection,' it means don't say another word. You don't get to just blab something," the judge admonished. "I'll allow this," growled the judge, looking crossly at me.

"Is it possible that it was because you had attacked your wife?"

"No."

"Nobody said anything to you about that? It was because your wife was the one who was ill, and she's the one who needed treatment?"

"Yes."

"Do you still think that?"

"Yes."

"Are your brothers siding with your wife?"

"Yes, they are siding with my wife."

"When you were looking for your wife, were you ringing various neighbors' doorbells?"

"I rang Caroline's doorbell. I wanted to wish my wife good luck with her treatment. That's the only doorbell I rang. No one answered, so I left."

"Have you been taking your medications at the hospital?"

"I only take Ativan. It's hard to sleep in that place. I have three roommates—some snore terribly; others come, go, and use the bathroom at all hours of the night. So I take it as needed to get enough sleep."

"Ativan is for sleep?"

"Yes. It also stops me from having seizures. I've tried Benadryl, too, but it doesn't work for me."

"Dr. Davis recommended that you take lithium?"

"Yes, but I'm not taking it."

"Thank you. That's all I have, Your Honor."

"Mr. Lermer, do you have anything more?" asked the judge.

"Just two questions, Your Honor. Mr. Dickson, have you ever attacked your wife?"

"No."

"Is one reason you are concerned about taking lithium the adverse effects it might have due to your recent surgery?"

"Yes."

"That's all."

"You may step down, sir."

"You rest, Mr. Lermer?" asked the judge.

"Yes, Your Honor."

"Ms. Cuomo?"

"Yes, Your Honor."

The attorneys then gave their closing arguments. Roger gave his first.

"Your Honor, I ask that you not impose a court order for treatment. Regarding Mr. Dickson's brother Dana's testimony, he was only in town for a short time and with Mr. Dickson in his home only one night. He did spend some time with him during that week but did not observe his brother every minute of that time. We heard that Mr. Dickson might have been acting a little differently.

There was no testimony that my client can't take care of himself, that he's persistently and acutely disabled, or that he was doing so poorly that he had to be taken away at the time that his brother was here. Violence and being a danger to himself or others are not questions. He testified that Mr. Dickson wasn't sleeping but admitted he didn't know his brother's sleep patterns.

"With regard to the crisis worker's testimony, she was there for a two-hour time period and was called without Mr. Dickson's knowledge. Mr. Dickson testified that he didn't know why she was there, which is understandable: the family called her without his knowledge. She testified that she explained why she was there, but my client does not have any recollection of that.

I didn't hear any specific testimony supporting him being persistently and acutely disabled. I did hear general observations from the crisis worker. His moving around a lot was a snapshot in time. Many people get like that. He was outside running around with his dog. She didn't specifically observe him having behavioral problems while he was outside.

I thought Mr. Dickson's testimony was very focused, and I believe that he understands why he's here. He doesn't want to take specific medications, and he has good reasons for that. He doesn't want to harm himself, or anyone else; he can take care of himself and is willing to address his issues as they come along. He just doesn't want to have medication forced upon him. For all these reasons, Your Honor, I'm asking that you not impose a court order, as very convincing evidence has not been presented. Thank you."

"Ms. Cuomo?" the judge said.

"I would just argue that Mr. Dickson is continuing not to take the medication that was suggested by his doctor in the hospital.

Though the defense argued that Mr. Dickson has a clear understanding of why he is here, we would argue that he doesn't have that understanding. He continues to say it's his wife that has the issue despite his testimony on the stand that there were nine people in his home concerned about his behavior and suggesting he get help. He somehow turns that into, well, it was his wife who needed the help, not him.

So, we would argue that he doesn't have insight. He continues not to follow through with his medications, although he is taking Ativan and is clearly calmer than he was earlier. He is not following through and is in need of a court order. Thank you."

Finally, the judge made a ruling.

"I've had an opportunity to review the petition that was filed on June the first, 2011, with the allegation of 'persistent or acutely disabled,' and I read both of the doctors' reports in the affidavits attached to the petition. I also reviewed the medication affidavit and the treatment plan. I've taken into consideration the testimony of the two witnesses for the petitioner and the testimony of the patient.

Based upon all the matters presented to the court, I find by clear and convincing evidence that the proposed patient is, as a result of a mental disorder, persistently or acutely disabled, in need of psychiatric treatment, and unwilling or unable to accept voluntary treatment. The court finds that court-ordered treatment is appropriate and that the patient is to be in an inpatient treatment program.

It is therefore ordered that Kenneth Dickson shall undergo treatment for up to one hundred eighty days at Gracewood until he is found to be no longer persistently or acutely disabled. It is further ordered that Mr. Dickson, having been placed under court-ordered treatment, shall not possess, receive, and/or purchase firearms, ammunition, or other deadly weapons. Mr. Dickson has the right to apply for restoration of firearms rights after court-ordered treatment has been terminated. This matter is adjourned. Thank you."

**

Beth's journal, June 7, 2011:

I don't really remember what I was feeling in the courtroom. I was numb, completely drained physically and exhausted emotionally. I was incredulous that we were in a courtroom with a judge deciding Ken's fate. I had no hope at that point in my life. I could not see how we would ever recover from such a horrible situation. I was fearful of what would happen to the girls and me in the future. How would I be able to support them and send them to college? Where would we live? What was going to happen to Ken?

In the end, I was relieved with the court's decision. I knew that Ken was not well enough to come home, but I was in no way happy. How could I be happy to have a judge rule that my love was persistently and acutely disabled? I fought so hard to protect him and felt that I failed miserably. It was Kaitlin's birthday today. What a sad birthday for her.

***

Back at Gracewood that evening, I fell in line with everyone else when the medication cart rolled in. When my turn came, instead of one pill, there were three in my cup. I asked what they were and was told Ativan, Risperdal (an antipsychotic), and Eskalith, a brand of lithium carbonate. I had no choice but to take them. If I refused, they would forcibly restrain me and give them by injection. I took the small paper cup of pills and dumped them into my mouth, then washed them down with water from a second cup. The nurse checked off my name on her list. Unbelievably Dr. Davis won. I walked away numbly as I contemplated a life in Gracewood for another 180 days.

Chapter 30

UTOPIA: LETTING GO

June 13, 2011: In my heart, I always believed that I was contagious, that I was the first person without negative emotions and would infect others and make everything and anything possible, including Utopia. If I was not contagious, none if it was possible, and Utopia would just be another failed social project like many before.

In 1984, Space Biospheres Ventures bought a convention center owned by the University of Arizona just outside of Oracle, Arizona. In 1986, the company started construction of Biosphere 2 on the property to research and develop self-sustaining, space-colonization technology. Why Biosphere 2? Because Earth is Biosphere 1, the only other currently known biosphere.

Space Biospheres Ventures' ultimate goal was to seal a team of Biospherians in the state-of-the-art structure, which housed everything they believed necessary for a fully balanced, self-sustaining ecosystem, and measure survivability of the inhabitants and system. When Biosphere 2 was completed, it was breathtaking. Within its glass walls were trees, plants, animals, bugs, fresh water, brand-new living quarters, clothing, cooking and eating utensils, beds, and too many other things to list.

The scientists and professionals involved worked long and hard on everything, including the selection of an ideally suited team of Biospherians. Through study and experimentation, they determined the makeup of an optimal team, and then chose the ideal people for that team: eight all together, both men and women. The team of Biospherians was overall one of the most technically, socially, and psychologically skilled teams ever assembled.

Finally, on September 26, 1991, with the media in full force and cameras recording, they sealed the team inside the beautiful, state-of-the-art structure for its first mission.

There were many catastrophes during that mission, but most importantly, before the mission was half over, the perfect team fractured. People who were intimate friends became ruthless enemies who could barely speak to each other.

With negative emotions, we are doomed to battle each other forever and my notion of Utopia would fail before it started. For that reason, I was constantly on the lookout for a sign of someone else that lost all negative emotions as I had. I watched the news and observed people around me. I found no one anywhere I looked. At one point, I wondered whether Tim and Dana were like me, but I eventually realized it wasn't the case. There was no one else like me. I was unique, alone. *I am the only one.*

It was torture to be the only one: to see all the opportunities and possibilities, to have them within reach and yet have it all be meaningless. Everyone thought I lost it, that I was completely gone when I talked about the things I did. I hated more than anything to admit that they were right. I hated it because what I wanted was for them. I wanted them to have those wonderful opportunities. I wanted all the people of the world to have them.

Reluctantly, I made the decision to let go of Utopia and things beyond it. I needed to get back to normal life: to be a good husband, father and provider, and stop dreaming of things that were impossible. Farewell, Utopia, you will always hold a special place in my heart, but the journey sadly ends here.

However, the subconscious mind, where dreams originate, cannot so easily forget manic visions...

Chapter 31

CREAM

It was June 14, 2011, my last night at Gracewood. Unbelievably, shortly after the court hearing, Dr. Davis informed me that he was willing to let me go as soon I complied with my medication and he was satisfied that I was medically stable. I had a rough time for the first few days. The lithium and Risperdal didn't agree with me at all. My heart frequently raced, my head ached, I was dizzy, and my mouth felt like someone poured dry desert sand into it. My blood pressure rose, and I was hot all of the time. Instead of getting better rest, I tossed and turned even more at night. Rather than feel cured, I felt poisoned, but my blood lithium levels were right on target and that was good enough for Dr. Davis. In his mind, he succeeded once more. Therefore, the next day, June 15, I was going home.

On top of the issues with my medications, helping Matthew was taking its toll. That last night, I lay in the dark in anticipation of his call, unable to sleep. I looked over at his still body lit only by the sliver of reflected light from under the room door. He seemed dead, but I knew it was only a matter of time before he needed me once again. In between helping him, minutes seemed like hours, and hours like days.

Just when I thought he wouldn't call out, he did, and I once more tracked down a nurse, and then crawled back into my bed only to lay sleepless. Finally, it grew light. I got up, used the bathroom, quietly slipped from the room, and made my way to the main area just in time to catch the morning news.

I took a seat on the sofa by the nurses' station as I had on many mornings as the world woke up. Two female patients joined me. Right on cue, one of the nurses pointed the TV remote through the glass of the nurses' station, powered on the TV, and switched it to CNN. "Turn it up!" the three of us yelled in unison. The nurse pressed the volume button on the remote, and when an indicator on the screen hit twenty-four, I gave a thumbs-up, however, I was quickly outvoted. As soon as the nurse stopped, the women both yelled "Turn it up!" in unison. I grimaced as the indicator continued incrementing, and then sighed with relief when they both gave a thumbs-up at thirty. *I can handle that.* I sat back on the sofa eager to learn what was new in the world.

***

"The relationship between the US and Pakistan is on the ropes this morning. I'm Christine Romans. The CIA informants who helped the US track down bin Laden have been arrested by a Pakistan military spy agency."

I always felt that Christine ran the show in this three-ring morning circus. She was the consummate professional, quickly reining things in whenever they got too far out of line.

Christine's dark blue pants were a departure from the short skirts she and Kiran usually wore. Pants or no, she still crossed her legs, predominantly right over left, as opposed to Kiran's left over right. I was glad I was a man and didn't need to worry about such things. I looked at Ali's knees at table level; they were a comfortable foot apart.

"The showdown with the president: I'm Kiran Chetry. House Speaker John Boehner is warning that the US could be breaking the law with its military operation in Libya. We're live at the White House with reaction."

"An anchorman lands an interview with the Dalai Lama. Then he decides to tell him a Dalai Lama joke. I'm Ali Velshi. The Dalai Lama didn't get the joke. We'll see if you do on this *American Morning.*"

"Good morning everyone, it is Wednesday, June fifteenth," announced Christine.

Christine, Ali, and Kiran then traded off stories. First Christine reported on the police use of tear gas and water cannons on demonstrators in Greece. A video clip showed the hapless protesters running amok after police blasted them with water jets and enveloped them in fog from tear gas canisters. Next Ali reported on a US drone strike that killed four suspected militants (according to intelligence officials). Supporting footage showed a compound and a barely visible vehicle in a video supplied by the military and used to confirm the strike. The video displayed a rectangular targeting box around the building and a vehicle with a bright spot at the center from the laser targeting system.

Suddenly a missile streaked into the image, and the screen went white. When the camera recovered from the flash and the smoke cleared, nothing remained but a hole and debris where the building and vehicle once sat. Though I secretly cheered for America every time I saw such a video, it was chilling how casually the media replayed peoples' deaths. The news was action packed to that point. It sure beat having to listen to Weinergate for days on end. I wished Congressman Weiner would resign and put us all out of our misery.

Kiran piped up next with a report about NATO air strikes targeting Tripoli. There was no information about targets or casualties, but there was a report of NATO aircraft dropping leaflets telling Moammar's forces to leave. *Yeah, I would leave if someone dropped leaflets on me.* Even though, like most Americans, I knew nothing about them, I rooted for the citizens of Libya.

Things quickly took a turn for the worse after that as the anchors focused on the fact that President Obama didn't get permission from Congress to carry out the bombing of Libya. That could have been an interesting story, but in this case, it just gave a few politicians an opportunity for some free airtime.

In a short while, I yawned. I needed sleep badly and, if CNN was going to deliver it, hallelujah. I curled up on the hard, gray, simulated leather sofa, rested my head on my arm, and closed my eyes.

"Ahem" *That sounds like someone clearing his throat.* Tap, tap. *Now he's tapping a stack of papers on edge.* I'd like to say I opened my eyes and sat up, but instead I found myself already sitting up on the sofa as before. The room was strangely quiet with no one there but me. I turned to look at the nurses' station: it was empty. Devoid of any living sound, the entire place seemed deserted. For some reason this was perfectly acceptable to me. I turned to the television, and Christine, Ali, and Kiran were still there. It looked like they were caught at the tail end of a break and didn't yet realize they were live.

"Hello and welcome back to this *American Morning* with Ali Velshi, Kiran Chetry, and myself, Christine Roman. In technology news today, we're excited to introduce a new software product called 'Cream' from Web Immersion Technologies. Here to discuss this exciting product is our special guest, the founder and president of Web Immersion Technologies, Mr. Tucker Hartford. Welcome, Mr. Hartford."

"Thank you. It's great to be here, Christine."

"Mr. Hartford," Kiran injected, "I understand that you have both a BS and an MS degree from Stanford."

"Yes, I have a BS in computer science and an MS in artificial intelligence," Tucker replied.

"Your location near Silicon Valley couldn't be better," said Christine.

"As a matter of fact, many business partners and several colleagues in the area are acquaintances from my school days. Being near Silicon Valley and Apple in particular, is extremely beneficial. Apple has helped almost from the start supplying iPads and technical support for beta testing. Many companies in the area provided input during product development."

Ali spoke next. "Mr. Hartford, can you tell us a little about Cream?"

"I'd be glad to. Cream is an artificial intelligence-powered web servant developed to ensure that everyone will have the best experience possible on the Internet."

Christine asked the next question. "Mr. Hartford, I didn't think artificial intelligence was invented yet. Are you the first to develop it?"

"My apologies, it's more of a specialized intelligence, nowhere near self-aware, and is nothing anyone should fear. It has one purpose: to better serve. It is pivotal to the future success of Cream."

"Excuse me, Mr. Hartford, but how did you arrive at the name 'Cream'? Is it an acronym?" asked Ali.

"Not at all, it pertains to cream being the best part, the part that rises to the top. When cream rises in milk, it doesn't do it instantaneously; it has to work over time. Cream works that way with the Internet: by allowing the cream of the Internet, the best of the Internet if you will, to rise to the top."

"I understand the rising to the top part," said Ali, "but what exactly is Cream?"

"Cream is an application that you download for free to your computer or smart phone. Once installed, you simply click on the Cream icon to open a 'Cream portal.'"

"A what? What's that?" asked Kiran.

"The Cream portal is the gateway to the Cream web."

"This is starting to sound a little too creamy," said Kiran. Everyone laughed.

"Bear with me; it's a good cream, I assure you," said Tucker as the laughter subsided. "Seriously though, the name grows on you. I guarantee that when you use Cream, you'll be thinking of that cream rising in the gosh-awful Internet we have now. That's the point, to motivate the Internet to get better."

"So how does it do that, or should I keep my mouth shut?" asked Christine.

"Do you really want us to answer that?" asked Ali, chuckling.

"OK, OK, go ahead, Mr. Hartford. Sorry for the interruption," said Christine.

"All right, getting back to the point where you've downloaded the app and pressed the Cream icon for the first time. You'll notice immediately that the interface is simple and clean, reminiscent of web browsers you use every day: Windows Explorer, Firefox, or Google, for example. The beauty of the Cream portal is that, from the beginning, it continually improves, becoming friendlier and smarter with use. Even better, it adapts to your specific likes and needs. Eventually, it will be the best and, dare I say, most perfect web interface that you've ever used."

"Is that all Cream does?" asked Ali.

"No, that's a part of the experience, but it's only the beginning. The real work happens in the Cream web: the heart of the dedicated intelligence. There, powerful servers continuously fend off the harsh realities of the real Internet to ensure Cream users have a friendly, positive experience."

"Like malware, pop-ups, spam, and viruses?" asked Kiran.

"Yes, and even more. Are you familiar with eBay and Amazon?" asked Tucker.

"Yes," all three answered in unison. "That was weird," said Kiran, laughing.

"Well, eBay created a safe environment for buyers and sellers by implementing a ranking system. By treating each other with honesty and respect, users improve their rankings. Amazon did something similar by using product ratings to ensure a good buyer experience. Those companies proved that when you reward people for good behavior and honesty, bad behavior and deception fade from the picture. The whole environment continually improves."

"The Cream philosophy," said Ali. Christine nodded.

"Exactly, Cream takes it to a new level by applying the same philosophy to every user and website utilizing our own proprietary rating and ranking protocols. As some websites and users rise in an effort to be the cream, others who refuse to improve sink. At a certain cutoff, Cream blocks those users, isolating them from the Cream web. The aim is to promote and reward good practices so that users of the Cream web will always have the finest, safest, least prejudiced, most trustworthy, fun, and productive environment conceivable. Within the Cream web, everyone will be freer and more equal than ever. Because of that, within the confines of the Cream web, you will be able to connect with people of the world like never before."

"Wow, that's really exciting. Is Cream available yet?" asked Kiran.

"It's in beta testing with some of our major clients and will be available for general use in a few months."

"Mr. Hartford, can you tell us the one thing you like most about Cream?" Ali asked.

"That's tough. I can think of at least ten things right off the top of my head. How about letting me share three?"

Ali laughed. "I should have expected that. You certainly are a bulldozer, there's just no stopping you once you get rolling. OK, but only three: we still have the rest of the show to do."

"What can I say? All right, the top three..." He hesitated in thought and the three anchors leaned closer in anticipation. "First, Cream continually learns from its user interactions and improves itself to make the Cream experience even friendlier and better. Second, Cream puts the best of everything right at your fingertips. You no longer have to suffer through hours of frustration and depend on chance to find what you're looking for. Finally, Cream is nondiscriminatory. Everyone is equal in the Cream web regardless of race, religion, nationality, size, shape, or color; if you are rich or poor, what your age is, or if you are pretty, ugly, handicapped, diseased, or disabled."

"Outstanding," said Ali. "I have just one final question: are you trying to control the Internet with Cream?"

"That's a valid concern, but not what Cream is about. We could waste our time trying to control a rapidly expanding and evolving technology and fail, or we can skim the cream for our users to create a virtual paradise: purified, organized, streamlined, and customized for each Cream user right now, leaving the Internet itself alone for others to deal with. We're happy to share with anyone the path to becoming a part of Cream. Shine. Be the brightest and best; be the fastest, most useful, most entertaining, most important, most educational, or the friendliest. If you shine, you won't need to come to us; our doors will already be open to you."

"Thank you for joining us on this *American Morning*," said Kiran. "We wish you and Web Immersion Technologies the best of luck."

"Thank you for having me. It's been a pleasure," said Tucker.

"Stay tuned for more news. We'll be right back after this break," announced Christine.

That was a fascinating product. I was amazed at how long the segment was. It was unusual for CNN to devote so much time to one topic. Suddenly, an unseen force shook me.

"Ken? Ken!" someone yelled. I opened my eyes, which surprised me because I thought I *was* awake. Instead, I was lying sideways on the sofa, my arm curled under my head and damp with drool. I blinked and looked around; not believing it was a dream. It was the most sophisticated dream I ever had. I guess that's how it is when your full brain comes back online.

"Sorry to wake you. I didn't want you to miss breakfast."

"No problem, Al. I guess I was really out. I can't believe I slept through all this noise," I said, now able to hear all the normal breakfast commotion.

"You must really be tired."

"Matthew kept me up all night. I can't wait to get out of here and sleep in a real bed without Matthew waking me all the time."

"I bet he'll really miss your help."

"I wish I could train someone to take over, but I doubt anyone else would care like me. What's for breakfast?"

"Breakfast burritos."

"Great, I love those things. Thanks for waking me. I have to go get something from my room."

I rushed to my room and retrieved two packets of hot sauce that I'd hid behind a sock in one of the shoes in my cubby. I loved the stuff. The last time they had breakfast burritos, I scored the unused packets from other patients. I ran back and waited to hear my name as they read them from the paperwork attached to each tray.

"Ken Dickson?" That was my cue. I rushed to the cart.

"Easy, boy, here you go."

"Thanks," I said, taking the tray. I sat at one of the tables and wasted no time peeling the tinfoil wrapper open, unrolling the burrito, and pouring three packets of fiery sauce on it. I took one bite and was in heaven. My tongue was on fire, my lips were on fire, my entire mouth was on fire: that was heaven to me.

As I savored my burrito, I pondered the point of the dream. Two thirds of the way through the burrito it came to me. The dream implied that through science and innovation, we could create a place that encourages the best of human interaction and fosters the finest of human ideas. We can create an environment free of everything that holds us back from reaching our full potential, an environment much like the real one I envisioned. The difference was that it would be a virtual environment, a virtual Utopia. Instead of humankind losing their negative emotions, Cream would circumvent them completely. Everyone would still have their negative emotions, but within the Cream web, they would be free of their effects.

I felt energized by that realization. No longer did I need to fret about changed people. Cream was so much more plausible, likely, even probable, that it seemed inevitable. It made much more sense than people randomly infected by some kind of un-disease that made them better instead of worse. Utopia wasn't dead after all; it simply underwent a metamorphosis. The stage was set for its opening show. There wasn't a changed person in the audience. Instead, it consisted of Internet users of every sex, shape, size, color, and religion, all waiting breathlessly for the show to begin. The lighting and sound crews were in place, the supporting cast was ready, and the stage crew was anxious to raise the curtain. The only thing missing is the real-world equivalent of Cream taking the stage so the show can begin.

Chapter 32

LOOSE ENDS

After finishing my breakfast, I asked Al if I could shower and shave. He nodded, rose from his chair against the wall of the main area, and walked to the storage room to fetch a razor and washcloth. He escorted me to my room's bathroom instead of the one in the quiet room that I usually used. That one had no hot water, and Al was letting me have a little luxury today. That was as close to heaven as I could get in Gracewood: shaving with hot water and a fresh single-blade plastic razor.

Next, I hit the shower. The foamy soap from the dispenser on the wall doubled as body soap and shampoo. I made the most of it, then dried off and dressed myself in a pair of brown dress slacks, a brown woven leather belt, a cream tropical-print dress shirt, and penny loafers that Beth brought. It felt so uplifting to be out of my cargo pants, scrubs, and running shoes.

Once dressed, I walked to the main area and paid homage to the day on Emma's calendar. I rested my hand on it for a moment longer than usual, dreading that it was the last time that I would do so and that it was the last day I would see Emma, perhaps for the rest of my life. That was a sobering thought. It seemed so uncanny that I could form a bond with her and then never see her again. As I stood by the calendar, the catcalls started:

"Hey, check Ken out. What a hunk."

"Woo-hoo, look at you."

"Where's the party, Ken?"

"Hubba-hubba."

I finished my homage and took a sweeping bow. "Thank you, young ladies," I said to women who were for the most part over forty and upward to their seventies. Then I joined them watching TV to pass the time until 9:25 a.m.

At that time, the call came for anyone wishing to go outside. Grace wanted to go and I offered to wheel her out. I considered it an honor to push her wheelchair. Everyone, including me, liked the cranky old woman's indomitable spirit, and I particularly enjoyed verbally sparring with her on the way out and back. I always won because I unfailingly responded with kind words to her malicious ones and broke through her tough armor.

Once outside, I parked her in her favorite shady place in the grass near the basketball court, and went to the hose reel to wait for Emma. Time passed and I wondered if she had the day off. Finally, the door to the yard swung open and Emma strolled out, smiling as she made her way to the hose reel.

"You look nice today," she said.

"It's my last day. I thought I'd dress up."

"Oh," she said. I didn't know what to make of that. It was so open ended. She said nothing else, just walked over to the faucet, unlocked the lock securing it, and connected the end of the hose. I unreeled the hose pulling it to full length as she turned on the faucet. We then proceeded to prune flowers and remove debris from the north garden. We didn't talk much, but Emma sang and that was fine by me; it was what I longed for the most and how I wanted to remember her. When we finished, I watered the flowers and she headed to the south garden to prune and clean it.

I loved watering the flowers. It was peaceful and calming. The nozzle had many settings, but I always turned it to the one marked "rain." I gave the flowers a few more raindrops than usual before shutting the nozzle off and pulling the long hose to the south garden. Emma was finished by the time I arrived, so I began watering it right away.

"I'm going to miss this. I really enjoyed taking care of the gardens with you," I said.

"I've really appreciated your help."

"I even helped on days you weren't here. Did you know that? The other recreational therapist did as you asked, but whenever possible I offered to water to make sure the job was done right."

"I didn't know that. Thanks."

If this sounds like a strained conversation, it was. Not that it was Emma's fault. Like the other patients, I was dangerous. As far as she or anyone else knew, I could snap without warning. I wasn't what you'd call good friend material. We probably would get along wonderfully if we met randomly outside, perhaps picking out six packs of young flowers at Home Depot. Maybe we could even have a good friendship, but in here, this was as good as it would get. In fact, during my weeks at Gracewood, this was the best anyone managed with me, even family. It made me wonder if things would ever be better. *What if this is how my life will be from here on out?*

"I just wanted to say one last thing, Emma. I hope that if we ever meet again, it will be under better circumstances." Once I said it, I felt that it was right up there with Emma's "Oh." It didn't begin to convey what I really felt—that it was difficult to imagine what life would be like without her in it. I wished there was a way we could remain friends after my recovery, but it seemed impossible in light of the circumstances that brought us together in the first place. Emma didn't respond; those were the last words spoken between us.

I finished watering and rolled up the hose, then went to wheel Grace in one last time. As my unit merged at the doorway and I led the pack inside (Grace was always first to go in), I paused, and looked back at Emma. Then, I removed my hand from the wheelchair handle and waved. She raised her hand slightly and waved back. I wheeled Grace through the doorway, and Emma vanished from my life.

After coming in from the recreation period, I went to my room to clean up and collect my things. I disassembled my stuffed pillow, stripped the bed, and took all the bedding to the hamper in the hallway. Next, I took the picture of the pretty, brown haired girl out of my left cargo pants pocket and put it in my left dress pants pocket. I then put all of my belongings in the well-used brown paper grocery bag with my name on it that I used for laundry. As quickly as that, I was ready to go. Everything I owned filled half the bag. It was hard to imagine that was all that I needed. It made me embarrassed to think of all the junk awaiting me in the normal world. I would never think of it in the same way again.

Before I left the room, there was one more thing I needed to do. I walked over to Len's bed, reached into my left pants pocket for the picture of the blue-eyed girl, unfolded it one last time, and silently said good-bye to her. Then, I folded the picture again and chuckling, placed it under Len's pillow.

As noon rolled around, I waited with everyone else for the lunch cart. Just after noon, George rolled Matthew up to a table in his wheelchair. I joined him at the table and sat down.

"Hi, Matthew, how are you feeling?" I asked.

"I'm great this morning. Hey, I have a special treat for you."

"What's that?"

"I ordered a Papa John's pizza for both of us, so don't eat anything else."

"Awesome, I could really use some pizza." Matthew had no idea that it was a dream of mine to share a pizza with him. It was inconceivable that he asked me to do that on my last day. "I'll supply the drinks. Bartender?" Al came over with a smirk on his face. "Can we have two of Matthew's signature drinks, apple juice?" Both Matthew and Al smiled, and he headed off to the snack room refrigerator to get the apple juice.

When the pizza arrived, Matthew and I clinked our juice boxes together in a mock toast. "Cheers," we said in unison. As I ate my lukewarm pizza, I swore it was the best I ever had.

After lunch, I noticed Jimmy sitting alone at a table. He looked impatient. I never saw anything but a huge grin on his face, so I sat down with him.

"Jimmy, what's up? You look worried." He looked at me and smiled—a real smile. I sensed it was meant especially for me. "Weren't you supposed to be released?"

"Yeah, my girlfriend couldn't pick me up. She had to work. She's coming to get me later today."

"That's great. I'm happy for you. It's my last day here, too. My wife is coming to take me home."

Jimmy nodded. "That's good."

It seemed like Jimmy had a lot on his mind that he needed to unload. He told me about his girlfriend, his mom, his cats, where he lived, and about his old job as an electronics technician. I couldn't believe how talkative he was. I'd never heard him speak so long or so well before. It seemed that he finally broke through all of his barriers and arrived at "normal." Finally, he stopped and sighed. Then he looked me straight in the eye and said, "You know, I really like you."

"I like you, too, Jimmy. I'm going to miss you. Good luck with your life." I extended my hand and we shook like two old friends. I was amazed at how far he came and so glad to have witnessed the miracle of his rebirth.

Normally I would expect Beth to visit at 2:00 p.m. This day was different: she was coming at 1:00 p.m. to take me home. The long days of counting Emma's calendar stick-ups were over. One by one, they fell until June 15 finally arrived. I waited for Beth on the same sofa I always sat on when she visited, the one directly facing the entrance. At 1:00 p.m., right on cue, the blue double doors swung open and she walked into the room.

I couldn't help but notice how fantastic she looked. It was more than just clothes or makeup: it was an aura. She was vibrant, happy, with a bounce to her step that was alien to her these past weeks. Instead of tentatively hugging me as she usually did, she wrapped her arms around me, pulled me close, and planted a warm kiss on my lips. Then she backed away with a sparkle in her eyes.

"What do I need to do to get out of this place?" I asked.

"I've got it all taken care of. You just need to come with me." She took my arm, hooked it in hers, and escorted me to the double blue doors that led to my freedom. Al waited there to let us out, all five foot six inches of his lean Mexican body. As we approached, he peered at me through his round, wire-rimmed glasses, extended his arm, and shook my hand. "You're a good man," he said. "Good luck with your life and God bless you."

We passed through the first set of doors and walked about thirty feet to another set. A security guard opened them as we approached. Only one set of doors remained: an unguarded set of glass ones through which I could see freedom. I paused there for a moment, remembering when I saw freedom through the doors at Pinecrest just beyond the janitor. I looked toward the concrete, asphalt and parked cars, and then stepped forward; the doors opened automatically.

Phoenix's summer heat enveloped me, ushering me into the real world where people were friendly and normal; a world full of traffic and streetlights, billboards and grocery stores, crying babies and jets roaring overhead; a world where I could do anything I wanted, anytime I wanted, and most importantly, be with the people I loved. With tears streaming down my face, I turned to Beth and smiled.

Chapter 33

THE LITTLE RED CAR

Father's Day, 2011: One thing I always wanted in my life was a perfect sale, one where I walked in, told the salesman exactly what I wanted, and after a perfect transaction, drove home in my dream car.

Wait a minute. Haven't I already gone down this path before? Yes, I have, but I learned that life isn't very generous with happy endings, and sometimes you have to create your own. So, after everything was said and done, I went back and bought that little red car all over again. I got the same salesman, made sure I had two bottles of water and finished every drop, right on cue, and purchased the same color, options, everything. It was the perfect sale all over again.

The only difference this time was that Beth was by my side the entire time, or I'm sure that everyone would have fled from me in panic. I received a generic thank-you e-mail from the salesman later, and I responded by telling him to feel free to tell potential customers that he had one customer who was so happy that he bought the same car twice. Not surprisingly, I never heard back from him.

Later that evening, as the sun faded to red on the western horizon, I drove west into the foothills of South Mountain for the sole purpose of being able to say, "In the end, I drove happily into the sunset in my little red car." It was just as it should be, and this time, Beth let me keep it.

Chapter 34

NORMAL SINUS RHYTHM

I believed that the little red car was the end. However, I was wrong: you can't force endings; they have to go their natural course. Life had another ending in mind for me, a much different and fitting one than I could ever conceive on my own.

On the evening of January 31, 2012, I again found myself restrained on a gurney headed toward an awaiting ambulance. Horrific visions of my last ambulance ride from the PDC to Gracewood played in my mind, but I wasn't making a trip because of another mental breakdown. The problem wasn't my mind, it was my heart. To make matters worse, I was on my way to the very same hospital emergency room that Beth told me to avoid at the beginning of it all. I hoped that wasn't a bad omen.

When I arrived at the emergency room of Chandler General, Beth was right behind me. She was a constant companion that evening, filling in whatever details I missed, and indeed doing all the talking at times as the emergency room doctors and nurses assessed the situation. It wasn't long before I was in a particularly spacious partitioned area of the emergency room filled with sophisticated medical equipment. It had an ominous aura to it, and I couldn't help but imagine scenarios of my heart stopping there and what events might transpire as experts took advantage of all the fancy equipment and space to save my life.

As if to further emphasize that prospect, a male nurse opened the hospital gown that recently replaced my clothes and started shaving the hair from my chest. When he finished, he placed five adhesive electrodes: one near my heart, two below my shoulders, and two more on the sides of my ribs. He then proceeded to place two large oval pads: one over my heart and the other over my ribs on my left side. They were unmistakable.

"Defibrillator?" I asked nervously.

"Don't worry; we're just placing them in case we need to pace your heart. If that's necessary, we'll sedate you."

I imagined my drugged body, jerking once-per-second in response to powerful electric shocks through those pads. After the nurse finished connecting the electrodes and plugging them into an EKG monitor, Beth and I saw the reason for my breathlessness and nausea. An electronic interpretation of my heartbeat scrolled across the EKG display. Even to a non-expert, something was obviously wrong. It was irregular, and sometimes there was no beat at all. Numbers on the right side of the screen, indicating my heart rate in beats per minute, varied between thirty-five and forty-two, but generally were under forty, nearly half my normal heart rate.

"See the big peak on this waveform?" the nurse asked, pointing to a large spike on the display. "It's missing a P wave, which normally precedes it. The P wave represents the electrical signal that initiates contractions of your right and left atriums, or the top portion of your heart. After that, the ventricles, or lower portion of the heart, contract at this time, just after the large spike on the waveform."

"So what does that mean? What happens if I don't have a P wave?" I asked.

"The P wave is the pacing event that controls your heart rate. When it's missing, the ventricles pace at a default rate."

"What about when there's no heartbeat, like that," I asked, pointing to a flat line on the waveform.

"That's called a pause. It can be caused by a premature beat or some other pacing anomaly."

"Is that serious?"

"It can be, but right now we're primarily concerned with your missing P wave."

A short time later, a doctor visited and showed us a copy of an EKG he obtained from Desert Hope, taken on April 18, right before my surgery. It was shocking to see the difference between the two waveforms. My heart was clearly in distress.

It was evident that despite how bad things looked, I was stable. The nurse unplugged the five electrodes from the EKG machine, and plugged them into a portable transmitter that he placed in a chest pocket of my hospital gown. The transmitter allowed remote monitoring of my heart twenty-four hours a day. They moved me to a room in the cardiac telemetry unit where I awaited further diagnosis by a cardiologist in the morning.

"You look exhausted." I said to Beth. "Why don't you go home: I'm in good hands here, and they're watching me all the time."

"OK." She squeezed my hand and kissed me. "I'll see you in the morning. Call me if you hear anything in the meantime." She placed my cell phone on a cart next to my bed. After she left, I tried to sleep, but my slowly beating heart barely provided enough oxygen to my body, leaving me nauseous and short of breath.

When I first moved to Arizona in 1990, I worked for Medtronic, a pacemaker manufacturer. I was very knowledgeable about pacemakers. That night all I could think about was the cardiologist telling me I needed one. The thought of surgery brought fears of new mania and further institutionalization. At least I was taking lithium to prevent such a scenario.

When morning arrived, I talked to Conner, the day nurse and mentioned with concern that I hadn't had my lithium since 6:00 p.m. the previous night.

"I take four three-hundred-milligram tablets a day, one at a time at morning, noon, dinner, and bedtime. I think they are CR, slow release," I explained to him.

"Where's your pharmacy? I'll call them to get more information, and then arrange to get some from our pharmacy. I think you'll be OK only missing one last night."

I gave him the pharmacy information, and he wrote it down and left. At 9:00 a.m., Conner returned with a small paper cup containing a single lithium carbonate tablet. I took the cup and tipped the tablet into my mouth, then accepted another cup of water and washed it down.

"I'll bring you another one at 1:00 p.m.," he said.

"Thank you," I replied.

At 9:30 a.m., Dr. Cree, the cardiologist, arrived. He was friendly and courteous. He walked to the side of my bed and extended his hand. I shook it firmly and prepared myself for the worst.

"Mr. Dickson, I'm Dr. Cree, your cardiologist. How are you feeling this morning?"

"A little sick."

"I'm sorry to hear that. That's a consequence of your low heart rate. As I'm sure you're aware, your heart is having some difficulties."

"Yes," I gulped.

"Essentially what we're seeing is that there is no conduction between the upper and lower chambers of your heart. As a result, the lower portion is beating at a default rate, which is very slow. It's also beating in an abnormal fashion, so it's very inefficient. As a result, you may have noticed that you can feel a stronger-than-normal beat as it tries to compensate."

It was true. I could often feel the slow pounding beats without even having to place my finger over an artery. I could almost hear them.

"This condition is called bradycardia," he continued.

Oh, just get it over with. I knew all about bradycardia. I didn't see any way around what I knew was coming next.

"It seems the source of this problem is the lithium carbonate you've been taking. You have lithium toxicity."

"What? I get my blood tested regularly for lithium levels, and renal and thyroid function. The tests always come back fine."

"That's true, and according to blood tests from last night when you arrived, your lithium levels are actually on the low side of therapeutic. The point is that these levels, even though they meet conventional standards of safety, are toxic to you. You need to stop taking lithium right away."

Whereas once I would have been ecstatic, now, I was concerned. "Is there a way we can quickly reduce the lithium in my blood, then wean me off the rest of the way gradually? I've read that if you go off cold turkey it can result in mania or depression."

"When did you last take a pill?"

"9:00 a.m."

"This is a life threatening condition. That pill was the last lithium you will ever take. Do you understand?"

I hesitated before responding. "Yes."

"Once we get the lithium out of your system, your heart should return to its normal rhythm and you'll be just fine."

"OK," I managed to muster. It was a lot to take in. I recalled months before standing up to Dr. Davis, taking the stand in court, and the court forcing me to take it, as well as the horrible months afterward. I hated being on lithium right from the start. It compressed my mood into a narrow band in which I never felt happy and was always on the verge of crying. I called it being "emotionally flat." It raised my blood pressure and frequently made me feel hot and uncomfortable. It caused me to toss and turn at night, and I drank water constantly to keep it from becoming toxic to my body.

Despite the side effects, I gradually accepted the fact that I would spend a lifetime on lithium. Whereas once it was all I could do to wash the pills down every day, I reached a point where I believed that if I didn't, I'd go manic again. It was fitting, however, that just as I was forced to take it, now I was being forced to stop taking it. I couldn't argue with fact: it was killing me. I had been right to fight Dr. Davis after all.

Despite my concerns over going manic, I was overjoyed to learn the simplicity of the solution to my problem. All that was necessary was to continue giving me saline solution through the IV already in place on the back of my left wrist and let my kidneys flush it out naturally. Nurses ensured I was safe in the meantime by monitored my EKG twenty-four hours a day.

I called Beth with the news immediately after Dr. Cree left and then relaxed. I wasn't going to die, I wasn't going to need a pacemaker, and, for better or worse, I was off lithium for good. I turned on the television and faced the same routine as at Desert Hope. I watched the required videos, took the test, then put the remote down, and tried to rest again. I was too nauseous to do anything else.

For much of the day, I lay in my room with the lights out, trying to find positions where I felt more comfortable. At lunch, I ate some mashed potatoes, but that was it. I spent a good deal of time going to the bathroom as my kidneys worked overtime. Occasionally someone knocked on my door.

"Come in."

"Just making sure you're OK. Are you all right?"

"Yes, fine. How's my heart doing?"

"Your heart rate has been really slow. It got down to thirty-three beats per minute. I wanted to check on you because your heart just paused for three seconds."

"Oh. Is that bad?"

"Bad enough that I need to check on you. I'm glad you're all right. Is there anything I can get you?"

"A fresh glass of water with ice would be nice."

That same exchange happened several more times during the day. When dinner arrived, eating half a carrot and a string bean nearly made me vomit. That evening, Beth visited. I reclined my bed and lifted my IV line so that she could slip under it and snuggle next to me. We watched a movie together on television. It was very comforting to have her there.

Unfortunately, Beth had to leave before the movie ended, which was probably for the best anyway. I really didn't feel well. I switched off the television and room light and lay uncomfortably in my bed. In the silence, I noticed the curious chuff, chuff, chuff, whirr sound that the IV pump made. I turned and looked at its glowing orange display through the darkness and tried to imagine what it must have been like with six pumps running at once, filling my body with chemicals and nutrients at Desert Hope. It must have made a real racket, but I didn't remember it at all.

As the evening progressed, it seemed that every time I got comfortable, someone turned on the lights, took a blood sample, measured my blood pressure or temperature, checked my oxygen saturation level, or asked me if I was OK. Finally, around midnight, I fell soundly asleep.

At 2:30 a.m., a gentle knock on my door woke me. "Come in," I responded. The night-shift nurse, Diana, opened the door and stepped excitedly into the room.

"I'm sorry to bother you, but I just had to tell you the good news: since midnight your heart has been in normal sinus rhythm."

"Thank you, Diana," I replied. She quietly shut the door and left me. I lay on my back for a while, repeating the words "normal sinus rhythm" to myself. I realized with great joy that my personal detour—my detour from normal—was finally over. The myriad cones, barricades, and reduced-speed-limit signs were gone, and there was nothing but open road ahead. I smiled. It was an unusually broad smile, a smile that I knew would be impossible on lithium.

I turned onto my side, careful to leave enough slack in my IV line and not dislodge any of my electrodes. I pulled the thin hospital blankets up around me, closed my eyes, and surrendered to a deep, blissful sleep.

Part 4

INSIGHT

Chapter 35

SIDE EFFECTS

I'm not a doctor, psychiatrist, psychologist, or neurologist, and I'm not an expert on other people's mania. But, being an engineer, I am a determined problem solver. After my mania ended, I spent years reviewing medical records, reading my wife's journal, interviewing friends and relatives and scouring books and the Internet, to better understand what happened to me.

Part three of this book was the end of my ordeal, but I'd be remiss not to share what I've learned since then, and I imagine that you may have many unanswered questions yourself. I hope that the following information will help to fill in the blanks and allow you to protect yourself or a loved one from experiencing what I did. I especially hope that this information will lead to more effective treatment and compassionate care by medical and mental health professionals.

From Simple to Unsolvable

February 20 2012, my fifty-sixth birthday: All the puzzle pieces fell into place, and I finally made sense of what happened to me. It took being off lithium and once again having full mental capacity. What I discovered is that any of the doctors or general practitioners involved with my illness could have saved me from months of suffering simply by addressing my only concern: sleep. No one dealt with it. Instead, they passed me from one professional to another without help.

As I moved from one place to the next, my medical records fell behind and the knowledge of what happened to me was effectively lost. As quickly as that knowledge faded, the prejudice of my caregivers grew. They looked at me once and knew my story: I was manic. Friends and family helping me then were taking desperate stabs in the dark, hoping to find the one doctor who could cure me. Their odds of finding that single person by chance were infinitesimally small. What they really needed was a team of doctors: a psychologist, a neurologist, and a medical doctor.

The psychologist would break through the smoke screen of my behaviors to better understand my disability and help me cope with my changes.

The neurologist would use his vast knowledge of the brain and nervous system, and tools such as a CAT scan, MRI, and EEG to isolate potential causes of my mania, seizures, and extremity pain.

The medical doctor would manage the insomnia and high blood pressure, and perform exhaustive tests to discover what toxins, chemicals, or hormones were at the root of my problems.

That's the scenario that we all envisioned, but sadly, there is no such team and it never happened that way. In reality, not one professional consulted with anyone else, ever. My problems became unsolvable by default because of the prejudice, bias, and shortsightedness of those involved.

My Mania

I experienced three distinct levels of mania. Although that may not be typical, the fact that my mania had distinct levels helped me to identify differences between stages of mania. When I was at my dentist's office waiting for my daughter, I was in very poor cognitive condition. In an instant, my mind placed me in a state I'll call "therapeutic mania." In that state my memory improved, my energy increased, and my earlier difficulties disappeared. It seemed a perfect solution for my mental disabilities at that moment. Aside from those improvements, I felt no different. Apparently, I sacrificed no abilities or memories. The mania was very subtle and beneficial.

At Pinecrest, during the night of my interaction with the big machine, I succumbed to a new level of mania I'll call "emergency mania." After describing it to my friend Tim, he mentioned that it sounded like something he experienced when he was in an automobile accident. I forgot that I also had an accident experience. The more I recalled about that event, the more I realized that he was right, hence the name "emergency mania."

In this second level of mania, much of my mental function partially or completely disconnected, and certain senses amplified to compensate for the loss of mental capabilities. In an emergency, one heightened sense can balance countless lost abilities and memories. In that state, my mind operated extremely fast due to the many things disabled. The effect was like traffic suddenly disappearing from a busy freeway, leaving all lanes open as my personal speedway. It seemed that all of the day-to-day chatter of my mind shut off, preparing me to make rapid-fire, life-saving decisions. The quality of those decisions suffered because of a lack of broad knowledge, but in an emergency, it is more important to make many decisions quickly and suffer through a few bad ones than it is to wait for one quality decision and risk injury or death.

Emergency mania could be compared to what an adrenaline junkie experiences when he BASE jumps, or what professional athletes experience when they are in the "zone." Psychologists call that mental state "flow." While in that level of mania, I felt euphoric. I felt no fear or worry, my instincts and senses were crisp, my energy was limitless, and my confidence and enthusiasm were boundless. Without doubt, people in that state are going to like it. You'll have a hard time convincing them that there is something wrong with them.

In fact, because of their changed perception, it may be impossible for them to recognize that there is anything wrong. That lack of insight is called "anosognosia," a condition in which the person suffering the disability is unaware of the existence of it. Unlike denial, which is a defense mechanism, anosognosia has physiological roots in the brain. When those people in my home tried to tell me I was sick, I had no clue what they were talking about, I *felt* great.

It's very confusing to suddenly become emergency manic. I spent days wondering how and why it happened. My reduced cognitive abilities weren't of much help, and besides, the answers to those questions weren't really pertinent to my emergency situation. I concluded that only a higher power could do such things. It was so completely outrageous; there was no other logical explanation. Not surprisingly, a common delusion among people who are manic is a sense of enlightenment of one kind or another. Many sufferers believe they are Jesus, are experiencing what Jesus did, or that God is calling them for some grand purpose.

I reached the height of my mania at Phoenix Mercy, a level of mania I'll simply call "peak mania." I cannot conceive of anything beyond that since it took so incredibly much for me to reach that level. For me, the main purpose of that state seemed to be conserving brainpower by allowing the brain to function only at the most primitive level. This was accomplished by disconnecting everything possible and compensating for the losses by boosting specific senses even more than in emergency mania. In this state, rational thinking took a back seat to intuitive thinking.

I'm convinced that peak mania is the last stop before your brain completely shuts down. If you think of your brain as a car battery, it would be like the final moment when the battery can barely turn the starter and you wait in dreaded anticipation for the clicking sound of the starter solenoid signaling the battery's final demise. My sleep deprivation by that time depleted all of my brain's reserves. There was literally nothing left. To give you an idea of what it's like being in peak mania, imagine if you were dropped in the wilderness and given a choice of three items to survive. You certainly would want the most useful items you could get. That's what I was given—the most necessary tools to survive and nothing more.

You'd think that rather than take away so much, my brain would have simply put me into a coma and taken some time to recover, keeping my function intact. Surprisingly, it seemed more important for me to stay awake. My brain sacrificed everything it could to give me even a few minutes awake. My body was clearly unable to fix its problems itself. I can only surmise that allowing me to be awake and functioning at any level provided opportunities for me to fix myself, whereas being in a coma provided no possible salvation.

In peak mania, I quickly learned to influence my environment to get what I needed by depending almost entirely on heightened senses and intuition. In the psychiatric ward of Phoenix Mercy, I secured the attention of doctors and staff, gained their trust, and convinced them that there was nothing wrong with me. They released me on my own recognizance in less than an hour, despite the fact that I was at the highest level of mania imaginable. That process would take hours for any normal person. Even though I was the least functional I could be, by design I was the most capable for my environment of the moment. In a few hours there, I discovered my heightened senses, studied and experimented with them, and put them to good use to gain my release.

When I was in peak mania, I felt just as I did in emergency mania, but the world took on a surreal quality. There was a feeling of tunnel vision, which might result from inhibited input from peripheral vision nerves. There was also a sense of quiet, perhaps because certain aspects of my hearing that didn't provide much useful information were inhibited. Streamlining sensory input would certainly present another opportunity for conserving brain function.

In all my levels of mania, I noticed that each seemed to set me up perfectly for a basic level of survival in the particular situation I was in at the time the mania changed. From there I could not tell if it adapted to new situations. I suspect there were continuous changes, but if there were, they were so subtle that I quickly adjusted. I only noticed the step function changes.

Sleep Paralysis

At Phoenix Mercy, I was in very dire straits. Due to extreme sleep deprivation, not only was I at the peak of my mania, I was having repeated seizure-like symptoms. What I refer to as a seizure is not exactly a seizure per se but a spontaneous shutdown of major muscle groups. An EEG technician told me it was an episode. I chose to call it a seizure because people rolled their eyes when I said episode: none of them knew what it meant. The mechanism for it appears identical to that of sleep paralysis, which affects the same muscle groups during REM sleep.

Although people believe that sleep paralysis occurs so that you don't flail about while in REM sleep, I believe it serves another important purpose: it silences billions of nerves, providing an opportunity for the brain to recharge all the chemicals needed for another full day of electrochemical communication. In my case, it was impossible to get any REM sleep. Once I reached a critical threshold, my mind forced me into paralysis regardless of what I was doing, perhaps so that it could recharge. I typically didn't remain paralyzed for very long, but without treatment, the paralysis reoccurred every fifteen or twenty minutes.

During paralysis, my sight and hearing remained intact, but I could not speak. When my body recovered from the paralysis, I felt pins and needles as you would if your foot fell asleep, most noticeably in my arms, hands, legs, and feet. The associated pain could range from mild to intolerable—from pins and needles to a thousand bee stings.

After many repeated seizures at Phoenix Mercy, it seemed the paralysis claimed even internal muscle groups, causing me extreme abdominal pain, retching and vomiting. To make matters worse, my arms and legs sometimes jerked as if nerves misfired (as sometimes happens when you are falling asleep).

I mention all this because it seems obvious that I was suffering from a neurological breakdown, yet all the hospital did was monitor my heart rate, respiration, and temperature. Had anyone thought to connect me to an EEG or similar equipment to monitor my brain waves, they might have been shocked. I don't know what their rationale was for giving me Ativan, but I'm thankful they did, or I could have ended up in much worse condition. Although doctors and psychiatrists generally prescribe Ativan for anxiety, for me it both stopped seizures in progress and prevented future ones by allowing me to sleep. It proved invaluable in my treatment, and I don't think anyone other than me recognized that.

Surprisingly, at Pinecrest I was able to prevent a seizure. I did it by "changing up," as I called it. By using extensive muscle groups and stimuli in a random and ever-changing fashion, I held the seizure at bay for literally hours until I was able to prevent it with Ativan. Had I not done that, I would have had another seizure within minutes of entering Pinecrest and repeated seizures every fifteen or twenty minutes.

During that struggle, there was a constant sense of "fighting the monster." I could literally feel how close I was to collapse at all times. I felt feverish, agitated, and desperate, well aware of what awaited me. In later stages of mania, I lost the knowledge of "changing up" by coincidence or design. I have a feeling that my body absolutely needed to shut down and didn't want me interfering again. In any case, at the next level of mania, that knowledge was the first thing to go.

Hypnagogic dreams

In Gracewood, there was a young woman that I occasionally talked to. She was attractive and acted normal. I couldn't help but wonder why she was there. I soon found out as she related a story that left me incredulous. She described being shot and the detailed efforts to save her life. First, her heart was removed and replaced by her boyfriend's heart, which was then replaced by her son's heart.

During the recounting of her story, she showed me the bullet entry and exit wounds on her thigh. I couldn't help but wonder if there was a real basis to her story.

It wasn't until many months later, when I was researching my own unbelievable visions of the flawless night that I learned of hypnagogic dreams. A hypnagogic dream is one where you can be awake and be dreaming at the same time. We've all had dreams so vivid we were thankful to awaken from them. Imagine if the dream continued, mixed with reality. Pinching yourself would result in the expected discomfort, and your senses would confirm your experience, even taste and smell. With such undeniable confirmation, it is impossible to distinguish dream from reality. Having experienced this firsthand, I can fully attest to the remarkable realism. Hypnagogic dreams are not uncommon in situations of trauma or substance abuse. Perhaps this explains some of the bizarre stories of the mentally ill and their certainty that they are true.

Micro-Emotions

When I was at the peak of mania, I sensed things about others like never before. I since learned of micro-emotions: involuntary movements of facial muscles, or "tells," which exist for less than a second. There are seven different micro-emotions: happiness, sadness, anger, surprise, disgust, contempt, and fear. Law enforcement officers train to recognize micro-emotions when dealing with criminals and routinely use that skill to uncover the truth during interrogations. When I was manic, my mind processed information much more rapidly, and with my elevated senses, these normally fleeting tells must have been very obvious to me. Though I had no idea what micro-emotions were at the time, I was able to recognize what I sensed as either good or bad and thereby manipulate people to accomplish my objectives.

Selective Hearing

You may recall a phenomenon that I called the "shield." I've learned that the correct term is "selective auditory attention" or, more commonly, "selective hearing." When we think of selective hearing, an image of a husband not paying attention to his wife comes to mind. In reality, it is much more common and dynamic than that, and we all use it frequently. In fact, it is such a common behavior that we work around it on a constant basis without even realizing it. When we start a question with someone's name or an affectionate term such as "honey" or "dear," it is often to reach past selective hearing to gain their attention, much as I did at Phoenix Mercy when I spoke kindly to people in order to secure my release.

The magic of selective hearing is that it allows us on one hand to hold a conversation with a single person in a noisy crowd, and on the other to block something entirely that we don't wish to hear, as when Rude Guy pestered the nurse. It is even possible to filter an entire conversation, letting through only critical bits of information. People filling out surveys or repetitive forms (social workers for example) frequently employ this technique. It's important to note that the sound enters our ears just fine, but the mind systematically filters out unwanted information, often without our being aware of it.

Collapse of the Ego

Many readers might be inclined to discount what happened to me during my encounter with the big machine. This is actually a well-known phenomenon, referred to as a "collapse of the ego." Several other authors have experienced this and written about it, including Eckhart Tolle, Byron Katie, Dr. Jill Bolte Taylor, and Sean Blackwell.

After years of near suicidal depression, Eckhart Tolle experienced a collapse of ego that permanently ended his depression. He then abandoned his secure life and lived simply and anonymously on the streets of London for several years. He subsequently published several top-selling books that radically improved readers' lives. He is now a highly regarded spiritual leader.

After ten years of self-loathing, rage, and depression, Byron Katie found herself at the lowest point of her life, abandoned at a halfway house by a family who lost all hope for her. She awoke one morning on the floor of the attic where she was confined and discovered that her world had miraculously changed. That event spawned a new purpose in her life, which she dubbed "The Work." She turned her focus to writing and speaking, and became a best-selling author and highly sought speaker.

Dr. Jill Bolte Taylor, a brain scientist, experienced a similar state of consciousness after a devastating stroke. Although her recovery and her discoveries about the mind are the primary focus of her book, *My Stroke of Insight,* she spends several chapters describing her experiences with this state and its potential benefits for humankind. Her book has sold millions of copies and at the time of this book's publication, is being made into a movie produced by Sony Pictures and directed by Ron Howard.

Sean Blackwell's book *Am I Bipolar or Waking Up?* details his personal collapse of ego due to psychological trauma and the inspiring changes it brought to his life. He believes that the collapse of ego will lead to a permanent cure for people suffering from various mental illnesses and is passionately spreading this message. He is very active on YouTube with dozens of videos and has a huge and growing following.

I described my personal collapse of ego in vivid detail in chapter eight: Inside the Big Machine, but haven't spent much time discussing how I felt or what it was like afterward. Moments after my collapse, my mind was crystal-clear, devoid of chatter and keenly alert. My body was completely relaxed and I felt a serene peace like never before. Without initially realizing it, I was freed from a lifetime of baggage: all my guilt, anger, shame, and doubt were gone; I was given a clean slate. My ties with the past and future were temporarily severed, and I was left with only the certainty of the present moment. If I were to describe how I felt in one word, that word would be reborn.

Lacking my previous inhibitions, I was happy to talk to anyone about my experience. What I explained to them initially was that I lost my emotions. "What about love? What about joy?" they asked. I still had those emotions, and that puzzled me. Then I realized that I hadn't lost all of my emotions, just the negative ones. Without them, I saw life in a totally new and euphoric light. Back then my family and friends wanted nothing more than to have their old Ken back; I can't imagine how mentally ill I must have seemed to them.

My collapse also resulted in a heightened awareness referred to in psychological texts as a "watcher" or "witness." Most of the time I feel like a regular person, but at times of heightened emotions, I feel as if I'm two people: one experiencing the emotion and the other weighing its validity. Having this newfound ability to detach from emotional situations not only allows me to retain a low level of negative emotions, it also helps me to dampen anger, block fear, and remain keenly alert in chaotic and frightening situations.

Though this may simply be a greater awareness and trust of my subconscious resulting from my experiences, I must admit that it feels markedly spiritual. That part of me is highly intuitive and recognizes subtle cues and synchronicities in my life that I would previously miss. It also gently nudges me toward a specific path without, unfortunately, giving any clues as to where that path might lead. Because of the positive effects of this phenomenon, many refer to it as a spiritual awakening.

This all sounds wonderful, but let me describe the reality of it with a few statements. It's a solitary journey; there is a sense of aloneness, of being the only one. People don't accept or believe you, and they suspect continued mental illness. Instead of voicing joy over your good fortune, you must remain silent about it. As a result I found myself in confusion as I struggled alone to make sense of a gift that became mine only by happenstance.

All the other authors I mentioned shared this solitary path. It took each of us years to understand and accept our gift. None of us searched for, or were prepared in any way for, the gift that we received. Remarkably, all of us awakened in much the same way and published books as a result, with the intention to lead others toward a better world.

I've learned that what happened to us can result from any number of traumas, from medications, and perhaps even by choice, but that it is little understood and rarely spoken or written about. I hope that by introducing readers to this subject, it will lead to open discourse and eventual acceptance. There are many trapped or soon to be trapped in the same cycle of confusion we all faced. Nothing would please me more than to smooth their transition through what I consider a normal and natural process, which, when better understood, may indeed lead to a treatment for many dysfunctions.

Making Sense of Crazy

Whenever I entered any new state of mania, it was extremely disorienting to be suddenly missing huge chunks of memory and abilities. I had no realization that I lost anything; I just could no longer do certain things that I could before, and I had to find different ways to do them.

Oddly, it seemed that my mind left facades of everything I lost, perhaps as placeholders or to make it less traumatic. Take the map I encountered at Pinecrest for example: I knew what the map was and its purpose, but I had no clue how to use it. The facade of map knowledge was there, but the knowledge behind it was disconnected. I had similar issues with camera memory cards, among other things. I knew what they were, but I had no ability to use them. I also could use the Internet just fine but I couldn't execute a program or find a file or directory on a computer.

Luckily, without negative emotions, I had a sunny attitude toward workarounds and was not embarrassed at all to ask someone to help me do something I no longer could.

Doubling my Seroquel at Pinecrest single-handedly knocked me to the next level of mania. When I received the same double dose the next day after my escape, I clearly showed many adverse reactions to the drug. Often during my institutionalization, it seemed that the treatment plan for me was completely wrong. At the same time, it seemed that no one consulted my medical history or listened to information Beth or I tried to convey. I later learned of the term "confirmation bias." That is the tendency to selectively favor information that confirms a hypothesis, while ignoring everything else. It was a favorite practice by Dr. Davis and one of the reasons I disliked him so much.

During emergency mania and peak mania, everything that was not necessary for survival was disconnected. In some cases that even involved the memory of my wife. While writing this book, I learned that she was by my side the entire day at Phoenix Mercy, holding my hand and comforting me, yet I have almost no recollection of her being there. I may have recognized that she was with me at the time and interacted with her, but my mind did not record that even though it was recording other information in vivid detail.

The most interesting realization was how important Dana was to me. It was as if I had reverted to childhood and he was once again the big brother fending off bullies. I would have followed him anywhere or done almost anything he asked regardless of the outcome. For my imploding mind, he was the only beacon of hope I acknowledged, although my wife was frequently at my side. It's clear that, even though love is strong, in a crisis, what your mind perceives will save your life is more important than emotions.

One of the most humbling discoveries I made from this experience is that I am not in charge of this machine that houses my small consciousness; I am simply a passenger. Not only do I not have conscious control over what's going on inside my body, when it comes down to it, I have very little control over what goes on in my mind.

On the other hand, I can't ignore the fact that there seemed to be a purpose to the things that happened to me. There was an organization to it, and the worst was consistently delayed as long as possible. Though my body and mind seemed to work in tandem to give me the best configuration possible in my extreme circumstances, my emotional reaction to what was happening was a very different story. As far as my body and mind were concerned, however, that reaction was merely an annoying byproduct. Their goal was to allow me to function and to protect me at the highest level possible.

On the day I went to Phoenix Mercy, I reached the summit of the mountain. My mind reached its narrowest functionality, my senses were at their peak, and my body was at its weakest. From there my mind and body slowly recovered, but other areas of my life continued to deteriorate because of people's reactions to my behavior and because no one involved had the necessary knowledge or skills to help me. I certainly wasn't out of the woods, but after that day, my mind slowly began expanding back to normal, and my senses dropped closer to where they were originally.

After June 3, when my heart rate and blood pressure finally started to drop, I was well on the road to recovery. If I wasn't in a situation where sleep was hard to come by, I could have gotten enough sleep without Ativan. I didn't need lithium; I just needed time. For whatever reason, it took time to turn all of my brain back on even though parts were of it disconnected in an instant.

I believe that once disconnected, those areas need to be stimulated to turn on by using them. It didn't seem to just happen automatically. The neural pathways apparently need to be exercised to build them back up to their previous levels. The writing of this book was originally an attempt to stimulate my mind to recover. When I look back at my earliest writing attempts, it's very clear that my mind was still compromised.

The Smoking Gun

Before everything began, I was a perfectly healthy, normal man with no personal or family history of mental health issues. One thing I haven't discussed is the link between my bowel surgery and my mania. Until July 22, 2011, there were no potential answers. On that day, I went in for a colonoscopy to evaluate the general health of my repaired bowels. While in prep, awaiting anesthesia, I asked the nurse if she ever heard of anyone going manic after a surgery.

"Why yes," she said. "In fact, I think I have some information I can print out for you. I believe it's called steroid psychosis."

I was excited to find a lead. It turns out that steroids given during surgery can result in mania within days or weeks. Genetics are not a factor; it can happen to anyone, even people who were given steroids previously with no ill effects. While I had my colonoscopy, the nurse printed and shared the information with Beth. Later, Beth dug through the thousand pages of medical records we obtained from Desert Hope, trying to find the suspect steroid.

She eventually found it: the corticosteroid Decadron, which was given to me during surgery to prevent inflammation. She called me with the news. We were both overjoyed. It meant that I wasn't just a random case of mental illness; there was a potential reason why I went manic.

Astoundingly, I learned there were twenty-seven drugs given to me during my hospital stay: twenty of them during my surgery. I researched all of them to determine their side effects. One drug, Levaquin, a powerful antibiotic, is in the top three of all drugs that cause adverse psychiatric effects. It is the focus of multiple lawsuits. Perhaps that was part of the reason for my surgeon's reluctance to be further involved with me—I must have received a gallon of Levaquin. It came in a large bag and I received several bags intravenously in the days preceding my surgery.

Serotonin, a neurotransmitter produced in the bowels, is another likely culprit. Since my bowels were certainly disturbed during my surgery, that may have stimulated the production of extreme levels of serotonin leading to serotonin syndrome or serotonin toxicity. Symptoms of serotonin syndrome include agitation, hypomania, mental confusion, hallucinations, high blood pressure and heart rate, nausea, tremor, twitching, seizures, dilated pupils, and inhibition of REM sleep.

Seroquel and other SSRIs (selective serotonin reuptake inhibitors) are particularly notorious for causing this syndrome. I was lucky that I got off Seroquel so quickly. Already in a compromised state, I went downhill rapidly when given that drug. Many patients react adversely to SSRIs, commonly prescribed for depression and anxiety. In extreme cases, they have been linked directly to violence, suicide, and even murder.

A final potential culprit is the inhibitory neurotransmitter GABA (gamma-aminobutyric acid). The brain becomes over stimulated when GABA levels are too low, resulting in rapid speech, insomnia, hyper sexuality, excessive spending, reckless decisions, risk-taking behavior, and grandiose ideas. You feel so euphoric that you may consider yourself a heavenly spirit, an intellectual genius, or in possession of extraordinary powers. In that state, impulsive behaviors aren't overruled by logic or reason. You may also suffer from seizures.

Here is the most eye-opening revelation of all: Ativan proved beneficial repeatedly during my ordeal. How does Ativan work? It acts on GABA receptors in the brain causing release of the neurotransmitter GABA. Another way to raise GABA levels is to consume alcohol. A test or even a temporary solution to my problems could have been the simple act of having a few beers. How unfortunate it may have been for me that I rarely drink.

Although I've pointed toward adrenaline often throughout the book, I suspect that low GABA levels could have been the real smoking gun. Sadly, I have no test results to confirm that theory. A NeuroBasic panel blood test will measure levels of both inhibitory and excitatory neurotransmitters including serotonin, GABA, dopamine, epinephrine, norepinephrine, and glutamate.

The Most Seductive Drug

Would I ever want to be manic again? Months after my mania ended, I went for a walk around my neighborhood. I found myself imagining the ideal breeze, stars too numerous and bright to be real, and perfect palm trees. I remembered the evening in my home when everything looked so pristine; how my dogs clung to me; and the afternoon my wife and I made love.

I cried when I walked that night. I cried because there were so many amazing things I experienced that I will never experience again. I cried because I knew that just as I fought against the use of drugs in my life, now I would have to avoid mania equally as hard. Ironically, something I never gave a second's consideration in my whole life is the most seductive drug I could imagine.

When I was manic, I had passion and enthusiasm by the truckload. Things I had trouble with in normal life were a breeze for me. I felt perfect, better than at any time in my life. Anything I may have had to give up in order to feel that way was far from my thoughts. The truth, however, was that it was all a lie. Mania took away my ability to recognize all that I sacrificed in order to feel good about a few things. It both stole my life from me and convinced me that my life was the best it had ever been at the same time. I fear that if I was ever under its full influence again, I would be equally powerless to regain my life. No matter how much you know or how smart you are, mania will take away your knowledge as it sees fit. Anyone will prefer being manic to being normal because it is such a perfect ruse.

Chapter 36

HOPE

Life Without Lithium

I had a conservative goal to begin weaning myself off lithium gradually under psychiatric supervision starting on the one-year anniversary of my court date: June 7, 2012. When I was instead told on February 1, 2012 that I took my last pill, I was very concerned that I might instantly relapse.

Instead, being off lithium was amazing. When I stopped lithium, there was a feeling that I was suddenly me again. For starters, I was no longer on the verge of tears all the time. Beyond that, I noticed that my positive emotions seemed unbounded. Within a few days, I experienced such heightened joy that I was in tears. I couldn't believe how wonderful it felt to experience joy again. I did grow a little concerned during some of the really over-the-top joyful experiences, until I realized that without drugs controlling my emotions, I was going to have to relearn how to regulate them myself.

Because I no longer had problems with my heart rhythm, I no longer felt out of breath going up stairs, and my lungs felt as if they were Roto-Rootered. The heart and lungs work in tandem, and when your heart has trouble, your lungs often do as well. My lung troubles were too subtle to notice until I stopped lithium. After lithium, taking a deep, clear breath gave me an immediate rush.

Overall, I had much more energy, endurance, and clarity. My mind was much faster and more creative, and my memory improved as well. Even some of the abilities I discovered when I was manic reappeared, but at a much subtler level, in particular, being "slapped in the face," recognizing when people are utilizing selective hearing and being more in tune with my intuition.

On top of everything else, I had deep and restful sleep. I also no longer had tremors. While on lithium I could put my hands under a certain amount of muscle tension, and they would shake uncontrollably. Sometimes the tremors interfered with writing or some fine motor skill such as screwing a small screw or threading a needle.

There was one thing overwhelmingly different about being off lithium: my mood was much the same as when I was manic yet my mind was fully functional. Apparently, my collapse of ego had lasting effects. What does that mean exactly? It means that it was perfectly natural for me not to worry about things like money, dying, or what happens after death. It means that I didn't feel a need to hold grudges or feel guilty over something from the past. I didn't dare tell anyone because of concern over being institutionalized again. After being that way for months, I grew used to it. It doesn't make me fundamentally different; I just live more in the moment.

I did come to realize that negative emotions are still part of the human experience no matter how immune you think you are to them, but once you are aware of them and the expectations that lead to them, you can stifle their impact. Whenever I do experience a negative emotion, it no longer feels authentic. Instead, it feels as if I'm standing beside myself watching the new me trying to act like the old me. Whenever that happens I refrain from reinforcing the emotion and it soon fades.

I know that my thoughts on the collapse of the ego and losing negative emotions are difficult to swallow. Not surprisingly, discussing those subjects with friends and loved ones makes them very uncomfortable. To keep from alienating them and making them worry that I'm still mentally ill, I avoid those topics even though I think about them often. If it makes it any easier to accept, I don't think of them as miracles; I think of them as rare reactions to severe trauma during which the mind has to shut down anything that gets in the way of lifesaving measures. Given enough physical or psychological stress, anyone could experience them.

Something else I've recently noticed is that I no longer have the same fight-or-flight response that I used to have. In situations that would normally get my adrenaline pumping and my heart racing, I've found myself instead in a controlled, heightened state of awareness, as if the fight-or-flight chemicals or hormones are flowing, but are intentionally "capped." I can't help but wonder if, while I was struggling with their effects before and during mania, my body figured out a way to regulate them, much like developing immunity to a disease. Perhaps that ability will one day prove to be a built-in insurance policy against experiencing mania again. I have read of others who went through mania without medication who developed such a resistance to future manic episodes.

Living with a Stranger

If your loved one becomes manic, don't assume that it's hereditary or by their own choice. In my opinion, there is *always* an underlying cause. The more aggressively you pursue that cause early on, the better. As time passes, medical evidence will be lost, and bias and prejudice will take over, making the search impossible.

Accept that there is no instant fix for mania, and prepare for the person to remain manic for several weeks, returning to normalcy gradually. Have all those involved educate themselves on mania. Don't blindly depend on professionals; their decisions may be counterproductive. If you have a sound understanding, you will make better decisions and your stress level will decrease.

In general, substance-induced mania will subside within four weeks. There is no consensus among the medical community regarding initiation of treatment for mania using medication, so it would be prudent to wait at least that amount of time without medicating unless behavior becomes too extreme. If medications are used, take a conservative and gradual approach, monitoring closely for negative side effects. Treatments that allegedly halt mania rapidly could be dangerous, catapulting the person to the opposite extreme: depression. In that state, they may attempt suicide, and will certainly be considered bipolar from then on. Bipolar disorder has a much greater stigma than mania alone, and after that diagnosis it will be difficult, if not impossible, to convince anyone that the person shouldn't be medicated for life.

Because mania sufferers talk fast, change subjects often, and conjure up unfamiliar ideas, people have a difficult time listening to them, leaving them feeling frustrated and isolated. Don't abandon or ignore them. Instead, interact with them much as you did before; be a rock for them. Ask questions about how they feel and what they're thinking or experiencing. It may be more educational than any amount of research and, if done early, will provide a baseline so you can monitor for signs of recovery. You might consider keeping a journal for future reference. It could be especially helpful if the person ever has a recurrence, particularly if you were able to solve any problems previously. My wife kept a journal, which was very helpful in writing this book.

Don't take offense at what the manic person says. They may no longer be capable of acting in the way you have come to expect. Common courtesy may in fact be blocked from their memory. At some point, I recognized that people reacted negatively to some of my actions. I called that recognition a "slap in the face." I had to re-teach myself common courtesy from scratch with only that phenomenon for feedback.

It may be difficult or impossible for manic people to get a full night's sleep. Encourage them to sleep whenever they can, and provide an optimum environment for them to do so. Even though I wasn't sleepy, I knew I needed sleep to prevent matters from getting worse. Sleep was such a priority for me that I mention various forms of the word "sleep" close to two hundred times in this book.

Spouses and friends of mania sufferers can easily be run into the ground. If friends or family are helping, take turns so everyone can recover and attend to his or her own needs. Watch each other for signs of physical or mental distress. Be prepared for the long haul; there's no telling how protracted the episode may be.

Prepare for extreme behaviors such as grandiose schemes to make money by taking early control of credit cards and finances.

Manic people frequently have a high level of sexual desire, and a heightened level of sensation and enjoyment of sex. They also have lowered inhibitions and therefore may seek out other sexual partners.

Manic people's minds work very quickly, and they may have increased creative capacity. They will have complex ideas that they've never had before. Let them explore their ideas as long as they don't hurt anyone.

Don't treat manic people disrespectfully. It was not their choice to become that way. Several people described me as "gone" or even "totally gone." With all the details I've included in this book, it is undeniable that manic people are instead highly functional. If you think at times they are speaking gibberish, consider that their minds are configured differently than yours. It may be impossible for you to keep up with the speed of their streamlined minds or comprehend their intuitive thought processes. Accept, too, that what they are experiencing is new to them, and they are doing their best to make sense of it. It is unimaginably confusing to experience things for which there are no explanations.

Avoid institutionalizing manic people as long as possible. Once your loved one is committed, you will have little or no control over his or her treatment, potentially worsening the situation. I was the only manic patient in the three psychiatric facilities, and there was no treatment at any of them geared toward mania. Their programs all focused on addiction.

Caring for someone who is manic may prove to be too challenging or dangerous, and you may have to commit the individual. Or medical insurance and short or long-term disability requirements may require you to. Regardless of the reason, research your options before making a decision. You basically have three options:

Voluntary: The person will go to the first bed that opens at any facility.

By petition: Patients will be held at a psychiatric holding facility (like the PDC) where they will await a bed at a more secure facility. Once there, they will be medicated and monitored for a minimum of seventy-two hours. If they refuse medication, they will be held until they are compliant or will be court-ordered to comply. If they still refuse, they will be forcibly restrained and the medication will be injected. They will then be monitored for progress.

Private care: This is generally not covered by insurance and could be prohibitively expensive. It may, however, provide the best transparency and quality of care. If you are considering such a facility, here are some things to look for.

- Opportunities to be outdoors to exercise, play, garden, or relax
- Reasonable sleep accommodations
- Chances to write or work on crafts
- Holistic treatment approaches with medications used sparingly and only when necessary
- Willingness to consult with outside experts
- Flexible meal plans for changing caloric needs
- An engaged and compassionate staff
- Classes in meditation, yoga, tai chi, etc. for exercise, flexibility, and stress reduction
- Groups geared specifically toward mania

I hope that you are able to provide your loved one with a better path toward recovery than I had. I sincerely believe that my recovery would have been faster and healthier had everyone been more knowledgeable. It would have greatly reduced their fear and helplessness as well. One thing to keep in mind: eventually the mania will end, and you will have your loved one back. In all likelihood, however, they will be different from before.

Rising from the Ashes

I originally wanted to talk here about all the broken relationships I have as a result of my mania—how my family is hurting, how my friends have built up walls or moved on, and how my relatives are holding their breath waiting for me to go mad again. I wanted to recommend counseling or support groups, but honestly those things weren't very effective for us and they may not be for you either. Instead, I'm going to take a leap of faith and recommend something that I believe is the truest and best advice I can offer, not just for those hurting in my life but for everyone.

My very first thought after my collapse of ego was, "Negative emotions are the source of all dysfunction." Why would a random manic person have something like that pop into his head? It wasn't the kind of thought you'd expect from someone who was manic—it was short, sweet, and to the point, and I never forgot it. It made me wonder about negative emotions. What are they exactly? They are baggage, every one of them.

To make matters worse, we can't seem to let go of that baggage. Over time, our pile of baggage continues to grow, except when we go on vacation, play sports, or party with friends. Why? Because at those times we live in the present. The way we feel then is the way we could feel all the time if we did one thing: learned how to live in the present.

All that baggage has one thing in common: it all involves the past or the future. You may feel hurt, angry, or worried at this very moment. But look around you. Is there anything actually making you feel that way, or is it something from the past or the future? The trick is that the past and future don't exist. They are fabrications of our mind. The only thing that truly exists is the present.

So what's my radical proposal? Start living in the present. When we do that, we stop worrying about the future, it doesn't exist. We stop feeling the pain of the past—the past doesn't exist. Only *this very moment,* the present, exists. Each of us spends an inordinate amount of time feeling guilty, sad, or angry about past events or worrying about things in the future over which we have little or no control. Consequently, we have all but forgotten the present, the most important, and real part of our lives. It's impossible to rid ourselves of all those past hurts or future fears one at a time, but that's what we typically try to do. To make matters worse, we create new pain and fear as quickly as we deal with the old.

The only way to stop the madness is to shift our focus to the here and now. By doing so, the pain of the past and worry of the future will eventually subside, and the joy of the present will fill our lives. Here are a few tips to help you live in the present.

- *Give:* Pass your unneeded possessions to your loved ones or the less fortunate.
- *Say no to fluff:* Stop buying things you don't need.
- *Forgive:* Stop living an illusion of pain and start living a real life. Most importantly, forgive yourself; you may be your worst enemy.
- *Focus:* Savor the sights, sounds, smells, touch, and taste of the moment as if it's your last.
- *Don't be the chatter:* Stop arguing—with others and yourself.
- *Tune out:* Shut off the media fear mongering of the day and instead enjoy the sunshine and breeze in your face.
- *Accept others:* Acceptance is one of the greatest needs of humanity and one of the most powerful tools for constructive change imaginable.

- *Be positive:* Don't just think positive, be positive. Begin by not cutting yourself down anymore.
- *Be honest:* Be truthful, straightforward, and to the point in all your communication. You'll find that it requires a lot fewer words.
- *Get off your duff:* Get off the computer, shut off the video game, and turn off the TV. Engage in your world by working in your garden, playing with your pets or children, playing a musical instrument, or exploring nature.
- *Stop wishing:* Be thankful for what you have instead of dwelling on what you wish you had.
- *Dream big a step at a time:* Stop planning and start moving on your dreams. Enjoy each step of the process instead of postponing your joy until the end.
- *Pack light:* Memory grows stronger when you replay it. By replaying past pain or future worry, you create baggage. Once those memories are strong, it's hard to get rid of them, so pack light by not replaying them to begin with.
- *Chip away:* Instead of procrastinating on responsibilities, chip away at them a little each day.
- *Conquer addictions:* They hold you hostage in another time and destroy the precious vessel that contains everything that is you.

These aren't just random trinkets of information; they are tools I use every day. You see, although I became the way I am by accident, there is no guarantee I will stay this way unless I make an effort to do so. In that sense, I'm no different than anyone else. I must take action to live in the present. It is work, but over time, it becomes a lifestyle that you will be glad you chose.

We Are People

Over the course of this book, you may have wondered if my concern for other patients was genuine or if it was simply a product of my mania. I don't know that I can ever answer that question with certainty. I never visited facilities like those before and never interacted with patients like them. Having only known them in a manic state, I can never be sure if I would feel the same compassion for them had I been normal. On the other hand, my feelings for them have not diminished over time. I think of those patients often and wonder what became of them. I can do nothing to help my fellow patients now, but I wish to submit the following recommendations in their honor to medical and mental health professionals.

First, view each patient as your spouse, mother, father, or sibling, and ask yourself what course of action you would take if that were the situation.

Second, eliminate bias and prejudice from your workforce through good hiring practices and training. When I was fighting medical issues at Desert Hope, the medical professionals were genuinely interested in my well-being. Everyone was compassionate, concerned, and engaged. When I became manic, it was completely the opposite—at the very same hospital. From then on, I experienced the impact of bias and prejudice from nearly every medical and mental health professional I encountered. Though well intentioned, medical and mental health professionals are only human and, without the right knowledge and training, they are prone to the same biases and prejudices as anyone else.

This last recommendation is mainly for mental health professionals. As I sifted through hundreds of pages of records during the writing of this book, I was astounded at how much information the staff wrote about me. Aside from a few minutes spent here and there with a psychiatrist, none of those people actually interacted with me. Instead, they spent nearly all of their time sitting at their desks writing verbosely about me and other patients based on a few casual observations from a distance.

My heart goes out to those people with their overwhelming paperwork requirements, but the truth is, if you really want to help patients, you have to interact with them on a personal level. Toss a Nerf football with someone like Grace. It's possible she may toss it back. When you meet a Carlos shuffling down the hall, give him a high five, and when you see him in the cafeteria, make sure he's getting a square meal. Perhaps one day he'll shake your hand and say, "God bless you." Have a chat with a Jimmy now and then. He may stop his babbling and tell you about his girlfriend and his cats. Play "crazy" beanbag with a Robert. You'll be overjoyed when his grumbles turn into laughter. Comfort a crying Jessie, knowing that sometime in the next few hours she'll be gone from your life and you'll never know if your act of compassion made any difference.

Be an angel to a Matthew, and perhaps one day he'll honor you by asking you to share some lukewarm pizza with him. Work your gardens with a Ken, and maybe he'll share the story of your kindness with others.

We are all people just like you, and you can make such a difference in our lives by getting to know us and accepting us despite our compromised state. I guarantee that if you do, those sorts of moments will not only be commonplace, they will light up your days and make all your efforts worthwhile.

Utopia.com

At the company I work for, I'm always amazed that everyone is able to get along despite living in different countries, speaking different languages, and having different cultures and religious beliefs, among other things. The reason is that, in order to reap the rewards of working there, we have to follow rules that neutralize the impact of our differences—rules that at the same time reward us for working together toward the common beliefs of the company.

During my ordeal, a perfect storm of disabilities and (arguably) enhanced abilities opened my eyes to how the world might be without negative emotions. The sudden loss of those emotions enabled me to recognize their impact on our daily lives. Being very creative, my mind went wild with all the possibilities. Not understanding why I had suddenly become the way I was, I believed that I was somehow given a gift by a higher power. Since the symptoms did not immediately resolve, I believed that it was a permanent condition. One thing led to another, and before long, I believed that I was seeing the same change in others and concluded that I was contagious. In a matter of days, I went from being a normal person to someone with completely unorthodox beliefs.

In a way, I was only being human, believing in things that could not be proven. I was no different than the many family members and friends who were struggling to help me. They each hold different beliefs of religion, politics, gun ownership, and child rearing, just to name a few things.

Just as I am unable to change what they believe, they were unable to change my beliefs despite the overwhelming truths with which they bombarded me.

When I became well again, that proved to be the biggest lesson of my life. I learned that believing in something doesn't make it true. My beliefs were temporarily shattered, but from that, I grew to appreciate the transitory and fluid nature of belief and its interaction with faith and truth.

Humanity tends to place belief on a pedestal while discounting truth, but it should be the other way around. Truth should be held in the highest regard, and belief should be an instrument for finding truth. Here is how I see things now…

Belief is unprovable, but it is a stepping-stone to truth.
Faith is unshakable. It is neither belief nor truth but lights the way between them.
Truth is undeniable. It is both the intention and the end of belief, and the reward of faith.

My experiences highlight how entrenched humanity is in our beliefs and how powerful an influence they are in our lives. At the same time, beliefs are responsible for our worst nightmares and our greatest achievements. Hitler built crematoriums and incinerated Jews by the millions because he believed them to be an inferior race. Thomas Edison tried and failed with thousands of lightbulb designs over a two-year period because he believed each design was the one that would work. John F. Kennedy shouted, "We choose the moon!" initiating a fury of technological development that landed Americans on the moon in only a few years because he believed we could do it.

Clearly, belief is both a bane and a blessing. It motivates us to create anything from bicycles to skyscrapers, or to strap a bomb to our body and kill countless innocents, hoping that will gain us favor in a believed-in afterlife.

Now that I'm well, I no longer believe that people will change, but I am still convinced that the possibilities I envisioned are viable. We just have to figure out a way to keep beliefs that isolate and destroy us from getting in the way. Even though I've seen efforts along those lines here and there, they never seemed to thrive. There is one exception: the Internet. It seems that there, everyone gets the message that to succeed they need to work around people's beliefs. In any area of our lives, if we can accomplish that objective, we can achieve things never before possible.

My hope for humanity is that whether by accident, by innovation, or by act of God, we are somehow provided with the means to mask our differences so that all of humanity can better work together and achieve things beyond our wildest dreams. I believe that will occur with the Internet. In many ways, it has already begun.

Chapter 37

NOTHING STOPS LIFE

I marveled at the perfectly shaped spring leaves of the small orange tree as I ran my fingers across one. They seemed almost as if they were made of plastic. The tree, covered with white blossoms, was barely over waist height. I didn't need to lean into it to smell the wonderful, sweet aroma of the blossoms, but I did anyway. I inhaled deeply and reveled in it. Nothing beats the smell of orange tree blossoms in my book. In Phoenix, I smell them everywhere in the spring. It may be another eleven months until I can pick my first orange from that tree, peel off the skin, and taste it.

Beside the little orange tree stood a taller tree, nearly twice its size—a nectarine tree. Wondrous pink blossoms covered it weeks before and now it sported dozens of reddish-green fruit, each the size of a small marble. I stepped over to it and began counting them, only to give up.

On April 10, 2011, there were two large holes in the caliche where these trees now stand, almost a year later, blossoming and ready to bear fruit. On that day, I nearly killed myself digging those holes with a shovel and a pick. The chain of events I started then was beyond unbelievable. I couldn't help but wonder that I was standing next to these two trees now. *Nothing stops life.*

AFTERWORD

Before I started writing this book, I was desperate to protect myself from ever experiencing these things again, and I began writing with that in mind. Initially I focused heavily on explaining my disorder and received little or no response from anyone involved. As I continued my efforts, I realized that the task was much more complex: it involved all aspects of my life surrounding the time of my surgery, illness, and beyond. As everything came together, I realized that I had a compelling story to tell, one that could protect others as well as me. As I recalled the other psychiatric patients trapped in the system, I could not stop myself from writing that story. Aside from Beth, Tim, and my mother, no one understood or supported me on this journey, and indeed, my dedication to this book seemed another symptom of ongoing mental illness.

I have not previously written or published anything, and what you are reading is the product of countless hours of learning, research, writing, rewriting, and tears of both joy and sorrow so that I could present this work from my heart to you. I hope that I've touched you and made you think of those less fortunate, opened your eyes to new ideas, and inspired you. More than anything, I hope that I have bettered your life in some small way. Thank you for allowing me to share my story with you.

ACKNOWLEDGMENTS

Dana, you will never know how much it meant to me that you traveled so far and spent so much time with me when I was medically and mentally ill. I am honored to have you as a big brother. Tim, you are an incredible listener and friend. It is a true testament of your courage that you are still around after everything you've seen and heard. Cole, I thank you and David for the heartfelt blessing when I was hospitalized and for your and Andrea's help throughout my ordeal. Bill, thank you for visiting me often at the hospital, and for all of your efforts to ensure that I didn't lose my job. Cynthia, thank you for guiding and comforting Beth at a time when she most needed it. Mom, I greatly appreciate your love, support, and letters of encouragement, which always seem to arrive when I most need them. It is rare and magical to receive handwritten mail in this age. Dad, thank you not only for teaching me how to survive life's challenges but also to see opportunity in them. I never realized how well prepared I was.

For all the other family, friends, and neighbors who were involved in a truly challenging situation, thank you from the bottom of my heart for your concern, kindness and good will when I was hospitalized and institutionalized. Finally, thanks to my children, Kaitlin and Hailey, who constantly remind me to live in the moment and who never cease to amaze and inspire me.

I especially wish to thank my editors, Dr. Elizabeth Lowry, Matthew Brennan, and Kent Corbin. Elizabeth, while I was still recovering, you accepted my crude manuscript. Instead of discouraging me from writing, you lit the path to a grand passion. Others might have thought me hopeless, but you transformed me by gently educating me, and encouraged me to look beyond my original vision. Your tutelage meant so much to me. Matthew, thank you for your infinite patience and suggestions as you struggled through my typos and grammatical errors. Kent, thanks so much for your valuable help on the book proposal, query, and book itself. You helped me to hone skills that I later utilized to improve and even rewrite chapters.

BIBLIOGRAPHY

Blackwell, S. (2011). *Am I Bipolar or Waking Up?* CreateSpace,
Bolte, J. (2008). *My Stroke of Insight.* Viking Penguin
Ekman, P. (2007). *Emotions Revealed*, 2nd edition. Holt Paperbacks
Eron, J. (2005). *What Goes Up.* Barricade Books Inc.
Hurd, R. (2010). *Sleep Paralysis.* Hyena Press
Jamison, K. R. (1997). *An Unquiet Mind.* Vintage
Katie, B. (2003). *Loving What Is.* Three Rivers Press
Tolle, E. (2004). *The Power of Now.* New World Library
Whitaker, R. (2011). *The Anatomy of an Epidemic.* Broadway Books

Made in the USA
Middletown, DE
15 October 2015